Problems
in
Retail
Merchandising

Sixth Edition

PROBLEMS
IN
RETAIL
MERCHANDISING

JOHN W. WINGATE, *B.A., M.S. in Retailing, D.C.S.*
Professor of Marketing Emeritus
The City College of the City University of New York

ELMER O. SCHALLER, *B.A., M.S. in Retailing, D.C.S.*
Professor of Retail Management Emeritus
Institute of Retail Management, New York University

ROBERT W. BELL, *B.S., M.A., Ph. D.*
Professor of Marketing
University of Arkansas

Prentice-Hall, Inc., Englewood Cliffs, New Jersey

Library of Congress Cataloging in Publication Data

Wingate, John Williams.
　　　Problems in retail merchandising.

　　　1.　Retail trade.　I. Schaller, Elmer Otto, joint
author.　　II. Bell, Robert W., joint author.
III. Title.
HF5429.W58 1973　　　　658.8'7'0076　　　　73-1606
ISBN　0-13-720680-1

Printed in the United States of America

10

Prentice-Hall International, Inc., *London*
Prentice-Hall of Australia, Pty. Ltd., *Sydney*
Prentice-Hall of Canada, Ltd., *Toronto*
Prentice-Hall of India Private Limited, *New Delhi*
Prentice-Hall of Japan, Inc., *Tokyo*

Contents

Preface

In an ever-changing world, and in an ever-changing industry, retail merchandise management must keep abreast of the problems evolving in the field. Statistical analysis and computer controls and forecasts are important new approaches to solving these problems. They have, in turn, led to new problems and to new statements of decision theories in retailing.

Five editions and fifteen printings reflect the contribution that *Problems in Retail Merchandising* has made over a 40-year span. With this, the sixth edition, the book will continue to provide a sound guide for training in merchandising.

Problems, discussion questions, and decision-making situations continue as the basic plan. Each problem is illustrated by a complete, step-by-step solution with ample additional problems to permit more than one semester's use. As in former editions, the term *problems* is used here in the narrow sense of a mathematical situation with the facts necessary for a specific calculation available. The term is thus contrasted with *case*, wherein the facts are seldom complete and judgment enters into the solution.

Managerial decisions are brought into the scope of the book so that students can learn to analyze and theorize concerning some of the main issues facing retailing today. This feature provides for discussion and participation of everyone in the class. Practice in decision-making helps to retain interest and brings out points that have not been presented through the problems. It allows the individual student to relate his own experience to a situation and to apply his knowledge and reasoning to the issue.

The sections in this book are numbered to correspond to the chapters in the companion text, *Retail Merchandise Management*, by Wingate, Schaller, and Miller. There are two exceptions: (1) Section 18 is devoted to Expense Control, whereas the text does not devote a chapter to that subject. But Chapter 18 in the text has to do with systems and procedures for which no mathematical problems are required. (2) Section 21 is a supplementary section devoted to Invoice Mathematics, a subject touched on lightly in the text but discussed fully in the text *Management of Retail Buying* by Wingate and Friedlander. If the

Instructor wishes to cover this section, it is suggested that he assign it after Section 3 has been studied.

The Budgeting Game that appears as sub-section C of Section 17 should be introduced near the start of that portion of the course dealing with Merchandise Control, since students are to be fed additional data from a computer at frequent intervals. This data does not appear in the Problem Book but rather in the accompanying Instructors' Guide. If two semesters are devoted to the subject matter included in this book, the second semester would logically be devoted to merchandise control and the Game would be "played" throughout that course.

Over the years, a great many teachers and merchants have made constructive suggestions in regard to the nature and design of the problems included. To these, the authors are profoundly grateful. We do wish to express our appreciation, in particular, to Mr. Abraham Cole, Merchandise Controller of the Interstate Department Stores; Dr. Theodore T. Ellsworth, Professor of Retail Management, Schools of Business, New York University; and to Mr. Joseph S. Friedlander, Retail Consultant, Stern Associates, New York.

J.W.W.
E.O.S.
R.W.B.

Problems
in
Retail
Merchandising

Part I   PROFIT DETERMINATION

1   Introduction

The chief technical equipment that young men and women entering merchandising should possess is a mastery of certain basic tools. First and most important of these tools is sales forecasting, since all of the other facts and figures developed depend heavily on a good forecast. Those other tools that will be used are buying, pricing, stock control, sales promotion, and expense control.

Persons new to merchandising should understand how an open-to-buy is calculated with all of its ramifications, how markup percentages are determined and how they affect the total outcome of the profit of the business, how expenses are classified and distributed, how the relationships between sales and stocks are controlled, and the importance of decision-making for all levels of management within the retailing industry.

A distinction may be made between a "case" and a "problem" as applied to retailing. "Case" is the broader term, including all types of business situations that require analysis and decision. Many cases have to do with matters of policy and accordingly have no clear-cut, generally accepted solutions.

A "problem" on the other hand, contains in its statement all facts necessary for a solution. It involves an accepted method of attack and a definite answer. Opinion is largely eliminated but may be a factor in problems that involve making budgets based on definite data in regard to performance to date. Policy cases and problems are essential tools in teaching retail merchandising. They are samples of the jobs to be performed in the store. Cases, however, involve top management and are often beyond the scope of junior executives and rank-and-file employees.

This book represents a collection of problems and decision-making situations covering various phases of retail merchandising. They are largely of a mathematical nature, but many involve the analysis of figures rather than their manipulation. The importance of policy is not neglected, in that there is a discussion question in connection with many problems and also numerous thumbnail cases involving managerial decisions.

The general plan of this book is to give an example and a solution of each type of problem presented, followed by an additional problem for the student to solve independently. At the end of many sections, additional practice problems for drill purposes are provided. Some of these are labeled "advanced problems" and may be reserved for students who are earning extra credit or making up missed work.

Parts I, II, and III have to do with the fundamental relationships among profit and loss figures. Parts IV and V deal with planning — they attempt to set up goal figures as a guide to operation.

Some planning procedures are introduced in the first three parts, however, so that the beginning student may promptly comprehend the significance of planning and the relationship of initial markup to gross margin.

The book is planned to cover a year's work in the field of merchandising. If only one term can be devoted to the subject, Parts I, II, and III will provide a sufficiently rounded course, since, as already indicated, they cover basic control procedures. Some teachers prefer to start the course with Part II, on markup, before presenting the Operating Statement, which is the subject matter of Part I.

In all sections of the book, the problems considered *basic*, in the opinion of the authors, are indicated by means of a bullet (●), to the left of *Example*.

A topic that is frequently treated in retail merchandising courses, but not included in Wingate, Schaller, and Miller's *Retail Merchandise Management*, appears in a supplementary section: "Invoice Mathematics" (Section 21), covering terms and datings.

A retail management game is introduced as a sub-section that can be used from the beginning of the text with its accompanying program that may be written in FORTRAN IV for the IBM 360. It has been used successfully in classes for a number of years and ties together the student's basic knowledge of accounting, statistics, finance, and retailing as they relate to budgeting.

DEFINITIONS

Merchandising is the planning and supervision involved in marketing the particular merchandise or service at the places, and prices, and in quantities that will best serve to realize the marketing objectives of the business.

Retail Merchandising. The planning done by retailers (1) to achieve an assortment of merchandise that is balanced to customer demand and (2) to maintain a balance among the factors of sales volume, costs, and expenses that will both promote growth and provide a profit potential. In a broad sense, many use the term to denote the buying and selling activities of a merchant.

Merchandising Division. The division of the store that is responsible for planning stock assortments, for buying, and for merchandise control. The merchandising division is often responsible for sales results, too, even though it may not supervise the selling and publicity staffs. Along with the controller and top management, it shares in the responsibility for balancing the growth and profit factors.

Merchandise Manager. The executive (sometimes called merchandising manager) in charge of the merchandising division of a store. In large stores, there are often divisional merchandise managers, each in charge of one of the major merchandise lines carried, such as women's ready-to-wear, men's wear, and home furnishings.

2   Basic Profit Elements

Profit is the excess of business income over the costs and expenses incurred to achieve that income. Profits are essential to a business because (1) they provide the remuneration for those who have invested equity (ownership) capital in the business, (2) they provide for increased inventory and equipment necessary in an expanding economy, and (3) they allow the replacement of inventory and equipment at prices that continue to be inflationary.

Although a merchant occasionally seeks profits in order to amass capital that may be removed from the business to satisfy unrelated wants, he more often keeps some or all of his profits in the business so that it may grow and expand its sphere of operations. Such expansion requires more than materials, merchandise, and equipment. It demands research. Although it is common to treat most outlays for research as current operating expenses, they may quite properly be regarded as an investment of profits to secure future business.

With population growing rapidly and with creeping inflation boosting the cost of replacements in inventory and fixed assets, profit is essential for business survival. Not to expand is to retrogress and to court ultimate failure. Without profit, a retail organization would soon perish.

It may be debated whether a merchant is motivated in his retailing activities primarily by (1) the desire to serve the community, (2) the desire for social recognition and status, (3) the desire to assure the survival and growth of his business, or (4) the desire to achieve a profitable return on his investment. But it is unlikely that the first three goals can be achieved unless a profit is realized. It becomes imperative, then, that every merchandising operation be measured in terms of its effect on profit. Immediate profit may be temporarily sacrificed for growth as reflected in sales volume, but growth itself over the long run requires profit for reinvestment. It thus becomes the responsibility of the merchant to seek effective ways in which to increase volume and profits.

The four basic factors that enter directly into the profit results are sales volume, cost of merchandise sold, operating expenses, and other income.

The following example indicates the interaction of the factors:

Factor 1.	Sales	$10,000
Factor 2.	Cost of merchandise sold	6,500
	Gross margin	$ 3,500
Factor 3.	Operating expenses	3,000
	Operating profit	$ 500
Factor 4.	Other income (net)	200
	Net profit	$ 700

Since the retailer has more control over his gross margin than he does over the cost of the merchandise he sells, he often thinks of his profit factors as consisting of:

Factor 1.	Sales	$10,000
Factor 2.	Gross margin	3,500
Factor 3.	Operating expenses	3,000
	Operating profit	$ 500
Factor 4.	Other income (net)	200
	Net profit	$ 700

But the retailer does have some control over this cost of merchandise sold: by astute buying he may obtain the goods at lower prices from his suppliers. By improving his merchandise mix he may reduce the cost of merchandise relative to sales, and by careful inventory control he may reduce the extent to which the value of his inventory depreciates in value because of obsolescence.

DEFINITIONS

Operating Statement. An analytical presentation in figures of the income, costs, and expenses of a business for an accounting period, such as a month, a season, or a year.

Profit. The financial gain a business realizes over a period, measured in terms of money. It is the excess of income over the cost and expenses of earning the income.

Operating Profit. The business gain realized from trading operations alone. It is the difference between sales income on the one hand and the cost of merchandise sold plus the operating expenses on the other.

Net Profit. The sum of operating profit and net other income. It is also called "net gain." It may be reported as "before Federal Income tax" or as "after allowance for Federal Income tax."

Other Income. Income from sources other than the sale of merchandise. Such sources include, among others, interest and dividends received and capital gains from the sale of securities and of real estate.

Deductions from Other Income. Disbursements or losses that pertain to the financing of the business. They include interest paid or payable and other expenses incurred in borrowing and investing funds, losses in the sale of securities and real estate, and other financial losses that are not incurred to earn current income.

Net Other Income. The difference between other income and deductions from other income.

Sales. The amounts received or accrued to the store in exchange for merchandise sold to customers during an accounting period.

Purchases. The amount of merchandise received by the retailer during a period (at cost or retail value). The term is distinguished from "orders" that represent the amount contracted for delivery during a period but not necessarily received in that period.

Total Merchandise Handled. The sum of the beginning inventory plus purchases. It must be calculated at cost and, if the retail method of inventory is used, at retail also.

Cost of Merchandise Sold. The cost to the store of the merchandise that has been sold during the period covered by the operating statement. This figure is also called "cost of sales."

Gross Cost of Merchandise Sold. The cost of merchandise sold *before* adjustment for alteration costs and cash discounts earned on purchases. It is found by subtracting the closing inventory at cost from the total merchandise handled at cost.

Total Cost of Merchandise Sold. The cost of merchandise sold *after* adjustment for alteration costs and cash discounts earned, when they exist.

Alteration Costs. The cost incurred in altering and finishing merchandise to meet the needs of customers at the time of sale.

Net Alteration Costs. The difference between the cost the store incurs in performing the alterations and the amounts, if any, paid by the customers for this service. It is treated as an addition to the gross cost of merchandise sold.

Gross Margin. The difference between the sales and the total cost of merchandise sold. This figure is sometimes loosely called "gross profit" or "gross profit margin."

Gross Merchandise Margin. A synonym for gross margin.

Operating Expenses. Amounts disbursed or incurred in order to operate the business as distinct from outlays to finance the business. They include: (1) cash outlays for services provided the business during an accounting period, such as payroll, advertising, and rent, and (2) imputed expenses or actual charges made against the business for services received during the period but paid for either earlier or later.

A. PROFIT CALCULATIONS

1. Profit calculation — cost of sales known.

● *Example*:*

   A small grocery store had sales for the year of $100,000 and other income of $1,000 and its operating expenses were $28,000. Its cost of merchandise sold was $68,000. What was its gross margin, its operating profit, and its net profit in dollars? As percentages of net sales?

Solution:

Sales	$100,000
Cost of merchandise sold	68,000
Gross margin	$ 32,000
Expenses	28,000
Operating profit	$ 4,000
Other income	1,000
Net profit	$ 5,000

$$\text{Gross margin } \% = \frac{\$32,000}{\$100,000} = 32\%$$

$$\text{Operating profit } \% = \frac{\$4,000}{\$100,000} = 4\%$$

$$\text{Net profit } \% = \frac{\$5,000}{\$100,000} = 5\%$$

ASSIGNMENT 1:

   A small light hardware store in your town had sales last year of $50,000; cost of merchandise sold, $30,000 expenses, $12,500; and other income of $1,500.
   Find the net profit in dollars and in percentage.

DISCUSSION QUESTIONS:

   Is it possible to make an adequate profit (in dollars) on a volume of $50,000? What other information is necessary to determine whether the hardware store profits are adequate?

---

*Problems identified by this symbol ● are recommended for inclusion in an elementary course in retail merchandising. Those not so marked should be included in a more comprehensive course.

2. Computing cost of merchandise sold.[1]

● *Example:*

A specialty shop operator wants to compute his cost of merchandise sold for his fall and winter season. His figures are as follows:

Sales	$85,000
Opening inventory (cost)	24,000
Closing inventory (cost)	26,000
Purchases (cost)	50,000
Transportation charges on purchases	1,500
Alteration costs (net)	2,500
No cash discounts.	

Find total cost of merchandise sold and gross margin, both in dollars and as a percentage of sales.

Solution:

Sales		$85,000
Opening inventory at cost	$24,000	
Purchases at cost	50,000	
Transportation charges	1,500	
Total merchandise handled at cost	$75,500	
Closing inventory at cost	22,000	
Gross cost of merchandise sold	$53,500	
Alteration costs (net)	2,500	
Total cost of merchandise sold		56,000
Gross margin		$29,000

$$\text{Total cost of merchandise sold in \%} = \frac{\$56,000}{\$85,000} = 65.9\%$$

$$\text{Gross margin in \%} = \frac{\$29,000}{\$85,000} = 34.1\%$$

ASSIGNMENT 2:

Purchases (cost)	$24,000
Sales	40,000
Opening inventory (cost)	14,000
Closing inventory (cost)	7,000
Alteration costs (net)	500
Transportation charges	1,000

---

[1] The element of cash discounts earned on purchases is taken up in the next section.

Find (1) gross cost of merchandise sold in dollars and percentage, (2) total cost of merchandise sold in dollars and percentage, and (3) the gross margin in dollars and percentage.

DISCUSSION QUESTIONS:

Is not the gross margin found in the assignment above unusually low? How might it be explained?

3. Computing gross margin, operating profit, and net profit.

● *Example:*

A young woman purchased a children's wear store, taking over an inventory for which she paid $30,000. She also earmarked for the business some surplus capital, invested in securities. At the end of the first year the following additional figures were available:

Sales	$60,000
Closing inventory at cost.	33,000
Purchases at cost	40,000
Transportation charges	500
Gross alteration costs	1,500
Alteration receipts from customers	300
Operating expenses	15,300
Gross other income	2,000
Deductions from other income.	200

Find (1) gross margin, (2) operating profit, and (3) net profit.

Solution:

Sales		$60,000
Opening inventory at cost	$30,000	
Purchases at cost	40,000	
Transportation charges	500	
Total merchandises handled		
at cost	$70,500	
Closing inventory at cost	33,000	
Gross cost of merchandise		
sold	$37,500	
Gross alteration costs	$1,500	
Alteration receipts.	300	
Net alteration costs	1,200	
Total cost of merchandise		
sold		38,700
Gross margin	$21,300	35.5%

```
Operating expenses . . . . . . . . . . . . . . . . . . . . .    15,300
Operating profit . . . . . . . . . . . . . . . . . . . . . . .  $ 6,000    10.0%
Gross other income . . . . . . . . . . . . . .  $ 2,000
Deductions from other income . . . . . . .       200
Net other income . . . . . . . . . . . . . . . . . . . . . .    1,800
Net profit . . . . . . . . . . . . . . . . . . . . . . . . . . .  $ 7,800    13.0%
```

ASSIGNMENT 3:

During the year just ended, a store has achieved the following results:

1. Income: sales, $95,000; alteration receipts from customers, $3,000; other income, $2,100.
2. Outlays: purchases, $58,000; transportation charges, $900; alteration costs (gross), $3,500; operating expenses, $25,000; financial expenses (deductions from other income), $2,000.
3. Inventories at cost: beginning of year, $53,000; end of year, $49,000.

Find (a) gross margin, (b) operating profit, and (c) net profit. Express all three in dollars and in percentages.

DISCUSSION QUESTION:

For a men's shoe store shop, would you consider the above results to be outstanding, normal, or subnormal?

B. PERCENTAGE AND INDEX COMPARISONS

4. Sales expressed in dollars and as a percentage of the preceding year's volume.

● *Example:*

A midwestern supermarket reports a decrease in sales of 8.2% this year from the year before. If sales this year are $750,250, what were the sales last year?

Solution:

Let last year's sales = 100%

Sales this year = 100% − 8.2% = 91.8% = $750,250

$$1\% = \frac{\$750,250}{91.8} = \$8,172.65$$

100% = $817,265 = the sales last year

ASSIGNMENT 4:

A store reports an increase of 2.3% in sales this year over last year. Sales this year were $1,221,705. What were the sales last year?

DISCUSSION QUESTIONS:

Would you consider this an adequate increase for a store from last year? If yes, why? It not, why not? (Answer with reference to a particular type of store at the present time in your community.)

5. Comparing changes in ratio of sales with percentage increase or decrease in sales.

● *Example:*

If sales this year in a men's sportswear shop have increased 130% over last year, this year's sales are how many times last year's?

Solution:

Let 100% = last year's sales
Then this year's sales are 100%
+ 130%, or 230%
230/100 = 2.3
Thus, this year's sales are
2-3/10 times last year's

ASSIGNMENT 5:

1. If sales this year show an increase of 600% over 5 years ago, what is the relationship between the sales of the two years?
2. If sales this year are 10% less than last year, what percentage would they have to increase next year to just offset this year's decrease?

DISCUSSION QUESTION:

Discuss what could cause such a large increase in sales over the 5-year period, as (1) above in assignment 5.

6. Changing the base of comparison and changes in physical volume.

● *Example:*

An independent druggist has kept a record of the increases and decreases in his sales year by year, compared with the year before. His figures are as follows:

```
1968 . . . . . . . . . . . . . . . . . . . . +5%
1969 . . . . . . . . . . . . . . . . . . . +4%
1970 . . . . . . . . . . . . . . . . . . . . -2%
1971 . . . . . . . . . . . . . . . . . . . . -1%
```

He wishes to express the changes that have occurred in terms of a fixed base and for this purpose chooses 1967.

  1. Construct the sales index from 1967 through 1971.
  2. If the druggist's retail prices were 10% higher in 1971 than in 1967, what has been the change in the physical volume of his sales?

Solution:

  1.   Let 1967 sales = $100 = index of 100

       Then 1968 sales = $100 + 5% of $100 = $105
         = index of 105
       And 1969 sales = $105 + 4% of $105 = $109.2
         = index of 109.2
       And 1970 sales = $109.2 - 2% of 109.2
         = $107 = index of 107
       And 1971 sales = $107 - 1% of 107 = $105.9
         = index of 105.9

  2.   His index of sales in dollars for 1971 was 105.9, indicating that sales in dollars were 5.9% above the 1967 figure.

But prices were 10% higher. If they averaged $1.00 in 1967, they averaged $1.10 in 1971. The price index in 1971 was 110. Dividing the sales-in-dollars index of 105.9 by the price index of 110 gives 96.32, the index of physical volume. This means that in 1971 he sold 3.7% fewer goods than in 1967.

ASSIGNMENT 6:

  The following is a consumer price index for food in New York City based on the average prices for the first 3 years:

1st year 95.5		6th year 113.7	
2nd year 104.2		7th year 111.4	
3rd year 100.3		8th year 111.4	
4th year 101.3		9th year 110.7	
5th year 112.0		10th year 111.5	

  1. Express the food prices each year as a percentage of the price

level of the year before. In what year did the largest increase occur? The smallest increase? The largest decline?

2. If the index of dollar food sales in New York in the last year based on the average sales in the 3-year base period was 156.1, how much would physical volume of sales have increased above the base period?

DISCUSSION QUESTION:

Why does a store manager need to study price indexes and price changes?

Managerial Decision

Based on the trend of total consumer-goods prices over the past 10 years, suggest how this information might affect your current pricing policy.

7. Adjusting current inventory values to a former price level.

● *Example:*

The inventory at cost at the first of the year was $10,000 and at the end of the year, $15,400. But the wholesale prices for the type of goods in the inventory have risen 10% since the first of the year. What is the value of the closing inventory in terms of the price level at the first of the year? How much has the physical inventory increased?

Solution:

Let 100% = price level at the first of the year

Then 110% = price level at the end of the year

Dollar stock = price $\times$ physical quantity

Therefore, $15,400 (the dollar stock at the end of the year) = 110% of the quantity measured in terms of first-of-the year prices.

$15,400 ÷ 110% = $14,000, the closing inventory in terms of first-of-the-year prices.

Since the opening inventory was $10,000, there has been a 40% increase in the physical stock.

ASSIGNMENT 7:

A store's inventory at cost at the first of the year was $50,000 and at the end of the year $40,000. Wholesale prices had dropped 5% during the year. What is the value of the closing inventory in term's of the price level at the first of the year? How much has the physical volume increased or decreased?

DISCUSSION QUESTION:

What practical value is there in such a calculation?

ADDITIONAL ASSIGNMENTS

8. Sales $280,000
    Operating expenses 80,000
    Opening inventory at cost $400,000
    Closing inventory at cost 420,000
    Purchases at cost 190,000
    Find the cost of goods sold, gross margin, and operating profit.
9. Operating profit .... $ 10,000
    Operating expense 70,000
    Cost of merchandise sold 210,000
    Find: (a) Gross margin.
          (b) Sales.

10. The March 1970 sales index, based on the average daily sales 1957–59, is 137. The 1969 index for the same period was 117. What is the percentage of increase over 1969?

11. Sales indexes based on 1967–69 are as follows:

	This Year	Last Year
January	116	110
February	118	112
March	137	117

(a) For the 3-month period, what percentage are sales ahead of last year?

(b) If retail prices for the first quarter this year are 2% lower than last year, how does physical volume for the 3-month period compare with last year?

12. If retail prices for home furnishings are 25% higher than 5 years ago and if sales in this line are up 20% during the same period, what has been the change in physical volume of sales?

3   How to Figure Profits

Since profits are essential for business survival, it is important that every merchant understand how profits are figured and how changes in the different factors affect the final profit. The problems in this section are more detailed than those in section 2. They take into consideration a variety of specific transactions that are reflected in sales, cost of sales, and expenses.

A standard arrangement of the figures in a profit and loss statement is important so that one store may compare the details of its operation with those of other stores. Particular attention must be given to the difference between earnings from operations and financial earnings.

DEFINITIONS

Gross Sales. The sum of all prices charged customers during a period for goods purchased by them, before deductions for returns from and allowances to customers. Gross sales include cash sales, open account credit sales, revolving credit sales, and installment sales in both owned and leased departmental lines.

Returns from Customers. Cancellation of sales. The returns for a period measured by the retail value of goods returned by customers to the store and returned to stock. Even exchanges, in which a customer returns one article for another of the same value, are usually not included in either gross sales or returns. Uneven exchanges, however, are generally included in gross sales and in returns.

Allowances to Customers. Price reductions resulting in refunds to customers "after" the original sales were made.

Customer Return and Allowance Percentage. The sum of returns from customers and allowances to customers expressed as a percentage of the *gross* sales for the period.

Net Sales. The difference between the gross sales and returns from and allowances to customers during a specified period.

Gross Purchases (Cost). The billed cost of merchandise purchased during a period for resale, including special charges made by the sellers. Costs of transporting the goods to the store may be regarded either as a part of the gross purchase figure or as an addition to it.

Billed Cost. The invoice cost of purchases less trade and quantity discounts but without the deduction of cash discounts.

Returns to Vendors. The value of merchandise returned to manufacturers and wholesalers during a period.

Allowances from Vendors. The rebates and credits granted by manufacturers and wholesalers on purchases made by the store. They may reflect defects in merchandise, substitutions, declines in wholesale prices, and payments for promotional services to be performed by the retailer.

Promotional Allowances. An amount granted to the store by the wholesale seller to cover all or part of the store's cost of advertising or otherwise promoting the sale of the merchandise to the consumer. If the store is allowed to deduct the allowance from the face of the invoice without giving any assurance that it will use the allowance, the allowance is simply a form of trade or quantity discount. Otherwise it may be treated as a credit to promotional expense and not be credited to the cost of the merchandise.

Consignment Purchases. Vendor's merchandise that is received into a retail stock under an arrangement whereby the store has the right to return to the vendor any portion of the lot unsold within a specified period. Consignment purchases are generally treated as a part of the store's purchase and inventory figures.

Landed Cost. The cost of imported goods at the port of entry (sometimes at the store). It includes foreign cost in dollars; rail, ocean freight, and cartage; insurance; commissionaires' fees; duty; brokerage; entry fee; and other direct costs necessary to land the merchandise.

Transfer In. Value of merchandise procured "from" another department or another unit of a chain or branch store system rather than an outside vendor.

Transfer Out. Value of merchandise conveyed "to" another department or unit of a chain or branch store system. It is not a sale in that it is not a source of profit.

Inventory. The goods on hand at a specified accounting date. The term may apply either to the physical goods or to the value at the time of an accounting.

Cost Method of Inventory. The calculation of the value of an inventory by first determining the original cost price of each item or group of items. Cost codes on price tickets are commonly used for this purpose but serial or reference numbers attached to the goods may allow the determination of cost from other records. The original cost prices may be depreciated if the current market value is deemed to be less than the original cost. Also, the cost of transporting the inventory to the store may be estimated and added to the value of the inventory.

Retail Method of Inventory. A method of determining the cost or market value of an inventory by listing and totaling the goods on hand at current retail prices and translating this retail value to "cost."

Costing Sales. Recording the cost price of each item sold on the sales record so that a continuous cost of merchandise sold figure may be available as well as a record of retail sales.

Cash Discounts Earned. The discounts for prompt payment of purchases earned on the goods sold during a period.

Stock Alterations. The cost of altering and renovating goods in stock as distinct from goods ordered by customers. The cost of the work on stock is to be treated as a part of the cost purchase figure, not as a part of alteration and workroom costs.

Maintained Markup. The difference between the net sales and the gross cost of merchandise sold. It is the margin on sales before making adjustments for cash discounts earned and alteration costs.

Net Cost of Merchandise Sold. The gross cost of merchandise sold less the cash discounts earned. It is the same as net cost of sales.

Total Cost of Merchandise Sold. The net cost of merchandise sold plus net alteration and workroom costs. It is the same as total cost of sales.

Direct Expenses. Expenses incurred separately for the benefit of a department within a store. They can be assigned to departments directly and immediately without the intervention of any element of judgment. Direct expenses common to most departmentized stores are selling payroll, salaries of buyer and assistants, newspaper and shopping news space costs, and delivery charges made by a consolidated delivery service for packages delivered for each department.[1] Normally, these four classes of direct expense total about 40% of the store's total expenses. Other expenses may also be directly charged to departments; these include interest on the merchandise investment, supplies consumed, buyers' traveling expenses, and even a rental for space occupied.

Indirect Expense. Expenses incurred for the benefit of the store as a whole or for a group of departments. They are often charged to the selling departments on a logical basis but many stores charge direct expenses only against the departments, determining a controllable margin or contribution for each. These departmental margins are totaled, and the indirect expenses are deducted to determine the whole store's operating profit.

Controllable Margin. The difference between the gross margin and the direct departmental expenses over which the department manager has a degree of control. It is calculated first for each department and totaled for the store. See Direct Expenses. Also called "controllable profit," "semi-net profit," and "department contribution."

---

[1] The annual Merchandising and Operating Results for Department and Specialty Stores (National Retail Merchants Association) follows this plan.

Imputed Interest. A figure for interest expense calculated by applying to the value of major assets a standard rate of interest, such as 6%. It is thus the equivalent of interest on both owned and borrowed funds invested in the business. The charge to expense for imputed interest is credited to "other income" and the interest actually paid or payable on borrowings is deducted from "other income" and not treated as an operating expense.

Note: This practice of imputing interest is not generally followed in retail store accounting, but it is becoming a standard practice to exclude interest paid or payable from operating expenses and to include it as a deduction "from other income." Thus, interest on borrowed moneys does not affect operating expenses but does reduce net profits.

EXAMPLE OF A PROFIT AND LOSS STATEMENT*

	Cash		*Percentage*
Gross sales		$110,000	
Less returns and allowances		10,000	9.09
Net sales		$100,000	100.00
Cost of Sales			
Inventory — first of period		20,000	
Gross purchases (billed cost)	$73,000		
Less returns and allowances	4,000		
Net purchases.		69,000	
Transportation charges on purchases		1,000	
Total merchandise handled		$90,000	
Inventory — end of period.		25,000	
Gross cost of merchandise sold		65,000	65.0
Cash discounts earned		3,000	3.0
Net cost of merchandise sold		62,000	62.0
Net alteration and workroom costs		1,000	1.0
Total merchandise costs		$63,000	63.0
Margin and Expenses			
Gross margin			
($100,000 – $63,000)		$37,000	37.0
Operating expenses		30,000	30.0
Operating profit		$ 7,000	7.0
Other income			
Miscellaneous other income	2,000		
Deductions from other income† . .	1,000	1,000	1.0
Net profit before Federal			
income tax		$ 8,000	8.0

*Reprinted from *Retail Merchandise Management*, by John W. Wingate, Elmer O. Schaller, and Leonard Miller. Englewood Cliffs, N.J.: Prentice-Hall, Inc., 1972.

†This figure includes interest on borrowed funds paid or payable.

A. ELEMENTS IN OPERATING PROFIT

1. Gross and net sales.

● *Example:*

Last year, the rug department in a high-class chain department store recorded sales of $600,000. But $50,000 worth of rugs at retail were returned by customers. Furthermore, because of various complaints, $2,000 was refunded to cash customers and $8,000 was credited to the accounts of charge customers.

Find the net sales and the percentage of returns and allowances.

Solution:

Gross sales		$600,000
Returns from customers	$50,000	
Allowances to customers	10,000	60,000
Net sales		$540,000

$$\text{Returns and allowances } \% = \frac{\$60,000}{\$600,000} = 10\% \text{ of gross sales}$$

ASSIGNMENT 1:

Net sales	$54,000
Returns from customers	5,000
Allowances to customers	1,000

Find (1) gross sales and (2) the returns and allowances percentage.

2. Computing net sales.

Example:

The gross sales, as totaled from sales checks during a month, are $10,000. During the period, goods sold originally at $800 are returned, with customers receiving full refunds (or credits to their account) of the original purchase prices.

During this period, customers also returned goods they bought for $200, but for which they received refunds or credits of only $150, because the goods were selling at a lower price at the time of the refund. These goods were put into stock at a total of $150. Furthermore, customers were granted refunds of $100 on goods that had to be put into stock "as is" at $60. Still others complained about poor wear of goods and received allowances of $120 even though they did not return the goods in question. Find the net sales.

Solution:

Gross sales		$10,000
Returns *A*	$800	
Returns *B*	150	
Returns *C*	100*	
Allowances	120	
Total returns and allowances . . .		1,170
Net sales		$ 8,830

*Markdowns were taken for $40 *after* goods were returned to stock at $100.

ASSIGNMENT 2:

In a shoe department, gross sales, except for one unrecorded transaction, explained below, are $5,000. Returns, except for the transaction in question, are $300.

The unrecorded transaction involves the exchange, but not the original sale, of a $30 pair of shoes. The customer complained that the shoes had failed to give satisfactory wear and the store granted her a new $30 pair at half price. The old shoes had no resale value, but were taken back so that the store laboratory could test them. What are the gross sales and net sales figures?

3. Applying the percentage of returns and allowances.

● *Example:*

According to reports, a store last year had net sales of $75,000 and its returns and allowances from customers were 15% of gross sales. Find (a) the gross sales, and (b) the returns and allowances in dollars.

Solution:

Let   100% = gross sales
and   15% = the returns and allowances
Then   85% = the net sales
$$85\% = \$75,000$$
$$1\% = \frac{\$75,000}{85} = \$882.35$$
$$100\% = \$882.35 \times \$100 = \$88,235 = \text{gross sales}$$
15% of $88,235 = $13,235, the returns and allowances in dollars

ASSIGNMENT 3:

> Net sales in a novelty shop are $54,000; returns, 10%; and allowances, 2%. What are the store's gross sales, its dollar returns, and its dollar allowances?

DISCUSSION QUESTION:

> Discuss whether this is a high rate of return. Would this be true if this were a women's dress operation rather than a novelty goods shop?

Managerial Decision

What managerial steps should be taken to help reduce the returns and allowances in any department within a store?

4. Computing purchases (all figures at cost).

● *Example:*

Gross purchases from domestic vendors	$50,000
Returns to domestic vendors	3,000
Allowances from domestic vendors	1,000
Landed cost of imports (net)	5,000
Transfers into the department from other departments . . .	4,000
Transfers out of the department to other departments	
or for expense purposes	7,000
Manufacturers' excise taxes charged to the store	100
Charges made the store by manufacturers for	
containers and for "prepacked" goods	60
Transportation charges on incoming goods paid by store. . .	300
Stock alterations	200

Find the total cost purchase figure.

Solution:

Gross purchases from vendors	$50,000
Other charges made by vendors (excise taxes,	
containers)	160
	$50,160
Returns and allowances	4,000
Net domestic purchases	$46,160
Foreign purchases	5,000
Net transfers − out ($7,000 − $4,000)	−3,000
Transportation charges	300
Stock alterations	200
Total purchases	$48,660

ASSIGNMENT 4:

A department shows the following figures at cost:

Gross purchases	$8,000
Returns to vendors	400
Rebates from vendors	100
Freight inward	100
Transfers in	500
Transfers out	450

Find total cost purchases.

DISCUSSION QUESTIONS:

What problems appear in transfers from one department to another department or from central store to branch? How can they be controlled?

5. Adjustments in cost of sales — maintained markup or gross margin.

● *Example:*

The net sales of a dress shop are $200,000. The cost of altering garments is $5,000, of which $3,000 is collected from customers. Expenses, not including the above, are $70,000. Cash discounts earned during the period are $6,000, purchases at cost $140,000, opening inventory at cost $40,000, and closing inventory at cost $50,000. Find the gross margin, maintained markup, and operating profit.

Solution:

Net sales		$200,000
Opening inventory	$ 40,000	
Purchases	140,000	
Total merchandise handled	$180,000	
Closing inventory	50,000	
Gross cost of merchandise sold	$130,000	
Less cash discounts earned	6,000	
Net cost of merchandise sold	$124,000	
Alteration costs	$5,000	
Less receipts	3,000	
Net alteration costs	2,000	
Total merchandise costs		126,000
Gross margin		$ 74,000
Expenses		70,000
Operating profit		$ 4,000

Maintained markup: sales – gross cost of merchandise sold =
$200,000 – $130,000 = $70,000

ASSIGNMENT 5:

From the following data, compute the cost of sales, the percentages of
maintained markup, gross margin, and operating profit:

Beginning inventory at cost	$30,000
Cash discounts earned	300
Net alteration costs	100
Purchases at cost	15,000
Ending inventory at cost	25,000
Sales	45,000
Expenses	4,000

DISCUSSION QUESTION:

Would maintained markup always be greater or could it be less than the
gross margin?

6. Relationship between gross margin and maintained markup.

● *Example:*

Gross margin	$4,000
Cash discounts earned	200
Alteration costs	125

Find the maintained markup.

Solution:

Maintained markup = gross margin – cash discounts earned + alteration
costs = $4,000 – $200 + $125 = $3,925

ASSIGNMENT 6:

1. Operating expense	$80,000
Operating loss	8,000
Alteration costs	3,000
Cash discounts earned	10,000

Find the gross margin and the maintained markup.

2. Maintained markup $50,000
   Cash discounts earned   5,000
   Alteration costs   1,000
   Expenses   29,000

Find gross margin and operating profit.

DISCUSSION QUESTION:

What is the relationship between the maintained markup and the gross margin and why is each important to the business?

7. Deferring profit on installment sales.

● *Example:*

An installment jeweler's sales were $250,000 for this year, of which only $50,000 was for cash. His gross margin on sales was 35%. Of the $200,000 installment sales, only $140,000 was collected during the year and $60,000 was still outstanding. Last year a reserve of $18,000 was set up for unrealized margin on installment sales. What adjustment should be made in this year's gross margin?

Solution:

Gross margin on all sales (35% of $250,000) $87,500
Less new reserve (35% of $60,000) . . . .   −21,000
Plus old reserve . . . .   +18,000
   Adjusted gross margin $84,500

(This solution should be checked against current Internal Revenue Service regulations)

ASSIGNMENT 7:

A clothing merchant sells largely on a 40-weeks-to-pay basis. His gross margin on all sales last year was 33-1/3% and this year, 32% of total sales of $45,000. His receivables at the end of last year were $15,000 and at the end of this year, $14,000. Find the adjusted gross margin for this year.

DISCUSSION QUESTION:

When is a profit really earned: when the sale is made or when payment is received?

Managerial Decision

A jeweler is tightening up his credit policy and expects to decrease his outstanding accounts at the end of the year. He has never deferred profits on installment sales. Income tax rates are going up. Would this be a good time to start?

8. Controllable margin (profit).

● *Example:*

The following figures are. available for a toy department:

Sales...................................	$100,000
Sales per square foot of selling space.............	$80.
Average inventory at cost....................	$13,000
Gross margin	35.4%
Newspaper advertising costs	2.2%
Selling salaries	6.9
Buyer and assistant salaries	3.5
Delivery services purchased	3.6
Rent and other space charges	6.0
Other "overhead"	12.0

Find:

1. Controllable margin as a percentage of sales and in dollars
2. Controllable margin per square foot of selling space
3. Controllable margin per dollar of cost inventory.
4. Operating profit in percentage and in dollars.

Solution:

1. Gross margin		35.4%
Direct expenses		
Newspaper costs	2.2%	
Selling salaries......................	6.9	
Buyer salaries	3.5	
Delivery	3.6	16.2
Controllable margin.....................		19.2%
		or $19,200

Note: Some stores include rent as a direct expense.

2. $100,000 ÷ $80 = 1,250, the number of square feet
                        occupied.

    $19,200 ÷ 1,250 = $15.36, the controllable margin per
                        square foot of selling space.

3. $19,200 ÷ $13,000 = $1.48, the controllable margin per dollar
                        of cost inventory.

4.   19.2% - (6.0% + 12.0%) = 1.2%, or $1,200, the operating profit.

ASSIGNMENT 8:

A major household appliance department has sales of $600,000, sales
per square foot of selling space of $150., and average cost inventory of
$100,000. Its gross margin is 22.4%; its newspaper costs, 2.2%; its
selling salaries, 5.6%; its buyers' salaries, 1.7%; its direct delivery
expenses, 2.2%; and other joint expenses charged to the department,
10%. Find:

1. The controllable margin in percentage of sales and in dollars.
2. The controllable margin per square foot of selling space.
3. The controllable margin per dollar of cost inventory investment.
4. Its operating profit or loss in percentage and in dollars.

DISCUSSION QUESTIONS:

1. Who controls a controllable margin and why is it so called?
2. Is it proper to include in direct expenses chargeable to the
   department any of the following: cost of space occupied, interest
   on the average merchandise investment, portion of the expenses
   of the merchandise office, portion of the expenses of the
   adjustment bureau?

9. Leased departments: standard accounting

Example:

The selling departments owned and operated by a store had total net
sales one year of $6,000,000 on which a gross margin of 35% was
realized. The store also had a number of leased departments whose net
sales totaled $500,000. On these sales, the store retained a commission
of 15%, paying the rest to the lessors.

Calculate the store's gross margin on all sales, including the leased
departments, in both dollars and percentage.

Solution:

Gross margin of owned departments	
(35% × $6,000,000)	$2,100,000
Gross margin of leased departments	
(15% × $500,000)	75,000
Total gross margin	$2,175,000
Gross margin % total sales	
($2,175,000 / $6,500,000)	33.5%

ASSIGNMENT 9:

A store's total sales are $10,000,000, of which 10% repesents leased-department operation. The total merchandise costs of the owned departments are calculated to be $5,760,000. Of the leased-department sales, the store retained $140,00 as commissions.

Calculate the gross margin on all sales, including leased departments.

B. OTHER INCOME

10. Other income — elementary problem.

● *Example:*

A small, incorporated department store's net sales for a year are $300,000 and its total merchandise costs $220,000. Its expenses are $75,000. During the year, the store received $5,000 in dividends and interest from outside investments and paid out $1,000 interest on borrowed money, not included in the expense figure above. What is the store's operating profit, other income, and net profit before Federal income tax?

Solution:

Net sales		$300,000
Total merchandise costs		220,000
Gross margin		$ 80,000
Expenses		75,000
Operating profit		$ 5,000
Other income:		
Income from outside investments	5,000	
Deductions from other income	1,000	
Net other income		4,000
Net profit before Federal tax		$ 9,000

ASSIGNMENT 10:

The gross margin is $40,000, operating expenses are $31,000, the financial earnings from outside and miscellaneous sources are $4,000, and the financial expenses including interest are $1,000. Find the operating profit, the other income, and the net profit.

DISCUSSION QUESTIONS:

Is it possible that the other income would be larger than the operating profit? If so, can you explain when and why this might be true?

11. Other income — composite problem.

Example:

From the following data, find the operating profit and net profit:

Gross purchases at cost	$250,000
Opening inventory at cost	125,000
Closing inventory at cost	115,000
Transportation charges	1,000
Returns to manufacturers at cost	2,500
Cash discounts earned on purchases	12,000
Gross alteration costs	800
Alteration receipts from customers	300
Gross sales	450,000
Returns from customers, including allowance	30,000
Salaries and wages	60,000
Advertising expenses	12,000
Rent	10,000
Imputed interest expense	8,000
Supplies consumed	4,000
Miscellaneous operating expenses	16,000
Income from investments	5,000
Income from carrying charges to customers on installment and deferred credit accounts	4,000
Interest actually paid out	2,000

Solution:

Gross sales		$450,000
Less returns from customers		30,000
Net sales		420,000
Opening inventory		$125,000
Gross purchases	$250,000	
Less returns	2,500	
Net purchases	$247,500	
Transportation charges	1,000	
Total purchases		$248,500

Total merchandise handled	373,500	
Closing inventory	115,000	
Gross cost of merchandise sold	$258,500	
Cash discounts earned	12,000	
Net cost of merchandise sold		$246,500
Gross alteration costs $800		
Less alteration receipts 300		500
Total merchandise costs		$247,000
Gross margin		$173,000

Operating expenses:

Salaries and wages	$ 60,000	
Advertising	12,000	
Rent.	10,000	
Interest computed	8,000	
Supplies consumed	4,000	
Other	16,000	
Less income from carrying charges	4,000	
Total		106,000
Operating profit		$ 67,000

Other income:

Imputed interest credit	$ 8,000	
Miscellaneous other income		
(Income from investments)	5,000	
Total	$ 13,000	
Less deductions (interest)	2,000	
Net other income		$ 11,000
Net profit		$ 78,000

Note: The practice of imputing an interest expense figure on major assets, particularly merchandise inventory and accounts receivable, is not the standard practice but some stores feel it is a useful device to help control the investment.

In regard to carrying charges on installment and deferred accounts, the former generally accepted practice was to treat them as "other income," but they are now commonly credited to expense, the expense of the credit operation.

ASSIGNMENT 11:

A men's store shows the following figures for a year:

Returns and allowances to customers	$ 12,000
Purchases of merchandise at billed cost	200,000
Merchandise returned to vendors at cost	17,500
Opening inventory at cost.	22,300
Inward freight, cartage, and express	1,000

Gross sales	275,000
Closing inventory at cost	18,100
Cash discounts earned	5,200
Net alteration costs	4,600
Expenses for store, not incl. interest	56,400
Income from carrying charges on credit transactions	2,000
Income from outside securities	4,800
Net income from carrying charges on installment sales	2,100
Unclaimed salaries and cash	300
Interest paid on borrowed funds	2,200

What are the percentages of gross margin, operating profit, and net profit?

DISCUSSION QUESTION:

Why are alteration costs not fully covered by alteration charges in the illustrative problem?

Managerial Decision

Why is interest paid out or payable not included with store expenses as it is in many industries? Could it be so included without affecting the net profit figure in any way?

ADDITIONAL ASSIGNMENTS

12. The figures for the year on the operating statement of a store were as follows: net sales, $500,000; operating expenses, $232,000; gross margin, $244,000; net other income, $3,2000. On what amount does the store have to calculate Federal income tax?

13. Expenses, $20,000; operating profit, $4,000; cash discounts, $3,000; alteration costs, $600; gross cost of merchandise sold, $51,500; returns from and allowances to customers, $6,000. Find gross margin, maintained markup, net sales, and gross sales.

14. Gross sales, $95,000; returns, 8.0%; allowances, 1.6%. Find the net sales.

15. Net sales, 5% below last year; gross sales, 8% below; returns and allowances to customers last year, 6%. Find the percentage of returns and allowances to customers this year.

16. A men's department with sales of $250,000 has buying expenses of 6%, direct selling expenses of 8%, advertising expenses of 7%, delivery expenses of 2.5%, and other expenses prorated to the department of 10%. Its gross margin is 35%. Find the department's controllable margin; its operating profit.

17. A chain has net sales of $1,460,500 and total merchandise costs of $766,740. The expenses and other income are itemized as follows:

Salaries and wages	$216,037
Tenancy costs, except rental on owned real estate	85,326
Light, water, and power	11,228
Depreciation on fixtures and equipment	8,252
Supplies	10,500
Property taxes	12,900
Imputed interest	18,200
Interest paid on borrowed capital including mortgage	4,300
Interest and dividends received	1,425
Miscellaneous operating expenses	23,900
Profits from outside investments in real estate	10,500
Carrying charges on certain credit transactions	8,500
Miscellaneous revenue	500

Prepare a profit and loss statement (1) with interest imputed; (2) without imputing interest.

Part II   PRICING

If the buyer is actually in the process of selecting merchandise, he has a number of arithmetical processes to perform:

1. He must be able to calculate the markup percentage.
2. He must be able to calculate the retail price to place on his proposed purchases — when he knows the cost and the predetermined necessary markup percentage
3. He must be able to calculate how much to pay for goods after he has estimated what they will sell for or after he has calculated his open-to-buy at retail.

A. CALCULATING MARKUP

DEFINITIONS

Retail. The price at which goods are offered for sale. In practice, there may be three different retail prices: (1) the original retail price placed on goods when first purchased; (2) the current retail price of goods in stock, which may be more or less than the original retail if the price has been changed; and (3) the sales retail, the price at which the sale is actually made, after markdowns, if any.

Cost. The price at which goods are purchased in the wholesale market. Technically, this includes the billed cost and the transportation cost. The billed cost is the amount asked or charged by the seller without the deduction of cash discounts. Transportation cost is the amount charged the store for delivery of goods, including insurance. This charge may be made either by the seller or by a transportation company. When the seller absorbs any cost of transportation, in the billed price, and delivers the goods without separate charge to the buyer, there is no separate transportation cost.

Thus, if goods are bought for $1.00 with a 2% cash discount and a transportation cost of 5 cents, the cost is $1.05. In practice, when the transportation cost is very small in relation to the billed cost, or when the transportation cost is not known at the time of purchase, the buyer regards the billed cost as the cost. When transportation costs are considerable, however, they should be added to the billed cost, for the standard practice in calculating markup on the aggregate purchases of a store or of a department is to include transportation costs in the cost.[1]

Markup. The difference between the cost and the retail price of merchandise. In equation form: Markup = Retail − Cost. If an article is offered for sale at $1.00 and cost 65 cents, the markup is 35 cents. When the term markup is used in this book, it is (unless otherwise specified) the initial markup, which is the difference between the original retail price placed on purchases and the cost.

Markup Percentage on Retail. The markup divided by retail. In equation form, it is $\frac{\text{Markup}}{\text{Retail}}$. If retail is $1.00, cost 65 cents, and markup 35 cents, the markup percentage is $\frac{\$.35}{\$1.00} = 35\%$. The term, percentage *of* retail, means the same as percentage *on* retail.

Complement of the Markup. The cost price as a percentage of the retail. It may be calculated as 100% minus the markup percentage on retail. Thus, if the markup is 35%, the complement is 65%.

Markup Percentage on Cost. The markup divided by the cost. In equation form, it is $\frac{\text{Markup}}{\text{Cost}}$. If retail is $1.00, cost 65 cents, and markup 35 cents, the markup percentage is $\frac{\$.35}{\$.65} = 53.8\%$. Markup percentage on cost is higher than markup percentage on retail. The generally accepted plan is to express markup on retail, even though markup percentage on cost is the older method.

Note: In all problems in this book, markup is expressed as a percentage on retail, unless there is a specific statement to the effect that it is a percentage of cost.

Supplement of the Markup. The retail as a percentage of the cost. It is calculated as 100% plus the markup percentage on cost. Thus, the supplement of 53.8% is 153.8%.

A Job Lot. An assortment of goods of different qualities and values, all offered at a single, reduced price.

Basic models

The most important concept in the area of learning how to determine markup is simply and clearly represented in the following basic model:

---

[1] Some retail organizations continue to treat transportation as an expense rather than as a part of the cost.

	$	%		$	%
Retail		100	Retail		
Markup			Markup		
Cost			Cost		100

to be used for calculations   to be used for calculations
with markup on retail   with markup on cost

The basic model can be used to find cost in dollars or percentages, to find markup in dollars or percentages, or to find retail in dollars or percentages. The model is very easy to use. For example, one immediately knows the percentage value of one cell when he knows whether the markup is calculated on cost or retail. (If the basis of the markup is not given, it is assumed to be on retail.) If the markup is on retail, 100 is put in the % column and the retail row. With two other cell values, one can fill in all other cells. A sample problem follows on the next page.

Example:

The billed-cost figure on an invoice is $400. The transportation cost is $8.00. The cash discount allowed is $25.00 and the retail value of the invoice is $510. What is the markup percentage on retail on the invoice?

Solution:

Using the basic model, the steps are:

1. Fill in 100 in the % column and the retail row. (Markup is to be on retail as stated.)
2. The dollar amount of $510 (retail) is filled in.
3. The dollar amount of $408 (cost) is filled in.
4. Find cost as a percentage of retail by dividing $408 by $510, or 80%.
5. After filling in this cell, one subtracts 80% from 100% to get the markup percentage of retail of 20%.
6. To get the dollar amount of markup, one either multiplies $510 by 20% or subtracts $408 from $510

		$	%				
							0.80
Retail	(2)	510	100	(1)		(4)	510 ⟌408.00
Markup	(6)	102	20	(5)	or	(6)	$510
Cost	(3)	408	80	(4)			0.20
							$102.00

1. Basis for markup.

● *Example:*

The billed-cost figure on an invoice is $342; the transportation charges to the store, $8.00; the cash discount allowed, $25.60; and the total retail value of the invoice, $540. What is the markup percentage secured on the invoice?

Solution:

Retail		$540
Billed cost	$342	
Transportation	8	350
Markup		$190

Markup percentage on retail: $190 ÷ $540 = 35.2%
Markup percentage on cost: $190 ÷ $350 = 54.3%

Note: The cash discount of $25.60 is not subtracted from the billed cost of $350.

ASSIGNMENT 1:

If goods cost $24.00 a dozen, with $2.40 a dozen transportation cost, and are marked $3.00 each, what is the markup percentage on retail? On cost?

DISCUSSION QUESTION:

What is the highest possible markup percentage: (1) of retail? (2) of cost?

TABLE OF MARKUP EQUIVALENTS

Markup % on Cost	Markup % on Retail
5.3	5.0
10.0	9.1
11.1	10.0
14.3	12.5
15.0	13.0
17.6	15.0
20.0	16-2/3
25.0	20.0
30.0	23.1

TABLE OF MARKUP EQUIVALENTS (cont.)

Markup % on Cost	Markup % on Retail
33-1/3	25.0
40.0	28.6
42.8	30.0
50.0	33-1/3
60.0	37.5
66-2/3	40.0
75.0	42.9
100.0	50.0
150.0	60.0
300.0	75.0
400.0	80.0

2. Calculating cost when retail and markup percentage on retail are known.

● *Example:*

A buyer inspects a woman's dress in the manufacturer's show room and estimates that it should retail for $17.50. He needs a markup of 42% on retail. How much may he pay for the dress?

Solution:

Dollars: $17.50
Equation: Cost + Markup = Retail
Percentages: 58 +   42   = 100
Since 100% = $17.50, Cost = 58% of $17.50 = $10.15

Alternate Solution:

Formula: Cost = Retail × (100% – Markup %)
Cost = $17.50 × (100% – 42%) = $17.50 × 58% = $10.15

ASSIGNMENT 2:

A buyer's planned purchases at retail are $21,600 for March and the planned markup for his department is 41%. What are his planned purchases at cost?

DISCUSSION QUESTION:

Is it better to plan an average markup percentage for a classification of goods or is it better to plan the individual markup percentage by item?

3. Calculating retail when cost and markup percentage on retail are known.

● *Example:*

A novelty is quoted by the manufacturer at $1.50 and the markup that a buyer needs in order to realize a fair profit is 40% on retail. At what retail price should he mark the novelty to obtain the desired markup?

Solution:

$$\text{Formula:} \quad \text{Retail} = \frac{\text{Cost}}{100\% - M\%}$$

$$\text{Retail} = \frac{\$1.50}{100\% - 40\%} = \frac{\$1.50}{60\%} = \$2.50$$

ASSIGNMENT 3:

A hat costing $6.00 is to be given a markup of 40% of retail. What should the retail be?

DISCUSSION QUESTION:

What factors in addition to planned markup should be considered in pricing the $6.00 hat?

4. Calculating cost and retail when markup on retail is known.

Example:

A buyer tells you that he realized a markup of $100 on a television set. You know that his markup is 25% of retail. What did the television set cost him?

Solution:

Dollars: $100
Equation: Cost + Markup = Retail
Percentages: (75) +   25   = 100
25% of Retail = $100
  1% of Retail = $4
75% of Retail = $4 × 75 = $300, the cost

Alternate Solution:

$$\text{Retail} = \frac{\$M}{M\%} = \frac{\$100}{25\%} = \$400$$

$$\text{Cost} = \text{Retail} - \text{Markup} = \$400 - \$100 = \$300$$

ASSIGNMENT 4:

The markup percentage of retail is 37-1/2% and the dollar markup is $20.00. Find the cost.

DISCUSSION QUESTION:

What is the advantage to having a good understanding of the markup percentage in a department instead of simply cost and retail?

5. Calculating retail when cost and markup percentage cost are known.

● *Example:*

A buyer was offered a refrigerator at $85 cost and he needs a markup of 42.8% of cost. What retail will provide the desired markup?

Solution:

Dollars: $85
Equation: Cost + Markup = Retail
Percentages: 100 + 42.8 = 142.8
100% = $85
142.8% of Cost ($85) = Retail or $121.38

Alternate Solution:

Formula: Retail = Cost $\times$ (100% + M%)
Retail = $85 $\times$ (100% +42.8%)
= $85 $\times$ 142.8% = $121.38

ASSIGNMENT 5:

Men's shirts cost $36.00 a dozen and are to be marked up 66-2/3% of cost. Find the retail per unit.

DISCUSSION QUESTION:

Is it easier to apply a cost percentage to a cost price than to divide the cost by the complement of the markup?

6. Calculating cost when retail and markup percentage on cost are known.

● *Example:*

A store wishes to offer children's hosiery at 69 cents per pair retail. The buyer needs a markup of 65% of cost. How much can he afford to pay?

Solution:

Dollars: $.69
Equation: Cost + Markup = Retail
Percentages: 100   65   (165)
165% of Cost = $.69

$$1\% \text{ of Cost} = \frac{\$.69}{165} = \$.00418$$

100% = 100 × $.00418 = $.42

Alternate Solution:

$$\text{Formula:} \quad \text{Cost} = \frac{R}{100\% + M\%}$$

$$\text{Cost} = \frac{\$.69}{165\%} = \$.42$$

ASSIGNMENT 6:

The open-to-buy in a department for the balance of June is $45,000 at retail and the planned markup for this department is 66-2/3% of cost. What is the open-to-buy at cost?

DISCUSSION QUESTION:

Is it more difficult to divide the retail by the supplement of the markup on cost than to multiply the retail by the complement of the markup on retail?

7. Calculating cost and retail when markup on cost is known.

● *Example:*

A store obtains a markup of $1.50 per shirt on a line on which the markup on cost is 50%. Find the cost and retail per shirt.

Solution:

Dollars: $1.50
Equation: Cost + Markup = Retail
Percentages: 100 +   50   (150)
50% of Cost = $1.50

$$1\% \text{ of Cost} = \frac{\$1.50}{50} = \$.03$$

100% of Cost = 100 × $.03 = $3.00
Retail = 150% of $3.00 = $4.50

Alternate Solution:

$$\text{Formula:} \quad \text{Cost} = \frac{\$M}{M\%} = \frac{\$1.50}{50\%} = \$3.00$$

$$\text{Retail} = \text{Cost} + \text{Markup} = \$3.00 + \$1.50 = \$4.50$$

ASSIGNMENT 7:

> Markup % on cost 75%
> $ Markup. $30
> Find retail.

DISCUSSION QUESTION:

How does assignment 7 differ from assignment 4?

8. Computing markup on cost when markup on retail is known.

● *Example:*

A buyer goes to work for a store in which markup is planned as a percentage of retail and the figure set for his department is 40%. But this buyer is accustomed to use markup percentages on cost. He wishes to convert his goal figure to the cost basis so that it will be more convenient for him to use it while buying.

Solution:

> Let 100% = Retail
> Markup = 40% of Retail
> Cost = 100% − 40% ·= 60%
>
> $$\text{Markup on cost} = \frac{40\%}{60\%} = 66\text{-}2/3\%$$

ASSIGNMENT 8:

The markup percentage in a grocery store is 22% of retail. What is this figure as a percentage of cost?

DISCUSSION QUESTION:

When is it helpful to be able to convert from markup on retail to markup on cost?

9. Computing markup on retail when markup on cost is known.

● *Example:*

A buyer of aprons is accustomed to mark up his goods 50% of cost and wants to compare this figure with that of a store in which markup is figured on retail.

Solution:

Let 100% = Cost
Retail = Cost + Markup or 100% + 50% = 150%
Markup on retail = $\dfrac{50\%}{150\%}$ = 33-1/3%

ASSIGNMENT 9:

A markup of 40% of cost is equivalent to what percentage on retail?

DISCUSSION QUESTION:

In moving up the markup scale, why does the markup on retail as a percentage increase more slowly than markup on cost?

Managerial Decisions

1. A merchant bases his markup percentage on cost rather than on retail. He defends this practice on the grounds that once the goods are purchased, the cost of that particular lot of merchandise remains constant although he may change the retail price frequently. Do you feel that stability of the markup basis is a convincing reason for adopting the same method in your store? Why?

2. What does a merchant gain by figuring markup as a percentage in view of the fact that expenses (which the markup must be adequate to cover) are paid in dollars?

B. PLANNING MARKUP

In every store or merchandise department, it is desirable to plan an initial markup to be used as a guide to check against the aggregate markup obtained in actual pricing. This planning is generally done on a 6-month or an annual basis. The initial markup should be high enough not only to cover all expenses and a profit, but also to allow for price reductions and alteration costs that are likely to occur as the season progresses.

Thus, to plan initial markup, it is necessary first to plan the probable expenses for the season, the profit goal, the probable reductions, the forecasted alteration costs, and the probable sales. But this markup must be expressed as a percentage, not of *sales*, but rather of the aggregate *original retail price* at which the goods are to be offered for sale. This is the same as sales plus reductions. For example, if sales are planned at $10,000 and reductions at $500, the goods, eventually to be sold for $10,000, must be introduced into stock at $10,500 and the markup needed must be expressed as a percentage of this total. Expenses plus profits equal gross margin, and if there are no cash discounts or alteration costs involved, this is the same as maintained markup.

The relationships among the three concepts of markup (Definitions follow on the next page.) — initial markup, maintained markup, and gross margin — are expressed by the following formulas:[2]

$$(1) \qquad \text{Initial markup \%} = \frac{\text{Maintained markup + Reductions}}{\text{Sales + Reductions}}$$

Note: Sales plus reductions equal the original retail price. Initial markup percentage is customarily expressed as a percentage of original retail price.

If all figures are in percentages, *sales* become 100% and the formula reads:

$$\text{Initial markup \%} = \frac{\text{Maintained markup \% + Reductions \%}}{100\% + \text{Reductions \%}}$$

(2)   By transposition, Maintained markup % = Initial Markup %
         - [Reductions % × (100% - Initial markup %)]

The maintained markup and gross margin relationships are expressed in numbers 3 and 4.

(3)   Maintained markup = Gross margin - Cash discounts earned
                              + Alteration costs.

(4)   Gross margin = Maintained markup + Cash discounts earned
                         - Alteration costs.

Note: When there are no cash discounts to be credited to the department and no alteration costs, maintained markup and gross margin are the same.

(5)   Gross margin = Expenses + Operating profit

(6)   Operating profit = Gross margin - Expenses

(7)   Since Maintained markup = Expenses + Operating profit
                      - Cash discounts earned + Alteration costs,

Initial markup % =

$$\frac{\text{Expense \% + Operating profit \% + Reductions \% - Cash dis. earned}[3] + \text{Alt. cost \%}}{\text{Sales (100\%) + Reductions \%}}$$

It should be noted that:

Reductions = Markdowns + Shortages + Discounts to
                 employees and customers

---

[2] Some teachers and students may wish to reverse the sequence of the formulas, starting with 7 and concluding with 1.

[3] Cash discounts earned are subtracted because they reduce the amount of initial markup needed to attain a certain profit goal.

Problems of planning involving these formulas are of three types:
1. Finding the necessary initial markup when the other factors are planned.
2. Estimating the probable profits that will be realized if a suggested initial markup is achieved.
3. Estimating the reduction allowance in view of a planned initial markup and gross margin.

DEFINITIONS

Initial Markup Percentage. The difference between the total merchandise handled at retail and the total merchandise handled at cost divided by the total merchandise handled at retail.

Cumulative Markup Percentage. The initial markup percentage as calculated from the beginning of the season to a later date or to the end of the season or year.

Maintained Markup Percentage. The difference between the net sales and the gross cost of merchandise sold divided by the net sales.

Gross Margin Percentage. The difference between the net sales and the total merchandise costs divided by the net sales. It may be found from the maintained markup percentage by adding the cash discounts earned as a percentage of sales and subtracting the alteration and workroom costs, also as a percentage of sales.

Retail Reductions. The sum of markdowns, merchandise shortages, and discounts to employees and customers. Merchandise shortages are equivalent to a price reduction to zero.

Markdowns. Retail price reductions caused by inability to sell goods at original or subsequently determined retail prices.

Merchandise (or Stock) Shortage. The discrepancy between the amount of merchandise that the store's records indicate should be on hand and the amount actually on hand. It reflects (1) physical loss and (2) errors in record keeping and in counting. Shortages may be calculated at cost value, retail value, or in units, but when they are included in Retail Reductions, they are always calculated at retail. Synonymous with stock shrinkage.

Discounts to Employees and Customers. Retail reductions taken not because of depreciation, but as a matter of policy to give a preferential price to certain favored groups.

10. Finding the initial markup when maintained markup and reductions are known. (No cash discounts or alteration costs.)

● *Example:*

A store has a gross margin (expense + profit) of 35% and reductions (markdowns, shortages, and discounts to employees) of 8%. What is the initial markup percentage?

Solution:

Since there are no cash discounts or alteration costs involved, the gross margin is the same as the maintained markup.

$$\text{Initial markup} = \frac{35\% + 8\%}{100\% + 8\%} = \frac{43\%}{108\%} = 39.8\%$$

ASSIGNMENT 10:

The expenses in a department store are 28.16%, the profit is 4%, and the reductions are 6%. Find (1) gross margin; (2) initial markup.

DISCUSSION QUESTIONS:

What sources would you use in forecasting expenses, reductions, and profit percentages for a store already in operation? A new store just starting in business?

11. Finding the initial markup when cash discounts and alteration costs are involved.

● *Example:*

The expenses in a department are 25%; the profit, 5%; the cash discounts earned, 3%; the alteration costs, 2%; the markdowns, 4%; and the shortages, 1%. Find (1) gross margin, (2) maintained markup, and (3) the initial markup.

Solution:

(1)   Gross margin = Expenses + Profit = 25% + 5% = 30%

(2)   Maintained markup = Gross margin − Cash discounts
        + Alteration costs = 30% − 3% + 2% = 29%

(3)   Initial markup = $\dfrac{\text{Maintained markup \% + Reductions \%}}{100\% + \text{Reductions \%}}$

$$= \frac{29\% + (4\% + 1\%)}{100\% + (4\% + 1\%)} = \frac{34\%}{105\%} = 32.4\%$$

ASSIGNMENT 11:

The following data are available for women's clothing store.

Expenses	31.5%
Profit	3.0%

Markdowns	5.5%
Shortages	1.0%
Net alteration costs	2.8%
Cash discount earned	1.2%

Find:
   (1) Gross margin
   (2) Maintained markup
   (3) Initial markup

DISCUSSION QUESTION:

Since the initial markup may be calculated without first finding the gross margin and the maintained markup, what is to be gained by determining both of the two other figures?

12. Finding maintained markup and profits when initial markup and reductions are known.

Example:

A store's initial markup is 40% and its reductions are 10%. (1) What is the maintained markup? (2) If expenses are 30% what is the operating profit? (No cash discounts or alteration costs.)

Solution:

(1)   Maintained markup % = Initial markup % -
          - [Reductions % × (100% - Initial markup %)]
   Maintained markup = 40% - [10% × (100% - 40%)]
                = 40% - 6% = 34%

(2) Since there are no cash discounts or alteration costs, the maintained markup is also the gross margin.

          Profit = Gross margin - Expenses = 34% - 30% = 4%

Alternate Solution:

$$\text{Initial markup} = \frac{\text{Expense \% + Profit \% + Reductions \%}}{100\% + \text{Reductions \%}}$$

$$40\% = \frac{30\% + P + 10\%}{100\% + 10\%}$$

$$40\% = \frac{P + 40\%}{110\%}$$

$$40\% \times 110\% = P + 40\%$$
$$44\% = P + 40\%$$
$$4\% = P$$

ASSIGNMENT 12:

The initial markup in a department is 38%; the markdowns, 4%; the shortages, 1%; and the expenses, 32%. There are no cash discounts or alteration costs.

Find:

(1) The maintained markup (also gross margin)

(2) Operating profit

DISCUSSION QUESTION:

Is it easier to exercise control of markup at the initial markup rather than the maintained markup level?

13. Finding gross margin and profits when initial markup and reductions are known. (Cash discounts and alteration costs involved.)

Example:

The initial markup in a shirt classification is 38.7%; the markdowns, 5.8%; the shortages, 1%; the cash discounts, 5.3%; the alteration costs, 0.5%; and the expenses, 27.9%. Find: (1) The maintained markup. (2) The gross margin. (3) The operating profit.

Solution:

(1)   Maintained markup % = Initial markup % − [Reductions %
                                              × (100% − Initial markup %]
                      = 38.7% − [6.8% × (100% − 38.7%)]
                      = 38.7% − 4.2% = 34.5%

(2)   Gross margin = Maintained markup + Cash discounts
                                      − Alteration costs

          Gross margin = 34.5% + 5.3% − 0.5% = 39.3%

(3)   Profit = Gross margin − Expenses
                  Profit = 39.3% − 27.9% = 11.4%

ASSIGNMENT 13:

Find the maintained markup, the gross margin, and the profit or loss from the following data for a furniture department:

Initial markup	45.0%
Markdowns	5.4%
Shortages	0.6%
Alteration costs	0.7%
Cash discounts	1.5%
Expenses	34.5%

DISCUSSION QUESTION:

> Why are shortages and markdowns two of the most difficult items to control in the profit and loss items given above?

14. Finding reductions when initial markup and maintained markup are known.

Example:

> The initial markup in a merchandise category is 40% and the maintained markup is 34%. What are the reductions?

Solution:

$$\text{Initial markup } \% - [\text{Reductions } \% \times (100\% - \text{Initial markup } \%)]$$
$$= 40\% - [\text{Reductions } \% \times (100\% - 40\%)] = 34\% \text{ Maintained markup}$$
$$40\% - 60\% \text{ of Reductions} = 34\%$$
$$6\% = 60\% \text{ of Reductions}$$
$$10\% = \text{Reductions}$$

Alternate Solution:

$$\text{Initial markup } \% = \frac{\text{Maintained markup } \% + \text{Reductions } \%}{100\% + \text{Reductions } \%}$$
$$40\% (100\% + \text{Reductions } \%). = 34\% + \text{Reductions } \%$$
$$40\% + 40\% \text{ of Reductions } \% = 34\% + \text{Reductions } \%$$
$$6\% = 60\% \text{ of Reductions}$$
$$10\% \text{ of Reductions}$$

ASSIGNMENT 14:

> The initial markup in a notions department is 42% and the maintained markup is 30%. What are the reductions?

DISCUSSION QUESTION:

> If the figures calculated above are the allowable reductions, what is meant by allowable reductions and why do many companies not want to put reductions into their plan?

15. Finding reductions when the initial markup and gross margin are given.

Example:

> In a fabric section, the initial markup is 48% and the gross margin, 46%; the cash discounts earned, 4%; the alteration costs, 1%; and the shortages, 1.2%. Find: (1) the maintained markup; (2) the reductions; (3) the markdowns.

Solution:

(1)   Maintained markup = Gross margin − Cash discounts
           + Alteration costs = 46% − 4% + 1% = 43%

(2)   Initial markup % − Reduction % × (100% − Initial markup %)
                     = Maintained markup

          48% − Reductions % × (100% − 48%) = 43%

          48% − 52% of Reductions = 43%

          5% = 52% of Reductions

          9.6% = Reductions

(3)   Markdowns = Reductions − Shortages = 9.6% − 1.2% = 8.4%

ASSIGNMENT 15:

In a maternity wear department, the initial markup is 39.9%, the expenses 30.6%, the profit 10.2%, the cash discounts earned 3.7%, the shortages 0.8%, and the alteration costs 0.2%. Find: (1) the maintained markup, (2) the reductions, and (3) the markdowns.

DISCUSSION QUESTION:

Should markdowns be thought of simply as the difference between reductions and shortages?

16. Effect of reductions on margin.

Example:

If the initial markup taken on a line of merchandise is 40% but markdowns taken on the line are 25%, what percentage of the potential margin is lost because of the markdowns? (Assume that there are no shortages).

Solution:

Maintained markup % = Initial markup % − Reductions % ×
                      (100% − Initial markup %)
Maintained markup % = 40% − (25% × 60%) = 40% − 15% = 25%

Assume cost of items in the line to be $6.00. At 40% initial markup, the original retail is $10.00. ($6/60%). at 25% maintained markup, the sales (retail) are $8 ($6/75%). With an initial markup of $4 and a maintained markup of $2, the potential margin is cut 50%.

ASSIGNMENT 16:

In a department with a 37-1/2% initial markup, markdowns are 8%.

What proportion is the dollar margin reduced because of the price reductions?

DISCUSSION QUESTION:

Since both are percentages of sales, why does the sum of the maintained markup percent and the reduction percent *not* give the initial markup percent?

Managerial Decision

You have set an initial markup for the fall season of 40%, based on planned 6-months sales of $100,000. By the end of December, with still 2 months to go in the season, you find that you have already sold $100,000 and that you have a markup of 40%. How would you price your merchandise during the last month of the season?

ADDITIONAL ASSIGNMENTS

A. *Calculating Markup*

17. Calculating cost when retail and markup percentages on retail are known. A buyer find a dress in a manufacturer's show room and estimates it should retail at $20.00. He needs a markup of 42%. How much should he pay for the dress?

18. Calculating retail when cost and markup percentage on retail are known. An item is quoted by the manufacturer at $1.50 and the markup that a buyer needs to realize a fair profit is 40% on retail. At what retail price should he mark the novelty to obtain the desired markup?

19. Calculating retail when cost and markup percentage on cost are known. A buyer finds a refrigerator at $75 cost and he needs a markup of 60% of cost. What must the refrigerator retail for to provide the desired markup?

20. Computing markup on cost when markup on retail is known. The markup for a department is 40% of retail. Convert this figure to the markup percentage on cost. Is the markup on cost greater or smaller than on retail?

21. Computing markup on retail when markup on cost is known. The markup percentage on cost is 35% in a department *A*. What is the equivalent markup on retail?

B. *Planning Markup*

22.

a. Maintained markup, 30%; initial markup, 35%. Find reduction percentage.

b. Reductions, 10%; maintained markup, 28%. Find percentage of initial markup.

c. Reductions, 8%; initial markup, 39%. Find percentage of maintained markup.

23. A merchant estimates that for the fall and winter season his sales in a certain category will probably be $12,000; his expenses, $3,500; and his reductions, $500. In view of former profits, the trend of business, and comparison with similar stores, he sets $1,000 as a profit goal. What initial markup should he achieve to assure this profit?

24. Last year, a buyer achieved an initial markup of 33-1/3% and is considering the same figure as this year's goal. His planned expenses for this year are 28% of planned sales, and his planned reductions are 5% and cash discounts, 4%. If these estimates prove correct, what profit percentage will be realized with a 33-1/3% initial markup?

25. A shoe department has been operating at a 40% initial markup. Its planned expenses are 34% of planned sales and its profit goal is 1%. How much may its reductions be if shortages are estimated at 1%. How much may be allowed for markdowns?

26. The initial markup in the glove department is set at 40% and allows for reductions of 6% of sales. In the novelty glove classification reductions are estimated at 10%.

(a) What markup should be taken on the novelty gloves to obtain the same maintained markup percentage planned for the department as a whole?

(b) If a style in this classification costs $19.00, what should be its retail at the markup in (a)? Round this out to a customary price line.

ADVANCED ASSIGNMENT

A merchandise manager is considering whether to set an initial markup of 38% or 40% for a department. With a 38% markup, reductions (markdowns, discounts to customers and employees, and shortages) are planned at 7%. If a 40% markup reduces sales 5% (from $200,000 to $190,000) with no change in dollar expenses but with an increase in the reduction percentage 8%, which markup will be the more profitable? How much more profitable?

5   How to Price Merchandise

In the actual pricing of goods, it is seldom possible or desirable to obtain the same markup on all lines of goods, or on all articles comprising a single line. On the cost side, expenses of handling and storing merchandise fluctuate; there are differences in the amount of sales promotion needed; and there are changes in the rate of stock turn. The probability of markdowns also varies with the fashion element. Thus, fast turning staples that require little advertising or personal selling may be sold profitably at a much lower- markup than slower turning stocks, subject to obsolescence and requiring considerable salesmanship. Again, in order to appeal to the bargain sense of customers, it is often desirable to hold "sales" at subnormal markups. If such sales are well planned and executed, the extra volume will not be accompanied by a proportionate increase in expenses.

As indicated in the preceding section, it is possible to determine the differences in the direct expenses of handling different classifications of merchandise but the technique used places major emphasis on cost rather than on the velocity of demand.

From the demand side, volume opportunities differ greatly at different price points. For example, competition has established customary prices and many articles and goods must be priced at or near these customary points for maximum sales, even though the markup percentages, at these points, may be considerably more or less than the desired markup goal. Furthermore, a limited number of price lines are desirable, since substantial jumps between prices, because of different qualities, help customers make intelligent selections.

In pricing individual items, although it may be desirable or necessary to deviate from the markup percentage planned for the store or department as a whole, great care should be exercised to insure that markups below average are balanced by markups above average; for, if the planned markup is not realized, the profit goal will probably not be reached. The exception to this rule is where below average markup leads to actual sales volume in excess of plan without a proportional increase in expenses and reductions. Under these circumstances a new lower markup may be planned.

DEFINITIONS

Break-even Retail. A retail price that will provide a markup just sufficient to cover the direct expenses incurred, or probably to be incurred, in stocking and selling the item. It is the price at which the item is expected to contribute neither to profit nor to loss; that is, it provides no controllable margin to help pay for the joint expenses of either the department or the store.

Break-even Cost. The cost price of an article for which the retail price has been determined that will provide a markup just sufficient to cover the direct expenses incurred, or probably to be incurred, by stocking and selling the item.

Variable Expenses. Operating expenses affected by changes in sales volume, increasing as sales increase and decreasing as sales decrease.

"Flat" Expenses. Variable expenses representing a specific dollar and cents cost for handling a single unit of merchandise or a single sales transaction. Thus, these expenses vary directly with the number of pieces or transactions handled and sold.

Value Variable Expenses. Variable expenses varying with the value of the unit or transaction handled, not with the number handled. Thus, if salespeople are paid on a commission basis, selling payroll varies directly with the value of sales. The expense is fixed in percentage, not in dollars.

Fixed Expenses. Operating expenses in dollars not affected by increases or decreases in sales volume.

Overhead. A synonym for fixed expenses. The term is sometimes used interchangeably with total expense but this use is to be discouraged.

Leverage. The influence of changes in sales volume on profits caused by fixed expenses. A relatively small increase in sales normally causes a relatively large increase in profits since many expenses are fixed. Conversely, a small sales decrease normally causes a large decrease in profits.

Averaging Markup. Adjusting the proportions of goods purchased at varying markups in order to achieve a desired average markup either for a certain period or on an individual lot.

Profitable merchandising often leads management to seek out opportunities to increase the average markup by increasing the proportion of high-markup goods, but in some lines competition is forcing lower average markups, which may increase profits if sales can be materially increased.

A. PRICING THE UNIT

1. Estimating the most profitable price.

● *Example:*

A merchant pays 60 cents a pound for butter and estimates that he can sell approximately the following quantities a week at each of the prices indicated:

Price	Pounds
$.60	1,000
.65	500
.68	300
.72	200
.75	150

Which of the above prices would be best?

Solution:

Price	Pounds	Margin Per Pound	Total Margin
$.60	1,000	$.00	0
.65	500	.05	$25.00
.68	300	.08	24.00
.72	200	.12	24.00
.75	150	.15	22.50

The 65-cent price yields the largest gross margin, but a 64-cent price might prove even better. However, direct expenses must be considered.

ASSIGNMENT 1:

You estimate that you can sell each week 9 yards of muslin at 95 cents, 18 yards at 83 cents, 24 yards at 71 cents or 5 yards at $1.00. If the material cost 50 cents a yard, which price will yield the largest margin?

2. Break-even retail.

● *Example:*

A careful analysis of the expenses incurred in connection with the physical handling and recording of the merchandise in a certain category of a department revealed a total of $20,000[1] during a period

---

[1] Under Merchandise Management Accounting technique, the direct costs would be broken down into narrower functions: (1) expenses fixed per unit and varying with the number of units such as receiving, warehousing, delivery, installation, and (2) expenses varying with the value of the unit such as selling, advertising, and inventory carrying costs. (If carrying charges are collected from customers, these may be subtracted from the sum total of this expense group.) The unit costs (1) in dollars and (2) in percentages are totaled to obtain figures comparable to the 40 cents and the 15% in the problem.

in which 50,000 units were sold. Other direct expenses, particularly advertising and selling payroll, were $30,000 and the total sales in the category were $200,000.

1. Find the "flat" expenses per unit and the value variable expenses per unit.
2. If an article in this category costs $3.85, what is its break-even retail and its markup at this point?
3. What is the break-even cost in this category for the $10 price line and what is the markup at this point?
4. What is the lowest retail price in this category at which a 35% markup would provide neither a profit nor a loss?

Solution:

(1) $20,000 ÷ 50,000 = $.40, the "flat" expenses per unit.
       and
       $30,000 ÷ $200,000 = 15%, the value variable expenses per unit.

(2) $3.85 (billed cost) + $.40 + 15% of Retail = Retail
       85% of Retail = $4.25

$$\text{Retail} \quad = \frac{\$4.25}{0.85} = \$5.00$$

$$\text{Markup} = \frac{\$5 - \$3.85}{\$5.00} = \frac{\$1.15}{\$5.00} = 23\%.$$

(3)   Retail – 15% of Retail – $.40 = Cost
       Cost = 85% of $10.00 – $.40 = $8.50 – $.40 = $8.10

$$\text{Markup} = \frac{\$10 - \$8.10}{\$10.00} = 19\%$$

(4)   Let X equal the lowest retail price
       Markup required: "Flat" per unit $.40
                              Variable   15% of X
                              Total   35% of X

       35% of X = $.40 + 15% of X
       20% of X = $.40
              X = $2.

ASSIGNMENT 2:

"Flat" handling expenses are estimated at 25 cents a unit and value variable direct expenses at 10% of the retail.

1. If an article costs 50 cents, at what figure should it be retailed to break-even?

2. If an article is placed in a $2 price line, what would be its break-even cost?

3. If a markup of 20% is obtained in this classification, what is the lowest retail price that would avoid a loss?

DISCUSSION QUESTION:

The demand curve at various price levels is much discussed by economists. Do you feel that the retailer can accurately estimate his volume at different prices?

3. Pricing by means of merchandise management accounting.

Example:

In a major appliance department, a particular product costs $540 including transportation. It is expected to turn 4 times a year. It will probably be sold on credit.

The store's accountant has set up the following estimates of direct charges applicable to goods in the classification into which this product falls:

Buying expense 2% of sales
Imputed interest 6% of average cost inventory
Accounts payable $3 per item purchased
Accounts receivable $6 per item sold on credit
Advertising expense 3% of sales
Selling salaries 10% of sales

(a) At what retail price would the item break-even (cover its direct expenses), with no contribution to overhead and profit?

(b) If management expects at least a 17% (of sales) contribution, at what figure might the item be priced?

Solution:

Calculation of total direct costs
Purchase price	$540.00
Imputed interest 6% of $140 (4 turns)	8.40
Accounts payable	3.00
Accounts receivable	6.00
Flat costs and expenses	$557.40

Variable expenses
Buying	2% of sales	
Advertising	3%	
Selling	10%	
Total	15% of sales	

Therefore: 85% of the break-even retail = $557.40
100% of the break-even retail = $656.00 (approx.)

Margin required for overhead, etc., 17%. Therefore: 83% of the minimum acceptable retail is $656 and 100% is $790 (Markup 31.6%).

ASSIGNMENT 3:

Another item in the same department and classification as the above costs $250, including transportation costs.

1. At what price would it break-even, making no contribution to overhead?
2. What would be the minimum acceptable retail price with 17% allowed for overhead?
3. Are the so-called direct expenses properly chargeable against the two items in question in the manner indicated?
4. Under what conditions might the items be doing better than breaking even if sold at the calculated break-even points?

DISCUSSION QUESTIONS:

1. What important factors are disregarded in merchandise management accounting?
2. What is the practical value of this method?
3. (*a*) Is it practicable for a store to calculate the fixed costs per unit and the variable expenses per unit for the different classifications in each department?

   (*b*) If done, is it sound to assume that these costs will be incurred on new contemplated purchases?

   (*c*) If recently it cost $20,000 to receive, mark, store, wrap, and deliver 50,000 articles in a classification, is it fair to conclude that each unit handled incurs a flat cost of 40 cents?

4. Break-even retail: Markdowns involved (Merchandise Management Accounting).

Example:

The flat or fixed expenses per unit in a merchandise line are 70 cents and variable selling and advertising expenses are 10% of sales. The reductions in this line average 6% of sales.

1. On an item in this line costing $2.00, what is the break-even original retail?
2. What is the initial markup at this point?

Solution:

(1) Break-even sales price = $2.00 + $.70 + 10% of break-even sales price ∴ 90% of break-even sales price = $2.70 and break-even sales price = $3.

Since reductions are expected to be 6% of sales, the original retail should be 6% higher or $3.18, the break-even original retail.

(2) Retail ($3.18) – Cost ($2.00) = Initial markup ($1.18).

$$\text{Initial markup } \% = \frac{\$1.18}{\$3.18} = 37.1\%$$

ASSIGNMENT 4:

1. If a retail price of $1.25 were planned for the above line, what would be its break-even cost and what would be the initial markup percentage at this point?
2. At a 30% initial markup, what is the lowest retail price that will permit the merchant to break-even?

DISCUSSION QUESTION:

Why cannot the reduction percentage be added to the variable expense percentage in calculating break-even points?

5. Analyzing the unit.

Example:

Analyze the profit in units if 50,000 units (pieces) are sold; each transaction is two units; gross margin is 35%; the average price per unit or piece is $2; value variable expenses are 10% of the average sale; flat expenses per transaction are 50 cents; and the fixed expenses are $10,000.

Solution:

$$\text{Profit} = \frac{50,000}{2} \times (35\% \text{ of } \$4 - 10\% \text{ of } \$4 - \$.50) - \$10,000$$

$$= 25,000 \times (\$1.40 - \$.40 - \$.50) - \$10,000$$

$$= 25,000 \times \$.50 - \$10,000 = \$12,500 \text{ (controllable margin)} - \$10,000$$

$$= \$2,500.$$

This analysis reveals that profits per transaction can be increased by:

1. Improving the gross margin ratio.

    2. Increasing the average sale.

    3. Reducing value variable expenses.

    4. Reducing "flat" expenses (by stream-lining handling operations).

ASSIGNMENT 5:

In the example above, assume that it is possible to increase the average unit of sale 5% (from $4 to $4.20) and the gross margin 1% from 35% to 36%); to reduce the value variable expenses 1% (from 10% to 9%) and to reduce "flat" expenses 5 cents (from 50 cents to 45 cents); also to increase units per transaction 5% (from 2 to 2.1) and units sold 10% (from 50,000 to 55,000).

    1. How would the controllable margin percentage compare with that in the solution above?

    2. How would operating profit compare, if fixed expenses remain at $10,000?

    3. If a particular item in the operation discussed in the example above sells only one unit per transaction, is priced at $1, and has a margin of 40%, how much does each item contribute to profit (controllable margin)?

DISCUSSION QUESTION:

How does unit profit analysis aid in (1) merchandise selection, (2) pricing, (3) sales promotion?

6. Controllable margin on a merchandise line.

Example:

A national brand shoe costs $9 and sells for $15 a pair. About 1,500 pairs are sold a year but of these about 200 represent styles that are marked down and closed out at an average of $10 a pair. An average cost inventory of $4,000 is carried in this brand and the inventory occupies 100 square feet of selling space. The department is charged (1) $4 a square foot a year for the space it occupies and (2) interest on its cost investment in merchandise of 5%. About half the shoes in this brand, are delivered to customers at a cost of 40 cents a pair and other flat expenses are estimated at 25 cents a pair. Value variable expenses include 6% for selling and 2% for advertising the brand after deducting advertising allowances from the vendor. Find the controllable margin for this brand, regarding space charge and interest expense as direct expenses, along with flat and variable expenses.

Solution:

```
Sales:  1,300 pairs at $15 . . . . . . . . . . . . . . . .   $19,500
          200 pairs at $10 . . . . . . . . . . . . . . . .     2,000
          Total . . . . . . . . . . . . . . . . . . . . . . .    21,500
Cost of merchandise sold: 1,500 pairs at $9 . . . . .    13,500
Margin . . . . . . . . . . . . . . . . . . . . . . . . . . . . .     8,000    37.2%
"Flat" expenses:
          $.40 X 750 + $.25 X 1500 . . . . . .  $  675
Value variable expenses: 8% of $21,500  .    1,720
Space charge: 100 X $4 . . . . . . . . . . . .     400
Interest on merchandise investment:
                        5% of $4,000      200
          Total direct expense . . . . . . . . . . . . . . . . .     2,995
          Controllable margin . . . . . . . . . . . . . . . . . . . .  $  5,005    23.3%
```

ASSIGNMENT 6:

After allowing for direct expenses, including interest on the merchandise investment of 6% and space charge of $3.50 a square foot a year, a department earns a controllable margin of 10% on its sales. The buyer is considering the addition of a branded line that will provide an initial markup of only 33-1/3% but markdowns of probably no more than 3%. Sales of the brand are likely to equal $10,000 a year or 2,000 units. Of these, 500 are likely to be delivered to customers at a unit cost of 50 cents. Other flat expenses are estimated at 10 cents. The brand will require 60 square feet of selling space, 5% of sales for selling payroll, $600 a year for advertising, and provide 5 stock-turns a year.
How will the controllable margin ratio from this brand probably compare with the departmental average?

DISCUSSION QUESTION:

What favorable factors in connection with a national brand are likely to offset a low initial markup and result in a satisfactory contribution to overhead and profit?

B. AVERAGING THE MARKUP IN PRICING

7. Averaging markup on purchases — purchases planned at retail.

● *Example:*

To reach his profit goal, a buyer needs to average a markup on retail of 40% on the purchases he is making on this buying trip. Of the $10,000 worth of goods to be purchased at retail, he has already bought 2,000 toys at $1.75 to be sold at $2.75. What markup is needed on the remaining purchases.

Solution:

Cost = Retail × (100% − Markup %) = $10,000 × 60% = $6,000

	Cost	Retail	Markup
Total planned purchases	$6,000	$10,000	40%
Purchases to date	3,500	5,500	
Balance to buy	$2,500	$ 4,500	

$4,500 − $2,500 = $2,000, the dollar markup needed

$2,000 ÷ $4,500 = 44.4%, the markup to aim at on the remaining purchases

ASSIGNMENT 7:

A furniture dealer plans to spend $10,000 at retail for merchandise during the month and needs a markup of 34% of retail. He totals his invoices during the month and finds that he has purchased $4,000 at cost and $5,500 at retail. What markup does he need for the remaining purchases?

DISCUSSION QUESTION:

When a buyer talks about the average markup, is he speaking about what he has obtained over a period of time within a department or is he referring to the markup obtained on one purchase?

8. Averaging markup on purchases — purchases planned at cost.

● *Example:*

Total planned purchases $750 at cost with a markup on retail of 25%, purchases to date, $400 at cost and $575 at retail. Find markup necessary on balance of purchases.

Solution:

If markup is 25% of retail, cost of $750 = 75% of retail and retail = $1,000.

	Cost	Retail
Total purchases	$750	$1,000
Purchases to date	400	575
Balance to buy	$350	$ 425

Dollar markup on balance = $425 − $350 = $75

Markup % on retail = $\frac{\$75}{\$425}$ = 17.6%

ASSIGNMENT 8:

A buyer plans to purchase $8,000 worth of goods at cost during the month and to average a markup on retail of 30% by the end of the month. He has purchased $5,500 worth at cost and $7,500 at retail. What markup on retail must be realized on the balance of purchases?

DISCUSSION QUESTION:

If you are in the market and the early purchases you have made have not allowed you to obtain the necessary markup, why do you suppose that the buyer in assignment 8 feels that he may be able to obtain a higher than average markup on late purchases.

9. Averaging markup on total merchandise handled (cumulative markup).

● *Example:*

In a men's clothing store, a markup of 37% is needed during the spring and summer season, February 1st to July 31st. The opening inventory for the season was $10,000 at retail with a markup of 36.5%. The planned purchases for the spring season are $50,000 at retail. The actual purchases during February and March are $20,000 at retail and $12,500 at cost. What markup must be realized on purchases during the last 4 months of the season in order to average 37%?

Solution:

Opening retail inventory plus planned˙ retail purchases = $10,000 + $50,000 = $60,000, the total planned merchandise handled.

	Cost	*Retail*	*Markup*
Total planned merchandise handled	$37,800	$60,000	37.0%
Opening inventory	6,350	10,000	36.5
Purchases to date	12,900	20,000	
Total merchandise handled to date	$19,250	$30,000	
Balance to buy	$18,550	$30,000	

$30,000 – $18,550 = $11,450

$11,450 ÷ $30,000 = 38.2%

ASSIGNMENT 9:

The cumulative markup planned for the entire fall season in a children's department is 42%. The inventory on August 1st is $126,000 at retail with a markup of 42.5%. The planned purchases for the season are $140,000 at retail. The purchases August through November, are $90,000 at retail and $46,000 at cost. What markup should be obtained during December and January in order to attain the needed average?

DISCUSSION QUESTION:

If the markup obtained so far during the season has been above plan, is it advisable to lower markup in order to just equal the expected goal and give your customers good buys at the end of the season or would it be preferable to maintain a fairly constant markup?

10. Averaging markup on total merchandise handled — markups known.

Example:

A buyer has planned an initial markup of 35% and is arranging for a sale of merchandise composed of special purchases on which a markup of only 25% will be realized. He expects to buy $1,000 worth of this merchandise at retail. How much regular merchandise will he have to stock at a 37-1/2% markup — the most he feels he can get — to attain the required average of 35%?

Solution:

Let X = the amount of regular merchandise to buy:

	Cost	Retail	Markup
Purchases planned to date	$750	$1,000	0.25 (25%)
High markup regular purchases	0.625X	X	0.375 (37.5%)
	$750 + 0.625X	$1,000 + X	0.35 (35%)

$$\therefore 0.65 (1,000 + X) = \$750 + 0.625X$$
$$\$650 + 0.65X = \$750 + 0.625X$$
$$0.65X - 0.625X = \$750 - \$650$$
$$0.025X = \$100$$
$$X = \frac{\$100}{0.025} = \$4,000, \text{ the amount of regular merchandise to buy at retail}$$

Alternate Solution:

	Regular Merchandise	*Special Purchases*
Amount	X	$1,000
Goal markup	35%	35%
Actual markups	37½%	25%
Over	2½% over	10% short
Ratio	1	4

$\therefore$ 4 times as much merchandise should be bought at 37-1/2% as at 25%
$1,000 × 4 = $4,000 ·

ASSIGNMENT 10:

A buyer of piece goods is expected to adhere to an initial markup of 42% of retail. Every month the controller notifies him of his markup to date. On March 1st, the report indicates that the markup to date is only 41% and that his total merchandise handled to date is $34,000 at retail. How much merchandise at cost must the buyer buy and mark up 45% of retail in order to attain his planned figure of 42%?

DISCUSSION QUESTION:

Discuss the advisability of such a method of planning as is used in Assignment 10.

11. Adjusting the markup goal to allow for changes in cash discount rate.

Example:

A buyer of women's garments has been obtaining a markup of 40% in a certain classification in which cash discounts have been 5% of billed cost. The vendors of this merchandise cut the discount to 2% with no change in billed cost. What markup should the buyer aim at in order to achieve the same over-all markup percentage as before?

Solution:

Let $2.00 = retail and $1.20 = billed cost
Take cost, $1.20 less 5% of $1.20, or $1.14
Over-all markup, $2.00 – $1.14 = $ .86 or 43%

$$\text{New cost, } \$1.20 \text{ less } 2\% \text{ of } \$1.20 = \$1.18$$

Necessary retail: $\$1.18 \div 57\% = \$2.07$

Billed cost	$= \$1.20$
$ markup	$= \$\ .87$

$$\% \text{ markup} \qquad = \frac{\$\ .87}{\$2.07} = 42\%$$

ASSIGNMENT 11:

A manufacturer elected to cut his cash discount rate from 6% to 1%. A merchant buying his product had been obtaining a markup of 42%. What markup should he aim at to offset the change in the discount rate?

DISCUSSION QUESTION:

In assignment 11, what problems are created by the decrease in the discount rate?

Managerial Decision

In millinery, a certain merchant always determines his retail by doubling his cost; thus, he has no need to average high and low markups. Is this policy of taking a uniform markup percentage on all millinery a wise one? Defend your answer.

ADDITIONAL ASSIGNMENTS

12. A standard raincoat is bought for $20 cost and there is no suggested retail price. The handling expenses are $1 a coat. At a retail as low as $24.00, it is estimated that customers would be skeptical of the value and buy no more than ten a month. But at $26 retail, sales should be 20 a month; at $27.50, 16 a month; at $30, 16 and at $32.50, 10.

Which retail price would provide the largest aggregate dollar margin?

13. In a grocery store, the average price per item is 1.38 cents, and the total expenses are 18% of sales. The average sale of butter is 80 cents, and the gross margin on butter is only 15%. The average turnover in the store is 7.5 times, but the butter turns 143 times. Of the total expenses, 40% depends on the number of transactions handled, 40% on the space occupied, and 20% on the value of the merchandise. Assuming that the average sale unit of butter occupies the same amount of space as the average for the store, find:

(a) The profit or loss realized on the butter in dollars and in percentage of sales.

(b) What general conclusions may be reached on a basis of this problem?

14. A buyer marks up most of his merchandise 33-1/3% of retail. His controller estimates that the flat costs of handling every article in his department are about 38 cents and that other expenses that vary directly with the retail value of sales are 13-1/3%. (a) What is the lowest price line the department should carry to avoid a loss? (b) If an item costs $1.65 and is marked up 33-1/3% of retail, how much controllable margin would it contribute?

15. In a department, it costs 30 cents to handle each transaction, not including expense items bearing little relationship to the volume of transactions handled. These other expenses average 25% of sales. If a markup of 40% is taken on all prices, what is the break-even retail price?

16. On total planned retail purchases of $8,500, a buyer plans a markup of 34%. On his first day in the market, he finds an unusual value — goods costing a total of $1,500 that he believes he will be able to sell readily for $3,000. What markup percentage does he need on the balance of his purchases to realize his markup plan?

17. On March 1st, you start the spring season with an inventory amounting to $18,000 at cost and $24,000 at retail. Your required initial markup for the season is 38%, and your planned purchases for the entire season amount to $96,000 at retail. (a) What markup percentage must you secure on the purchases for the season? (b) If in March through April you purchase at cost $24,600 worth of goods and mark them up 35% of retail, what markup would you have to obtain for the last 4 months of the season?

18. The markup on $500 worth of stock at cost is 45% of retail and the markup on $1,000 worth of stock at cost is 30%. What is the average percentage of markup on retail?

19. One-half of a stock of merchandise is composed of goods having a markup on the average of 38% of retail and one-fourth is made up of goods with a markup of 40% of retail. The average markup on the whole stock is 39.75%. What markup does the last one-quarter of the merchandise carry?

20. The planned markup in a rug department is 38% for the fall season, but on November 1 the following is the situation:

	Cost	Retail
Inventory, August 1	$31,000	$50,000
Purchases, Aug. 1 to Nov. 1	17,500	27,000

The buyer feels that he can obtain an average markup of 40% on his purchases during the next few months. How much merchandise will he have to mark up 40% to get back his planned figure of 38%?

21. A store with a volume of $2,000,000 a year estimates that 20% of its sales result in a markup of 40%, 50% in a markup of 33-1/3%, and 30% in a markup of 20%.

(a) If the percentage of sales at the various markups is changed as follows, what is the difference in the average markup?

22% of sales take 40% markup

51% of sales take 33-1/3% markup

27% of sales take 20% markup

(b) How can a store increase the percentage of high-markup goods sold and lower the percentage of low-markup goods?

6   How to Set
and Control Price Lines

In addition to the problem of setting suitable price lines, the merchant is faced with the task of analyzing sales by price as a preliminary to both purchase-control and sales-control. Pertinent examples of such analysis are presented in this section, with special attention to the averaging of markup on different price lines so as to achieve a planned markup goal.

DEFINITIONS

Price Line. A specific price at which a representative stock assortment is carried.

Price Zone. A range of prices all appealing to customers in a certain income group.

A Full Line Price. A price line at which a relatively complete stock assortment is carried. Three such price lines are often sufficient.

Secondary Price Line. A price line at which a lesser assortment is carried, but one that is adequate to meet the requirements of some customers.

B.B. An item carried in a price line that is a *best buy* from the angle of the customer who is interested in intrinsic quality.

M.P. A item carried in a price line that is *most profitable* from the standpoint of the merchant.

A. PLANNING PRICE LINES

1. Dollar and unit stock distribution by price line.

● *Example:*

The dollar stocks within a classification of merchandise are distributed as follows by price line:

Price Line	Dollar Stock
$2.50	35%
3.50	40
4.50	25
Total	100%

Find the percentage of stock distribution by units and the average value of the unit.

Solution:

Let $1,000 equal $ stock.

	Units	% of Total Units
$350 ÷ $2.50 =	140	45
$400 ÷ $3.50 =	114	37
$250 ÷ $4.50 =	55	18
Total Units	309	100%

$1000 ÷ 309 = $3.22, the value of the average unit of stock.

ASSIGNMENT 1:

1. Dollar sales are distributed over four price lines as follows:

Price Line	% of Dollar Sales
$16.00	30%
20.00	40
25.00	20
35.00	10
	100%

Find percentage distribution of sales by units and the value of the average unit of sales.

2. If the percentages in (1) above represent percentages of unit sales, find the percentage distribution of dollar sales and the value of the average unit sold.

DISCUSSION QUESTION:

In distributing open-to-buy to price lines, is it easier to use percentages of unit sales or of dollar sales?

2. Analysis of price lines.

● *Example:*

The total net sales volume of a popular-priced hosiery department was approximately $100,000 last year. The initial markup was 34%, the markdowns were 3.1%, and the stock turnover was 10 times. Sales volume of the entire store was about $5,000,000. Early this year, it was found the hosiery volume was not keeping up with sales of the year before. The trend required not only a decrease in stock, but also a more adequate assortment in the best-selling price lines. It was also found that the rent or space charge allotted to the hosiery department was larger than normal percentage to sales. The large number of price lines carried required much floor space.

An analysis of last year's sales by price lines revealed the following:

Price Line	Percentage of Sales in Units
$1.00	11.0%
1.25	2.5
1.35	9.0
1.50	3.5
1.75	3.0
1.95	54.0
2.50	7.5
3.00	8.5
3.50	1.0
Total	100.0%

1. Are the jumps or intervals between price lines in accordance with the principles of good price lining? Should the intervals be approximately equal, or should they be wider in the higher price lines or narrower?

2. Revise the price lines, reducing their number, and if desirable, creating new price lines.

   If price lines are correctly planned, will the middle price line always account for more sales volume than any other?

3. How can a knowledge of the purchasing power of consumers be used in setting price lines?

Solution:

1. The jumps or intervals between price lines are not in accordance with the principles of good price lining. The intervals should be wider in the higher price lines than in the lower.

2. Revised price lines: $1.00, $1.35, $1.95, and $2.95. However, there is merit in adding a new lower price line, as 89¢. The middle of the three best-selling price lines should account generally for a larger sales volume than any other. If the largest volume is done at the lowest price line, it may indicate a need for a still lower price if merchandise of good quality is obtainable. If the largest

volume is done at the highest of the major price lines, it may indicate that a still higher price should be carried or that assortments at the lower prices are incomplete.

3. A buyer should know the income of the majority of the group his store is catering to. The income can be broken down into the various items of food, clothing, and so forth. Knowing the average to be spent for clothing, it is possible to approximate the amount available for hosiery. The price lines should be adjusted to the purchasing power of customers. Other factors should also be considered, such as the willingness, as opposed to the ability, to buy.

ASSIGNMENT 2:

Sales of women's coats.

Price	Classification A			Classification B		
	May	June	July	May	June	July
$10.00	6	18	12	82	79	87
12.50	20	1	2	51	50	17
15.00	4	3	3	11	7	17
16.75	0	0	0	3	5	0
17.50	3	1	3	13	0	1
19.75	1	5	30	22	8	17
20.00	9	0	0	17	0	0
25.00	31	16	20	84	46	59
29.50	18	9	14	45	20	11
32.50	2	1	9	0	0	1
35.00	45	17	8	26	28	10
39.50	62	16	15	66	25	17
45.00	4	3	6	3	1	0
49.50	80	29	16	76	12	7
55.00	1	1	0	0	0	0
59.50	16	6	3	4	1	4
65.00	40	16	11	14	3	1
69.50	3	0	1	1	2	1
75.00	29	5	1	0	7	5
79.50	0	0	0	4	0	0
89.50	2	0	0	0	0	0
95.00	1	0	0	0	0	1
98.50	7	0	0	2	0	1
110.00	1	0	0	0	0	0
165.00	0	0	0	1	0	0
Total	385	147	154	525	294	257

Which of the above price lines should be eliminated?

DISCUSSION QUESTION:

What other suggestions can you make on the basis of the above report?

Managerial Decisions

1. As the merchandise manager of a store, you make an analysis of the sales by price lines in one of your departments and find the preponderance of *dollar* sales in the lowest regular price line of dresses. When the latter is discussed with the buyer, he defends the sales distribution on the grounds that there are more low-income customers than those in any other group and that his lowest price line should, accordingly, produce the greatest volume. Do you concur with his opinion?

2. A women's wear store catering to the middle-income class has been pricing most of its skirts in the $12 to $20 range with the emphasis at $14, $16, and $18. Markup has averaged 45% but sales volume has shown only a slight increase in spite of a favorable fashion trend.

Trade reports reveal that nearly 60% of the entire skirt market represents skirts selling for $8 or less. Much of this consists of skirts made to their own specifications by the great chains, such as Sears, Roebuck and Co.

Should the management change its price line policy? If so, what price lines should receive major emphasis?

B. AVERAGING MARKUP BY PRICE LINES AND GRADES

3. Averaging markup on price lines — two costs and one retail.

● *Example:*

A buyer is trying to develop a strong price line for pants at $15.90 retail. Merchandise available for this price line in the wholesale market is priced at $9.50 and at $11.50. To buy only $9.50 pants would assure a large markup, but would not make it possible to have outstanding values and broad assortments of styles and materials at $15.90. To buy only $11.50 merchandise would make the values at $15.90 outstanding, but would yield an inadequate markup. Accordingly, the buyer decides to buy pants at both costs, but in a proportion that will achieve the needed departmental markup of 38%. What should this proportion be?

Solution:

	$9.50	$11.50
Actual costs	$9.50	$11.50
Average costs	9.86	9.86
Variation of actual from average	−.36	+ 1.64

Since a cost 36 cents lower-than-average must be balanced by a cost $1.64 higher-than-average, 164 pants at $9.50 and 36 pants at $11.50 provide the correct proportions, since the number of units to buy at each price is in reverse ratio to the deviation from the average price. Proof: $.36 × 164 (units at $9.50) = $1.64 × 36 (units at $11.50). Since these proportions add to 200, the answer may be stated as 82% of purchases at $9.50 to 18% at $11.50. Roughly, of every five pairs of pants bought for the $15.90 price line, four should cost $9.50 and one $11.50.

A simpler method of solving is by adding the two differences together and this becomes the denominator for the fractions as illustrated below:

$$.36 + 1.64 = 2.00$$

then each becomes as follows:

$$\frac{.36}{2.00} = 18\% \qquad \frac{1.64}{2.00} = 82\%$$

Then these percentages are reversed in applying or multiplying them times the total needed. For instance, in the problem illustrated above, 18% of all purchased would be at $11.50 and 82% would be purchased at $9.50, as indicated by the arrows.

ASSIGNMENT 3:

A buyer has a price line of $130.00 for women's suits that he buys for $75.00 and $84.00. In what proportions should they be bought so as to average a markup of 40%?

DISCUSSION QUESTION:

What are the advantages in being able to include two cost lines in one retail line?

4. Averaging markup on price lines — one cost and two retails.

● *Example:*

A buyer has been marking most of the goods he buys for $1.20 at $2.00. But the wholesale prices go up 10%. The buyer is unwilling to drop his $2.00 price line since it is well established and in active demand by customers. Accordingly, he decides to retail the most attractive of this merchandise at his next higher price line, $2.30. In what proportions should he retail his purchases at the two prices, so as to average his former markup of 40%?

Solution:

Actual retail	$2.00	$2.30
Average retail required ($1.32 ÷ 60)	2.20	2.20
Variation of actual from average	.20	.10

Variation ratios $\quad\dfrac{.20}{.30}=\dfrac{2}{3}$ and $\dfrac{.10}{.30}=\dfrac{1}{3}$

The figure 1/3 or 33-1/3% may be regarded as the quantity to sell at $2.00 retail price and 2/3 or 66-2/3% as the quantity to sell at $2.30. This is because 20 cents "short" on ten items will just equal 10 cents "long" on twenty items. Thus, ten should be bought to sell for $2.00 for every twenty bought to sell for $2.30. This is the proportion of 1 to 2. Thus, the $2.30 price must become the major one for such goods, but the $2.00 price may be continued.

ASSIGNMENT 4:

Pants suits costing $67.00 are to be retailed at $100.00 and at $110.00. In what proportion should the suits be priced in order to average a markup of 37%?

DISCUSSION QUESTION:

Other than changes in wholesale price, what causes are there for setting two retail prices for a single cost?

5. Averaging markup on price lines — one cost and three retails.

Example:

A buyer purchased a job lot of 400 girl's coats at $5 each. He estimated that 100 of the lot were worth at retail only the $5 cost but the rest could be sold at a good profit, some for $8 and some for $12. How many should be priced at $8 and how many at $12 to average a 40% markup on the entire lot of 400?

Solution:

400 × $5 = $2,000, the entire cost
$2,000 ÷ 0.60 = $3,333, the necessary retail to average a 40% markup
100 × $5 =   500 the retail of the least desirable coats
                $2,833 the retail to be realized on 300 coats
$2,833 ÷ 300 = $9.44, the average retail price needed

Actual retail	$8.00	$12.00	
Average retail	9.44	9.44	
Variation	$1.44	$ 2.56	1.44 + 2.56 = 4.00

$1.44/$4.00 = 36% and $2.56/$4.00 = 64%

36% of 300 = 108, the number to price at $12

64% of 300 = 192, the number to price at $8

ASSIGNMENT 5:

A buyer inspects a job lot of 754 pairs of jeans priced at $8.00 a pair. He estimates that 100 pairs are worth at retail only $4.00 a pair but that the rest should sell at $14.00 and $16.00 a pair. In what proportion should he price these jeans in order to realize an average markup of 42% on the entire lot of 754 pairs?

DISCUSSION QUESTION:

Is it possible to determine the buying ratios for three retails with a single cost if the quantity to sell at none of the retails is known?

6. Averaging markup on price lines — both costs and retails different.

Example:

Packages of gum costing 6 cents each are to be sold for 10 cents each and those costing 14 cents, for 20 cents. In what ratio should they be stocked and sold in order to average a markup of 35%?

Solution:

$.06 ÷ 0.65 = $.09.23 the average retail needed for 6-cent gum

$.14 ÷ 0.65 = $.21.54 the average retail needed for 14-cent gum

Average retails	$.09.35	$.21.54
Actual retails	.10.00	.20.00
Variation	$ .77	$ 1.54

0.77 at 20 cents to 1.54 at 10 cents

This is the same as 1 at 20 cents to 2 at 10 cents

ASSIGNMENT 6:

Brand *A* infant's shirt costs 50 cents each and sells for 75 cents. Brand *B* costs 62½ cents each and sells for $1.00. In what ratio should the two brands be stocked and sold in order to average a markup of 35%?

DISCUSSION QUESTION:

In assignment 6 suppose that both brands sell equally, even though stocked in the desired proportions. How would this distort the markup?

7. Combining grades.

Example:

A food buyer wants to mix two grades of coffee to sell at 98 cents a pound. One grade sells for 80 cents and the other grade for $1.10. In what ratio should the two grades be mixed to assure the same margin that is obtained when the grades are sold separately?

Solution:

Actual retails	$.80	$1.10
Average retail	.98	.98
Variation	$.18	$ .12

18 parts of $1.10 coffee
12 parts of 80-cent coffee
30
    18/30 = 60% of $1.10 coffee
    12/30 = 40% of 80-cent coffee

ASSIGNMENT 7:

In drawing up specifications for women's wool suits, a chain store buyer decides that the material for the suits should cost no more than $10.00 a yard. The yarn accounts for 50% of the cost; labor and overhead accounts for the rest. The buyer decides to specify a combination of wool and rayon. The yarn to make a yard for the former costs $7.00 and the yarn to make a yard of the latter costs $4.00. In what ratio should the yarns be specified?

DISCUSSION QUESTIONS:

Why should a suit buyer be interested in the cost of the suit material? Isn't this the manufacturer's problem?

Managerial Decision

A friend of yours who is not in the retailing business questions the ethics of your practice of setting different retail prices on dresses that cost the same amount. Defend your practice.

ADDITIONAL ASSIGNMENTS

8. The dollar sales of living room lamps are distributed as follows:

$15.00	35%
20.00	50%
25.00	15%
	100%

Find the unit sales distribution of these lamps.

9. A dress buyer wishes a maintained markup of about 40% on his best-selling wholesale price line of $12.50. He plans the following five retail prices at which to sell this merchandise:

(a) A major regular price for 70% of his unit purchases.

(b) A high-profit price line for the 20% of his unit purchases that represent unusual style or quality.

(c) A promotional price for 10% of his purchases that he believes he can occasionally buy from his key resources at a discount that will make possible about the same markup as that to be realized at his major regular price.

(d) A first markdown price for goods that fail to sell at either the major regular price or at the promotional price. About half the markdowns from the high profit price will also be to this markdown price, the rest to the regular price.

(e) A final clearance price for dresses that fail to sell at the first markdown price.

From past experience, he believes that 20% of his regular stock will have to be reduced and about 30% each of his high markup and his promotional goods. Of the markdown goods, 80% should sell at the first markdown.

(a) What five prices would you recommend?

(b) Demonstrate that, with these prices, the maintained markup goal will be realized (use 100 units as a base).

10. Fall season report of sales in a men's clothing department, arranged according to price lines.

PRICE LINES

Total $35.00 $39.50 $44.50 $49.50 $55.00 $65.00 $75.00 $85.00

% $ sales at each price to total $ sales	Total	$35.00	$39.50	$44.50	$49.50	$55.00	$65.00	$75.00	$85.00
% $ sales at each price to total $ sales	100	14	2	27	26	10	1	11	9

PRICE LINES (cont.)

	Total	$35.00	$39.50	$44.50	$49.50	$55.00	$65.00	$75.00	$85.00
% of suits sold at each price to total suits sold......	100	16	3	28	27	10	1	9	6
% of suits sold at original retail price in each price line	68	96	51	85	70	65	0	50	40
% of suits sold at a markdown price in each price line	32	4	49	15	30	35	100	50	60
% of suits sold above cost in each price line	96	100	60	100	99	100	60	95	92
% of suits sold at less than cost in each price line ...	4	0	40	0	1	0	40	5	8
Original markup % ..	35	32	29	37	33	39	27	34	35
Maintained markup, % ..	32	32	15	34	32	31	8	29	28
Department expense, % ..	31								
% of average $ stock to total average stock	100	16	7	18	24	11	3	7	14

(a) Study the above figures and, on a basis of the analysis you have made, indicate the appropriate action that should be taken, particularly with regard to the elimination of price lines.

(b) What is the percentage of markdown for the department as a whole?

11. Price-line analysis of a women's coat department.

Price	Total Sales in Pieces	Sales at Original Prices	Sales at Markdown Prices	Total Originally Marked at Price Indicated	Markdowns from Prices Indicated
$23.50	165		165		
27.50	230		230		
29.50	2,700	2,000	700	2,000	
31.50	250		250	35	35
34.50	800	800		1,250	450
36.50	505		505		
39.50	800	800		1,150	350
44.50	595	350	245	700	350
49.50	200	200		700	500
54.50	205	150	55	300	150
59.50	100	100		250	150
64.50	50	50		165	115
69.50	25	25		75	50
Total	6,625	4,475	2,150	6,625	2,150

(a) What suggestions can be made for the marking of women's coats in the immediate future?

(b) What price lines should be eliminated and why?

12. A buyer purchased 1,000 pairs of an item at $1.90 per pair to retail at $2.78 at a special sale. At the same time, he bought 1,200 pairs for regular stock at $2.50 a pair. At what price must he retail each pair for regular stock in order to have an average markup of 36% on the day's purchases?

13. You are open-to-buy 50 pairs of slippers to sell for $4.95. When you arrive in the market you decide to purchase the slippers from two manufacturers. Manufacturer *A's* price is $2.75 and Manufacturer *B's* price is $3.25. If you wish to obtain an average markup of 39%, how many pairs of slippers should you purchase from each vendor?

14. The cost price for a line of men's shirts is $4.00 and the necessary markup is 34%. The nearest established retail prices are $5.50 and $7.00. The buyer decides to price the new and unusual styles at $7.00 and the rest at $5.50. In what proportions should he mark these goods at the two prices?

7   How to Establish
                      Competitive Prices

Setting policies for pricing goods relative to competition and to the average expense ratio is based on considerations of psychology and human relations. Nevertheless, the policy-setter should be able to calculate the short-run effect of various policies on markup and profits.

DEFINITIONS

Market Price. The price at which a product handled by competitors is generally sold.

Market Plus Price. A price set by a dealer that is higher than the market price for similar merchandise.

Market Minus Price. A price set below the customary market price in order to attract customers. It may be temporary to meet competition or it may be permanent, made possible by lower-than-average expenses per transaction.

Leader. A selected item that is deliberately sold at a price lower than the one at which the largest total profit on the item could be realized, in order to attract customers.

Loss-Leader. A selected item that is deliberately sold at less than "cost" in order to attract customers.

Cost (as used in connection with leaders). May mean any one of the following: (1) billed cost; (2) actual net cost (less all discounts); (3) billed or actual cost plus flat handling expenses; (4) billed or actual cost plus a proportionate share of all expenses of doing business.

"Fair Trade" Laws. State laws and the supporting Federal Miller-Tydings Act and amendments, giving sellers the right to set minimum resale prices for their products under certain conditions.

Equating Velocity. Determining the increase in sales necessary at a lower price to provide the same aggregate dollar margin obtained at the higher price; also the decrease in sales at a higher price that will provide the same aggregate dollar margin obtained at a lower price. The margin may be calculated at the initial markup level, the maintained markup level, the gross margin level, or the controllable margin level. (In this section only the initial markup level is considered except in #6.)

A. EQUATING VELOCITIES

1. Retail price changes expressed as markup changes.

● *Example:*

A merchandise line with a 30% markup is cut 5% in price to meet competition. What is the new markup?

Solution:

Let $1.00 equal the retail price. Then 70 cents equals the cost. Since price is cut 5%, the new price is 95 cents, and the new dollar markup, 25 cents. The new percentage of markup, then, is 26.3%.

ASSIGNMENT 1:

With a markup of 40%, a merchant cuts the price of every item in stock 30%, for a sale. Find markup percentage after the cut.

DISCUSSION QUESTION:

Is the relative change in a price always greater than the corresponding change in the markup percentage?

2. Changes in markup percentage expressed as a change in price.

● *Example:*

A department has operated at a 50% markup, but to stimulate volume, a 45% markup is being considered. Wholesale prices are not changing. A cut of 5% in the markup percentage is equivalent to what average cut in retail prices?

Solution:

Let $100 = old retail price; therefore, the cost is $50.00.
New retail $50 ÷ 55% = $90.90, a reduction of 9.1% from $100.

ASSIGNMENT 2:

A department has been operating at a 48% markup, but a change to 50% is being considered. If wholesale prices are constant, what average increase in retail prices will this require?

DISCUSSION QUESTION:

> In view of the growth of successful low-margin retailers, are there many opportunities today to increase retail prices that are not necessitated by an increase in wholesale prices? Explain.

3. Increases in sales volume to offset lowered retail prices.

● *Example:*

> A department has been selling an article for $2.00 that costs $1.10. A 10% cut in price is contemplated to stimulate volume. What percentage increase in unit volume is necessary so that the lower price will result in as much dollar markup as before? What percentage increase in dollar volume is necessary?

Solution:

> Formula: former dollar markup ÷ new dollar markup = the new unit volume in terms of the old. This is called the equating velocity.

$$\text{Markup at } \$2.00 \ldots \ldots \ldots \ldots \$.90$$
$$\text{Markup at } \$1.80 \ldots \ldots \ldots \ldots \$.70$$

Since each sale will bring in only 70 cents, whereas it brought in 90 cents before, the unit volume will have to be $\dfrac{\$.90}{\$.70}$ or 1.286 times the old volume. This is an increase of 28.6% in the number of units. Since expenses will probably increase somewhat with the increase in units, the necessary increase in business should be somewhat greater than 28.6% to justify the price cut.

To find the increase in dollars, 1.286 (the increased units) may be multiplied by the new unit value of $1.80. Thus, $1.286 \times \$1.80 = \$2.314$, the new dollar volume. Since the old volume was $2.00, this is an increase of 15.7%.

The percentage increase in dollar sales required may also be found by the formula: old markup % ÷ new markup %. The old percentage is 45% and the new is $\dfrac{\$.70}{\$1.80}$ or 38.9%. $\dfrac{45\%}{38.9\%} = 1.157$. Thus a dollar increase of 15.7%, which is equivalent to a unit increase of 28.6%, is necessary to provide the same dollar markup as before.

ASSIGNMENT 3:

A price line in a department has been operated at a 40% markup and a cut of 5% in this price is contemplated from $100 to $95. How much increase in unit and dollar volume is necessary to produce as much dollar markup as before?

DISCUSSION QUESTION:

What other conditions would have to be satisfied to justify the cut in price determined in assignment 3?

4. Composite problem.

● *Example:*

In a department with a 40% markup, a 35% markup is being considered. (1) What increase in dollar volume is necessary to offset the cut? (2) If wholesale prices are constant, what average reduction in retail prices would result? (3) What increase in unit volume is necessary?

Solution:

(1) Formula: old markup % ÷ new markup % = new dollar volume as a percentage of the old. 40% ÷ 35% = 114%. Thus, dollar sales would have to be increased at least 14% to realize the same gross margin as before. (2) Let $1.00 = old retail and 60 cents the cost. Since the new markup is 35%, the new retail is $\frac{\$.60}{65\%}$ = $.923. Thus, a 7.7% reduction in retail price would result. (3) With $1.00 as the old retail, the old dollar markup was $.40 and the new dollar markup $.323 ($.923 - $.60). The new unit volume as a percentage of the old, then, is $\frac{\$.40}{\$.323}$ = 123%. Thus, unit increase in volume required is 24%.

This result may also be found by dividing the new dollar volume, $1.14, by the new retail of $.923. Thus, $1.14 ÷ $.923 = 1.24 or 124%, an increase of 24%.

ASSIGNMENT 4:

In a department with a 35% markup, a 37% markup is under consideration. What decrease in dollar and in unit volume will result in the same dollar markup as before? If wholesale prices are constant, what would be the average increase in retail prices?

5. **Increase in sales volume to offset an increase in cost with no change in the retail.**

● *Example:*

As a sales promotion device for a week, a buyer wants to offer a free pair of $2.00 hosiery for every 6 pairs purchased. The hosiery costs $1.20 a pair. This hosiery normally sells at the rate of 24 pairs a week. How many pairs would he have to sell to avoid any cut in his dollar margin?

Solution:

Present gross margin per pair: $.80
The cost of the free pair must be spread over the 6 pairs sold that cost $1.20 each. Thus, 20 cents must be added to the cost of each pair, making it $1.40.

$$\frac{\text{Former dollar markup \$.80}}{\text{New dollar markup \$.60}} = 1.33$$

Thus, the unit sales would have to increase one-third from 24 to 32 pairs during the week. The increase would have to be more than this to justify the promotion from the point of view of immediate profit.
Note: Since the retail price is not being changed in this case, the ratio of the old markup percentage to the new markup percentage (40% to 30%) is the same as the ratio of the old dollar markup to the new dollar markup.

ASSIGNMENT 5:

You have been buying a line of clothing for $16 a unit and selling for $30 a unit. The manufacturer raises his price to $18 but you do not want to change your retail price since it is well established and you hope to undersell competitors who are raising their prices for similar goods.

What percentage would your sales have to increase to maintain the same dollar margin you are now realizing?

6. Equating velocities at different levels.

Example:

An article costs $1.91 and the normal initial markup in the department is 40% with reductions 6-2/3% (of sales). Direct variable expenses chargeable to each item sold in the department are estimated at 30 cents.

The buyer is considering a price of $2.98 rather than $3.19, the price at which he would obtain a 40% markup. But he recognizes that at the $2.98 price he would need to have a considerably higher sales

velocity to obtain as large an initial markup in dollars. However, at the
$2.98 price, he estimates that his reductions would be only 5% rather
than 6-2/3% and that his direct expenses might be only 26 cents rather
than 30 cents, since some of them (particularly selling and promotional
expenses) would tend to decline with the reduction in the value of the
unit of sale.

What percentage larger would his sales have to be at the $2.98 price
compared with the $3.19 price to provide:

1. The same total initial markup in dollars?

2. The same maintained markup in dollars?

3. The same controllable margin in dollars?

Note: Assume no cash discounts or alteration costs, so that
maintained markup and gross margin are the same.

Solution:

Levels	Normals	Proposed	Equating $ Velocities ###
Retail	$3.19	$2.98	
Cost	1.91	1.91	
1. Initial markup. .	1.28 (40%)	1.07 (36%)	1.28/1.07 = 1.20
Average Sale # .	2.99	2.83	
2. Maintained markup ##. .	1.08 (36%)	.92 (32.5%)	1.08/ .92 = 1.17
Direct expense .	.30	.26	
3. Controllable margin.	.78 (26.1%)	.66 (23.3%)	.78/ .66 = 1.18

The average sale figures are found by dividing the original retail prices by
100% plus the reduction %, since reductions are based on sales, not on original
retail price. At $3.19 reductions of 6-2/3% are expected. If the average final sales
price is called 100%, the original retail is 106-2/3%. Since this is $3.19, the average
selling price will be $3.19/106-2/3% or $2.99. Similarly, $2.98 is divided by 105%
to obtain $2.83. Thus, the reductions at the $3.19 price are estimated at 20 cents
and at $2.98 at 15 cents.

The maintained markup or gross margin in both instances is found by sub-
tracting the cost of $1.91 from the average sale (after reductions).

The equating velocities are found by dividing the normal margin at each
of the 3 analysis levels by the proposed margin at each level.

The equating velocity of 1.20 at the initial markup level means that
20% more items would have to be sold at $2.98 to yield the same initial
markup in dollars that is obtained at $3.19. The velocity of 1.17 at the
maintained markup (gross margin) level means that a 17% increase in
unit sales is needed at $2.98 to achieve a total dollar maintained
markup equal to that realized with a $3.19 original price. Similarly, the

velocity of 1.18 at the controllable margin level means that 18% more units must be sold to bring in an equal amount of controllable margin dollars. The slight difference among the velocities at the three levels of analysis suggests that it is often sufficient to make comparisons only at the initial markup level. From the shortrun profit point of view, the buyer should be reasonably sure that he will be able to sell at least 20% more at $2.98 than he could at $3.19. However, he might logically decide upon the $2.98 price, even if only a 10% sales increase were anticipated, in order to strengthen his competitive position and thus contribute to growth. The maximizing of immediate profits is often sacrificed in order to move more goods and to attempt to insure future acceptance by the public and by suppliers.

ASSIGNMENT 6:

An item costing $6.50 may be retailed at either $11 or $10. At $11, reductions are likely to be 10% of sales but at $10 only 5%. Handling and other expenses growing out of the stocking of the item are expected to be $1 at the $11 price and 96 cents at the $10 price. Determine the equalizing velocities at the (a) initial markup level, (b) the gross margin level, and (c) at the controllable margin level.

DISCUSSION QUESTIONS:

Does it seem likely that a $10 rather than an $11 price will increase velocity more than that required at the controllable profit level? Is such an increase more likely to be achieved in staples or in fashions?

Managerial Decision

You recognize the value of equating velocities as a basis for intelligent pricing but feel that it would be very costly and even inaccurate for your controller to determine handling costs per item, and you very much doubt whether probable markdowns can be estimated with any degree of accuracy. What use might you make, nevertheless, of the velocity concept?

7. **Volume necessary to offset changes in markup and expense.**

Example:

A staple item priced at $15.00 sells at the rate of 12 a week and at a markup of 46%. It is advertised once during a 13-week season at a cost of $130. It is proposed that the article be repriced at a 40% markup (same cost) and that it be advertised every month at the same cost per insertion as before. The unit handling cost is now $1.00 but can be reduced to 80 cents if the goods are sold in considerably larger quantities. What increase in unit volume is necessary to give the same controllable profit as is now being earned? Are you in favor of the proposed changes? Defend your answer.

Note: This is a problem in equating velocities but must be solved somewhat differently than above because the planned advertising expense is expressed neither as a per cent of the new sales unit nor as a flat amount per unit. Since it is planned as a total amount, it must be added to the total controllable margin goal and the sum divided by the planned unit controllable margin *before* advertising.

Solution:

Present weekly sales volume:

$15 × 12 = $180.   Markup = 46% of $180. . . . or . . . $82.80

Weekly advertising expense: $130 ÷ 13 = $10
Weekly handling cost: $1 × 12 =   12

Total direct expense $22.00

Controllable margin now earned. $60.80
New planned weekly advertising $130 ÷ 4 1/3 = ...   30.00

Margin that new volume must contribute to cover both
    advertising and margin goal $90.80
Cost of each item $15 × 54% = $ 8.10
New retail: $8.10 ÷ 60%   =   13.50

New markup. . . . . $ 5.40
Unit handling cost 80

Net margin per unit . . . . $ 4.60
Total units necessary a week: $90.80 ÷ $4.60 = 20 (approx.).

Thus, weekly volume must increase from 12 to 20 a week to justify the changes. If the buyer believes that a $13.50 price rather than $15.00 will increase volume more than 66-2/3%, the changes can be justified.

ASSIGNMENT 7:

A staple item that costs $3.00 is retailed at a markup of 25% and sells at the rate of 50 a week. It is not advertised, but each sales transaction costs about 25 cents to handle. In view of the investment and of the space occupied, the buyer feels that the amount this item contributes to department expense is inadequate. He is considering marking up the goods 33-1/3% of retail and advertising them once in 4 weeks at a cost of $20 an insertion. If he aims at a 50% increase in the contribution from this item, how many would he have to sell a week at the new price?

DISCUSSION QUESTION:

Has he a reasonable chance of selling this many?

Managerial Decision

In view of recent developments is it very important that each buyer be provided by the controller with "flat" and variable expenses for each category of merchandise as a basis for his pricing?

B. PROBABILITIES IN COMPETITIVE PRICING

8. Application of baysian statistics to competitive pricing.

Example:

In order to qualify for a substantial rebate based on the number of units sold of a certain brand handled, the merchant is planning to cut the price of the product substantially for the balance of the season from the present price of $10. He is considering either a $9 price or a $7.50 one. Even at the latter price he would more than cover his direct expenses.

But he recognizes that price cutting on his part may lead to retaliatory price cuts by his chief competitor on a very similar product that the competitor handles. The merchant makes the following estimates:

At $9 sales should increase 25% if his competitor does not retaliate. But if his competitor does, his sales will probably increase only 5%.

At $7.50 sales should increase 40% with no retailiation but only 10% with retaliation.

Next, he made estimates of the probability of retaliation;

At $9, an 80% chance that the competitor will not and 20% that he will.

At $7.50, a 10% chance of no retaliation; 90% chance of retaliation.

In view of these expectations and probabilities, should the merchant cut his price to $9 or to $7.50?

Solution:

Assume current sales of 1

	At $9 Sales	Proba-bility	Weighted	At $7.50 Sales	Proba-bility	Weighted
No retaliation	1.25	0.8	1.00	1.40	0.1	0.14
Retaliation	1.05	0.2	0.21	1.10	0.9	0.99
			1.21			1.13

Thus, the $9 price has the better chance of increasing his volume substantially.

ASSIGNMENT 8:

A merchant wants to maximize his unit sales without incurring a loss. He estimates that (1) a 15% cut should increase his unit sales 20% and (2) a 25% cut should increase his unit sales 40% *if* his competitors do not also cut prices on the same or similar goods. If they retaliate, the 15% price cut is likely to increase his sales only 10% and the 25% cut, only 15%. The chances of retaliation when he cuts 15% are estimated at only one in five, but if he cuts 25% they are four in five.

Which price cut is likely to result in the larger sales increase in units?

DISCUSSION QUESTIONS:

1. Is it possible for a merchant to estimate sales under various probabilities with sufficient accuracy to make this method of value in actual price determination?

2. What other reasons may a merchant have for putting more emphasis on increasing unit sales than on increasing immediate profits?

3. Can the same method of analysis used here be applied where the goal is profit and the profitability of different price points under various conditions is estimated, instead of the change in sales?

ADDITIONAL ASSIGNMENTS

9. A line of merchandise has been priced at $4.95 with a cost of $2.50. A cut in price to $4.50 is contemplated to increase volume. What increase in both units and dollars is necessary to yield the same dollar markup as before?

10. Dresses costing $4.00 each have been retailed for $6.00, but a $7.00 retail price is under consideration. How much of a loss in both dollar and unit volume can be contemplated without reducing the dollar markup now realized from the sale of this merchandise?

11. If a markup of 40% is reduced to 37% with no change in wholesale prices, how much will prices be reduced? How much increase in both dollar and unit volume is necessary to yield the same dollar markup as before?

How to Analyze Markdowns

The inability to sell all purchases at the original retail price presents a major merchandising problem. Its solution requires an analysis not only of techniques of buying, selling, and stock control, but also of the policy of original pricing.

Since much analysis is done in terms of percentages, the prospective merchandiser must understand the significance of the various ways of stating the percentages.

DEFINITIONS

Markdown Timing. Selecting the time to take markdowns relative to the length of the selling season still remaining.

One-Price Policy. A policy to sell to all customers at the same price. This does not preclude (1) the taking of markdowns so long as the reduced prices are available to all customers; (2) the offering of multiple prices; and (3) the granting of discounts to employees.

Multiple Price. A price placed on a number of identical or similar articles or on a set of related articles that is less than the sum of the unit prices of the articles. Example: tennis balls — 3 for $1.50 or 55 cents each.

"Two for" Plan. A multiple pricing plan in which two articles in a price line or at different price lines are sold jointly for less than the sum of the individual prices. Example: Two $29.95 dresses for $56.

Markdown Percentage. The net markdowns taken during a period divided by the net sales. Although this percentage is widely used for internal analysis, it is not the public's understanding of the term.

Markdown Goods Percentage. The dollar sales of goods marked down divided by total sales. Assuming carryovers of markdown goods in opening and closing inventories are the same size, the markdown goods percentage may be found by subtracting the dollar markdowns from the original retail prices of markdown goods and dividing by the total dollar sales. For example, if $90 in markdowns are taken on goods retailed at $900, the goods are sold for $810; and if total sales are $3,200, the markdown goods percentage is 25.3.

Markdown Off Percentage. The dollar markdowns divided by the original retail price of the goods marked down. This relationship is the one that the general public regards as the markdown percentage.

MARKDOWN PERCENTAGE RELATIONSHIPS

1. Relationship between markdowns on sales and off original retail.

● *Example:*

A buyer has in stock a supply of articles retailing at $12 each, which he wishes to mark down 20% of sales. He expects to sell all of these articles at the markdown price during the current accounting period. How much markdown should be taken in dollars and in percentage of original retail?

Solution:

Let 100% = sales
Then 100% + 20% = 120%, the original retail
120% of sales = $12

$$\text{Sales} = \frac{\$12}{120\%} = \$10$$

$12 − $10 = $2, the markdown.
$2 ÷ $12 = 16-2/3%, the percentage off original retail.

ASSIGNMENT 1:

A buyer plans to offer a lot of merchandise for sale. The present retail is $7,000 and he does not want the markdowns to exceed 15% of sales. How much may he reduce the goods?

DISCUSSION QUESTION:

Why are markdowns usually stated as a percentage of sales instead of original retail?

2. Relationship between markdown off original retail and markdown on sales

● *Example:*

If a buyer takes a blanket reduction of 15% on a stock of goods and sells the goods at the reduced price (and no other goods), what is his markdown percentage?

Solution:

Let $100 = original retail
Then, $100 - $15 = $85, the sales
Markdown percentage = $15/$85 = 17.6%

ASSIGNMENT 2:

If goods are reduced 25% in price and sold, what is the markdown percentage?

DISCUSSION QUESTION:

If other goods in addition to the reduced goods are sold, would the markdown percentage be larger or smaller?

3. Calculating markdown percentage relationships

Example:

A shoe merchant marked down all his $10 shoes to $8 for clearance. In dollars, his markdowns were $400. Twenty pairs failed to sell at $8 and they were cleared at $6 each. The total shoe sales during the period at all prices were $20,000.
Find:

1. the markdown percentage.
2. the markdown percentage off retail.
3. the markdown goods percentage.

Solution:

(1) $8 – $6 = $2, the second markdown per pair
$2 X 20 = $40, the second markdown
400, the first markdown
$440, the total markdown
$440 ÷ $20,000 = 2.4%, the markdown percentage on all shoes

(2) $10 - $8 = $2, the first markdown
$400 ÷ $2 = 200, the number of pairs reduced
200 X $10 = $2,000, original retail of reduced shoes
$440 ÷ $2,000 = 22%, the markdown percentage off retail.

(3)   Sales at $8:

$$\$8 \times (200 - 20) = \$8 \times 180 = \$1,440$$

Sales at $6:

$$\$6 \times 20 = \underline{\qquad 120}$$

Total sales of markdown goods $1,560

$1,560 \div \$20,000 = 7.8\%$, the markdown goods sold as a
percentage of total sales.

ASSIGNMENT 3:

A buyer of millinery kept the following records for a season:

Net sales $75,000
Net markdowns   12,000
Original retail values of all goods marked down   36,000

Find:

1. the markdown percentage.
2. the percentage off retail.
3. the markdown goods percentage.

DISCUSSION QUESTION:

Explain the significance of the following:

1. A decrease in the markdown percentage with an increase in the percentage off.
2. An increase in the markdown goods percentage with a decrease in the markdown percentage.
3. An increase in the percentage off with a decrease in the markdown goods percentage.

4. Relationship among (1) markdown percentage, (2) markdown off percentage, and (3) markdown goods percentage

Example:

In one department, during a season, markdowns were 5%. Analysis of sales showed that of the total dollar sales, 30% were markdown goods. Find the average percentage reduction from the original retail found necessary to move goods. (Assume that the markdown goods unsold at the end of the season are just balanced by the markdown goods unsold at the beginning.)

Solution:

Let $100 = sales

∴ $5 = markdowns and $30 = sales of markdown goods
Original retail of markdown goods, then, $5 + $30 or $35.
$5 ÷ $35 = 14.3%, the markdown off percentage.

ASSIGNMENT 4:

1. Markdowns, 5% of sales; 15% of sales at markdown prices. Find markdown off percentage.
2. Markdowns, 8% of sales; percentage off original retail, 30%. Find markdown goods percentage.
3. Markdown off, 25%; markdown goods, 20%. Find markdown percentage.

DISCUSSION QUESTION:

Which one of these three factors is generally found only by derivation from the other two?

5. Markdowns allowable.

● *Example:*

An oriental rug buyer is anxious to maintain a markup of 40% on all rugs after markdowns have been taken. He buys a lot of 50 rugs for $150 each that he retails at $265 each. After 40 are sold he decides to clear out the remaining 10. How much can he mark each one down and still realize his markup objective?

Solution:

Total cost: 50 × $150 = $7,500
Retail = $7,500 ÷ (100% – 40%)
$7,500 ÷ 60% = $12,500
Retail to date, 40 × $265   10,600
Balance of sales needed on 5 rugs $ 1,900
Retail per rug = $1,900 ÷ 10 = $190
$265 – $190 = $75, the allowable markdown per rug.

ASSIGNMENT 5:

A buyer purchased 70 lamps for $10 each. His maintained markup goal was 40%. After 60 lamps had been sold at $17.75, it was necessary to reduce the remainder to $12. Six were sold at this price. How much markdown could the buyer take on each of the remaining 4 to realize his markup objective?

DISCUSSION QUESTION:

Will a knowledge of the markdown that will protect his markup objective be of help to the buyer in repricing the last 4 lamps? Explain.

ADDITIONAL ASSIGNMENTS

6. How much may a buyer reduce the present retail price of certain goods in order to have a markdown of 9% of sales?

7. In a department, markdowns are 12% of sales, and 30% of the total sales are at markdown prices. What is the percentage of reduction from original retail price of the goods reduced?

8. Markdowns, 10%; percentage reduction from original retail, 20%. What percentage of the sales represents reduced merchandise?

9. Percentage reduction from original retail, 20%; sales at reduced prices to total sales, 25%. Find the markdown percentage.

10. One hundred items costing $4 each are retailed at $5.75. Eighty-five sell at this price but the last 15 become slow-selling. How much markdown per item may be taken to average a maintained markup of 25%?

11. A lot of one gross of handbags, costing $36 a dozen, are retailed at $4.50 each. After 124 have been sold, the remainder became slow-selling. How large a markdown may be taken on each to realize a maintained markup of 30% on the lot?

Managerial Decision

You ask one of your buyers to analyze, by reason, the markdowns he has taken during the past season. You provide a standard list of reasons to be used for this purpose. The buyer reports that "special sales from stock" is the major reason for his markdowns, whereas "overbuying" appears near the bottom of the list. Will you accept this analysis as conclusive? Why?

Part III   INVENTORIES

9   How to Take Physical Inventory

Counting an inventory is chiefly a matter of accuracy and completeness rather than one of problem-solving. Counting involves determining the quantity of each unit on hand and the value of each unit. The value may be the cost value or the retail value. When cost values are used, they are often in terms of dozens (or of other quantity units in which the goods are bought). There is, then, a problem of converting them to selling units.

DEFINITIONS

Physical Inventory. The quantity or the value of merchandise on hand at a given time as determined by an actual count.

Physical Inventory at Cost. The value of an inventory at aggregate cost prices.

Physical Inventory at Retail. The value of an inventory at aggregate retail prices.

Invoice Cut-off. Setting a specific time after which invoices received will not be included in the calculation of the inventory on hand. After this time, the merchandise corresponding to these invoices will not be included in the physical inventory count.

Inventory Sheet. A form for recording the inventory count that provides for listing a large number of items on a single form.

Inventory Tag. A form for recording the inventory count that provides for listing the quantity of a single item on hand.

Inventory Floor Plan. A diagram of the layout of the stock fixtures in a store or department with each fixture and subdivision (drawer, shelf, or bin) assigned a distinguishing number. Inventory sheets or tags are assigned to each fixture and a central record is maintained so that, if an inventory sheet or tag is missing, merchandise not yet included in the count can readily be spotted.

1. Cost codes.

● *Example:*

A buyer of toys wishes to select a suitable cost code to use on price tickets. He has a choice of three types:

Alphabetical – example: 12345   67890
                          Bacon   Fries (code phrase)
Numerical   – example: year, cost in dollars and cents, month
Symbolical – example:

(1)	(4)	(7)
(2)	(5)	(8)
(3)	(6)	(9)

X = 0

1. Indicate cost codes for a doll costing $2.50, bought on June 3, 1972.
2. If the code for a doll is 72055–10, what is its cost?

Solution:

1. Alphabetical: ANS
   Numerical: 7225006
   Symbolical: ⌐ □ X
2. $.55, bought in October, 1972.

ASSIGNMENT 1:

Using the same three codes given in the example, 1. Code the following: $27.32; 2. decode the following: (a) BOCS; (b) 7212003; (c) ⌐ ⊔ ⊏ □

DISCUSSION QUESTIONS:

Which of the three types of codes is likely to prove to be most satisfactory? Why?

2. Taking physical inventory.

Example:

In a notions department most merchandise is sold singly, but some is sold by the dozen, some in sets, some by the yard, and some is multiple priced. The following are examples of merchandise to be included on one sheet of the inventory. The quantities are determined by count, and the prices, units, and season letters are taken from the price tickets. This is the end of the *C* season of six months; the preceding season was *B* and the one before *A*.

21 garment bags at $.91 each, Season *A*.

16 garment bags at $.79 each, Season *B*.

65 hair nets at $1.42 a dozen, Season *C*.

19 dish cloths sold 6 for $.51, 3 for $.27, or $.10 each, Season *B*.

19 sets of hangers at $1.50 a set, Season *A*.

27 yards of ½″ elastic at $.20 a yard, Season *B*.

150 buttons sold 12 for $.45 or $.05 each, Season *C*.

34 spools of thread at $.99 a dozen, Season *A*.

Enter this information on the inventory sheet below and make the extensions.

Solution:

MERCHANDISE INVENTORY
END OF SPRING SEASON: *C*   DEPT. 21

Description	*No. of Units*	*Kind of Unit*	*Price per unit* $	*cents*	*How priced*	*Season Letter*	*Extension**
Garment bags	21	ea.		91	ea.	A	
Garment bags	16	ea.		79	ea.	B	
Hair net	65	doz.	1	42	doz.	C	
Dish Cloths	19	ea.	6 for	51	M.P.	B	
Hanger	19	set	1	50	set	A	
Elastic	27	yds.		20	yd	B	
Buttons	150	ea.	12 for	45	M.P.	C	
Thread	34	ea.		99	doz	A	
Seasons	A		B	C	D		Total
Totals							

*The student should make the extensions for each article and find the totals by seasons.

ASSIGNMENT 2:

A hardware store takes inventory at both cost and retail prices. Goods are listed on large sheets and the price information is taken from price tickets, where both the retail prices and the costs in code appear. The code used is MONEY TALKS. M stands for 1, O for 2, N for 3, and so forth, and S stands for 0.

Quantity on hand	Item	Buying Units	Cost Code (Buying Unit)*	Retail Price Selling Units	Season
5	H.S. steel wool	Doz	MYS	.40	X
51	Wick sets	Gr	OEN	.05	Y
4	Cast dampers	Doz	MOY	.15	Y
15	Copper rings	Doz	EOY	.50	Y
1	Cake box	set of 3	NAY	2.00	Z
73 qts	Royal polish	Gr	ENOS	.50	Y
3 qts	Royal polish	Free	SS	.50	Y
30 gals	Bulk oil	Lb.**	MMY	1.50	X
91 lbs	Nails	100 lb.	MNSS	.15	Z
42	1501 water sets	ea.	ON	.39	Y
7 gal	Special paint	special	YSSS	3.50	Y
14 half-gal	Special paint	deal of		1.85	Y
4 qts	Special paint	78 qts. in		1.00	Y
10 pts	Special paint	assorted size containers.		.60	Y

*In many lines, the cost code is readily applied to the cost of the selling unit, and calculating the total cost of an inventory is then simpler than in the above problem. In some stores, the cost is always expressed in terms of selling units and is carried out to five decimal places. Thus a cost of 34 cents a dozen is written $.02833 each.

**7½ pounds of oil to the gallon.

Fill in the inventory sheet from the information given in the table. Insert the decoded costs; calculate the total cost and retail value of this merchandise and the markup percentage on the inventory. Note that the quantity on hand and the retail prices are per sales unit, not per buying unit. Cost codes are in buying units.

DISCUSSION QUESTION:

Is it desirable to record all cost codes in selling units, rather than in buying units, so as to avoid error in inventory calculation?

Managerial Decision

From a merchandise management viewpoint, what useful purposes are served by recording the cost in code on price tickets?

INVENTORY SHEET

Description	Number of Selling Units	Kind of Unit (Selling)	Price per Selling Unit	Kind of Buying Unit	Cost per Buying Unit	Season	Retail Extension	Cost Extension
Total	—	—	—	—	—	—		
Season	X	Y		Z				
Totals (Retail)						Total		

3. Disposing of slow-selling goods.

● *Example:*

When the physical inventory is taken at the end of the year, there are in stock 200 items that are over 6-months old and in need of clearance. These cost $3 each and are in stock at $5. The buyer's goal is to dispose of the entire lot before the next semi-annual inventory. (1) To what retail price should he immediately reduce the goods? (2) If a month hence, 150 are still on hand, what action should then be taken?

Solution:

1. The first markdown should be substantial enough in the buyer's estimation to move well over half the supply promptly. If this is the first markdown on the goods, he will try to recover his cost, including direct handling. He might mark the goods $3.50. This is 30% off the original retail price.
2. Since he succeeds in selling only a quarter of the supply in the first month, another substantial cut is in order, and now with little consideration for the cost. The goods might be priced at $2.49. Unless most of the remaining lot is sold in the next 2 months, it may be wise to offer the goods to a jobber or at an employee sale at half the cost and perhaps as low as $1 a unit.

ASSIGNMENT 3:

A style of woman's blouse is clearly going out of fashion. Seventy pieces are on hand at the time of physical inventory, priced at $25 each. Make a plan for the coming 3 months, indicating the price you would set for the first of each of these months and the number you would hope to sell each month?

DISCUSSION QUESTION:

If in a $50 price line consisting of 100 pieces you locate only five that may be classified as slow-selling, ready for clearance, how would you dispose of them?

ADDITIONAL ASSIGNMENTS

4.

a. Develop an alphabetical code that includes the month and year of merchandise receipt as well as the billed cost.

b. Develop a numerical code that indicates the exact date of merchandise receipt as well as the billed cost.

c. Should the date of receipt be kept secret or be recorded in "plain English"?

5. The price per gross for an item in the inventory is $72 and 28 units of this item are on hand. Transportation charges in this classification average 2% of cost purchases. What is the cost of the quantity on hand? Would you figure transportation for each item or only for the inventory as a whole?

6. A 57-piece set of china costs $36 a set but is also sold as an open-stock item. The following table indicates the composition of the 57-piece set, the number on hand of each item when physical inventory was taken, and the retail price of each item when sold separately:

Item	Units in the set	On hand in inventory	Retail price per unit
Tea cup	12	10	$1.35
saucer	8	5	.75
Dinner/salad	8	14	1.00
Dinner plate	8	9	2.10
Soup plate	8	8	1.25
Fruit dish	8	3	.80
2 pc. sugar	1	0	3.00
Cream pitcher	1	1	2.10
Platter	1	0	6.00
Open veg. dish	1	2	3.10
Covered butter	1	1	3.40

There are also on hand in the inventory 2 unbroken sets. No separate cost figures are available for the individual items. What cost price would you put on the inventory on hand?

10   How to Determine Book Inventories and Stock Shortages

Merchandise shortages can be determined only by comparing the physical inventory with the book inventory. Accordingly, it is important to be able to calculate book inventories both readily and accurately. The book inventory also provides a guide to intelligent merchandising between inventory dates.

DEFINITIONS

Book Inventory. The amount of inventory, in dollars and cents, as determined from records rather than from actual count. Basically, the formula used is: opening inventory + purchases − sales = closing book inventory.

Shortage. The difference between the book and the physical inventories, when the former is the larger. It may be calculated at cost or retail value or in terms of units. It represents (1) clerical errors in calculating the book and/or physical inventories, and (2) physical merchandise losses, caused by such factors as shoplifting, pilferage, breakage, and charging customers for less merchandise than is actually delivered to them.

Overage. The difference between the book and physical inventories when the latter is the larger. Nearly all overages are caused by clerical errors.

Estimated Physical Inventory. Book inventory minus an estimate of the shortages that probably occurred during the period involved. If the estimate is exactly correct, the estimated physical inventory and the actual physical inventory are the same size.

Derived Sales. A sales figure obtained from records of purchases and of opening and closing inventories.

A. BOOK INVENTORIES

1. Book inventory at cost — estimated markup.

● *Example:*

Opening physical inventory at cost, February 1st	$20,000
Purchases at cost, February	10,000
Sales at retail, February	23,000
Last year's markup on sales, spring season	30%

It is assumed that this year's markup is the same as last year's. Find the closing book inventory at cost.

Solution:

Opening inventory at cost	$20,000
Purchases at cost	10,000
Total merchandise handled	$30,000
Estimated cost of goods sold ($23,000 × .70)	16,100
Estimated closing book inventory at original cost	$13,900

ASSIGNMENT 1:

The December 31st physical inventory at cost in a certain store is $34,500. Purchases during January and February at billed cost are $16,400 and the transportation charges are $200. Net sales during the 2 months are $24,300 and the estimated markup on sales, based on last year's experience, is 24%. Find the book inventory at cost on March 1st.

DISCUSSION QUESTIONS:

To determine the estimated cost of goods sold from the sales, which markup should be used: initial, maintained, or gross margin? Why?

2. Book inventory at cost — "costing" sales.

● *Example:*

The opening physical inventory at cost for a gift shop is $8,000, and the subsequent purchases at cost are $14,000. By means of cost codes on price tickets, the cost of each item sold is recorded at the time of sale along with the retail price. The "cost of goods sold" so determined is $17,000. What is the closing book inventory at cost?

Solution:

Opening inventory at cost	$ 8,000
Purchases at cost	14,000
Total merchandise handled	$22,000
Cost of goods sold	17,000
Closing book inventory at original cost	$ 5,000

This closing book inventory is valued at original cost, not at the current replacement price. To determine the present market value in this problem, it would be necessary to determine what depreciation in value has occurred.

ASSIGNMENT 2:

A store keeps a sales audit of sales checks at cost. The sum of the items at cost appearing on the sales checks is $3,400. The purchases at cost during the period are $4,650 at cost, and the opening inventory at cost is $3,000.

1. Find the book inventory at original cost.
2. If a physical inventory is taken and reveals a stock of $4,000 at original cost, what is the amount of shortage in dollars.

DISCUSSION QUESTIONS:

When shortage is determined at cost, should it be expressed as a percentage of sales or of the cost of merchandise sold? If expressed on the latter base, would the percentage be the same as it would be if the retail of shortages are expressed as percentage of sales? Explain.

3. Book inventory at retail.

● *Example:*

Opening inventory at retail	$18,000
Purchases at retail	29,000
Net sales	27,000
Net markdowns	6,000
Discounts to employees and customers	500

1. Find book inventory.
2. If a physical inventory reveals a stock of $12,000 at retail, what is the amount of retail shortage in dollars and in percentage?

Solution:

1. Opening inventory at retail		$18,000
Purchases at retail		29,000
Total merchandise handled		$47,000
Net Sales	$27,000	
Net markdowns	6,000	
Discounts to employees and customers	500	
Total retail deductions		33,500
Closing book inventory at retail		$13,500

2. Shortages at retail = $13,500 - $12,000 = $1,500 = 5.6% of net sales.

ASSIGNMENT 3:

Net sales	$212,000
Net retail purchases	206,000
Opening retail inventory	100,000
Net markdowns	20,000
Discounts to employees and customers	3,000

1. Find closing book inventory at retail.
2. If a physical inventory reveals a stock of $69,000 at retail, what is the shortage percentage?

DISCUSSION QUESTIONS:

In calculating profits, when should book inventory be used? When should physical inventory be used?

4. Estimated physical inventory at cost.

● *Example:*

Purchases at cost	$16,500
Cost of goods sold — from saleschecks	13,200
Opening inventory at cost	9,000
Shortages estimated at 2% of cost of goods sold.	

1. Find estimated physical inventory.
2. If a physical inventory is taken and reveals an actual count of $12,100 at original cost, what is the amount of actual shortage?

Solution:

1. Opening inventory at cost . . . . $ 9,000
   Purchases at cost   16,500
   Total merchandise handled $25,500
   Cost of goods sold — from saleschecks   13,200
   Book inventory at original cost $12,300
   Estimated shortages (2% of $13,200)   264
   Estimated physical inventory at original cost $12,036

2. Actual shortage is $12,300 − $12,100 = $200. Shortages were over-estimated by $64.

ASSIGNMENT 4:

> Estimated shortages 1% of cost of goods sold as determined from saleschecks.

Purchases at cost $44,000
Cost of goods sold   27,000
Opening inventory at cost   14,000

Find estimated closing physical inventory at original cost.

DISCUSSION QUESTION:

> How does the cost of merchandise sold as usually determined differ from the cost of the articles sold as determined by costing sales?

5. Estimated physical inventory at retail

● *Example:*

Opening inventory at retail $14,000
Total purchases at retail   62,100
Net sales   46,000
Net markdowns   2,400
Discounts to employees and customers   650
Shortages estimated, 2% of net sales.

Find estimated closing inventory at retail.

Solution:

Opening inventory at retail		$14,000
Total purchases at retail		62,100
Total merchandise handled		$76,100
Net sales	$46,000	
Net markdowns	2,400	
Discounts to employees and customers	650	
Shortages estimated	920	
Total retail deductions		$49,970
Estimated closing retail inventory		$26,130

ASSIGNMENT 5:

Net sales	$74,950
Shortages estimated, 1% of net sales	
Markdowns	4,000
Opening retail inventory	23,000
Discounts to customers and employees	2,000
Retail purchases	72,000

1. Find the estimated physical inventory.
2. If a physical count is taken and reveals an actual stock of $12,500, what are the actual shortages?

DISCUSSION QUESTION:

What is to be gained by estimating shortages between physical inventory dates to arrive at estimated physical inventory figures?

6. Detailed calculation of book and estimated physical inventories at retail.

● *Example:*

(All figures at retail):

Opening inventory	$ 63,000
Gross purchases	149,000
Returns to vendors	3,500
Transfers out of the department	6,600
Transfers into the department	4,600
Gross sales	157,000
Returns and allowances to customers	13,000
Net markdowns	7,600
Discounts to employees and customers	500
Shortages estimated, 2% of net sales.	

Find closing book inventory and estimated physical inventory at retail.

Solution:

```
Opening inventory. . . . . . . . . . . . . . . . . . . . . . . . . . . . . . $ 63,000
Gross purchases  . . . . . . . . . . . . . . . $149,000
Returns to vendors . . . . . . . . . . . . .      3,500
Net purchases. . . . . . . . . . . . . . . . . . . . . . . . . . $145,500
Transfers in . . . . . . . . . . . . . . . . . . $  4,600
Transfers out . . . . . . . . . . . . . . . . .    6,600
Net transfers out. . . . . . . . . . . . . . . . . . . . . . .      2,000
Total purchases. . . . . . . . . . . . . . . . . . . . . . . . . . . . . .   143,500
Total merchandise handled . . . . . . . . . . . . . . . . . . . . . . $206,500
Gross sales . . . . . . . . . . . . . . . . . . . $157,000
Returns and allowances . . . . . . . . . . .    13,000
Net sales . . . . . . . . . . . . . . . . . . . . . . . . . . . . . $144,000
Net markdowns  . . . . . . . . . . . . . . . . . . . . . . .      7,600
Discounts to customers and employees . . . . . . . .        500
Total retail deductions . . . . . . . . . . . . . . . . . . . . . . . . . $152,100
Closing book inventory  . . . . . . . . . . . . . . . . . . . . . . . . $ 54,400
Shortages estimated, (2% of $144,000) . . . . . . . . . . . . . .    2,880
Closing estimated physical inventory. . . . . . . . . . . . . . . $ 51,520
```

ASSIGNMENT 6:

```
Gross purchases at retail . . . . . . . . . . . . . . . . . . . . . . . . . .  $8,400
Gross sales . . . . . . . . . . . . . . . . . . . . . . . . . . . . . . . . . .   9,200
Net markdowns  . . . . . . . . . . . . . . . . . . . . . . . . . . . . . . .     460
Returns to vendors  . . . . . . . . . . . . . . . . . . . . . . . . . . . .      320
Returns from customers . . . . . . . . . . . . . . . . . . . . . . . . . .      700
Transfers in at retail. . . . . . . . . . . . . . . . . . . . . . . . . . . .     165
Transfers out at retail. . . . . . . . . . . . . . . . . . . . . . . . . . .      300
Opening inventory at retail . . . . . . . . . . . . . . . . . . . . . . .    2,175
Discounts to customers and employees . . . . . . . . . . . . . . .      135
Shortages estimated, 3% of net sales.
```

Find book and estimated physical inventories.

DISCUSSION QUESTIONS:

Assume that in assignment 6 the period in question is 4 months and a physical inventory will not be taken for another two months. In drawing up an operating statement for the four-month period, should the book inventory or the estimated physical inventory figure be used? Why?

7. Computing markup on aggregate purchases from inventory and sales data.

Example:

A small store owner kept no record of the markup obtained on his purchases, but during his annual inventory he did count his stock at retail value and he also kept a record of his sales at retail. Although he kept no record of markdowns, they were comparatively small in his line and he estimated them at 3% of his sales. His sales for the year were $70,000; his purchases at cost, $50,000; his opening inventory at retail, $19,000; and his closing inventory at retail, $18,200. Find the markup percentage obtained on his purchases.

Solution:

Closing retail inventory	$18,200
Plus sales	70,000
Plus markdowns, 3% of sales	2,100
Total	$90,300
Less opening retail inventory	19,000
Purchases at retail — derived	$71,300
Purchases at cost	50,000
Markup on purchases	$21,300

$$\text{Markup \% on purchases} = \frac{\$21{,}300}{\$71{,}300} = 30\%$$

ASSIGNMENT 7:

Purchases at cost	$20,000
Opening inventory at retail	7,000
Closing inventory at retail	6,000
Sales	38,000
Markdowns	1,400
Shortages	420

Find markup percentage on purchases.

DISCUSSION QUESTION:

Would the markup on purchases determined in the example above be overstated or understated if there were a merchandise shortage in addition to markdowns?

Managerial Decisions

1. In your grocery supermarket, shoplifting by customers is excessive. What precautionary steps can you take?

2. You took a careful physical inventory, but found it to be greater than the book inventory; thus you have a stock overage. What action, if any, should you take?

B. DERIVING SALES

8. Deriving sales.

● *Example:*

In a certain department, sales are kept only for the department as a whole, but inventories are taken monthly by classification and purchases are similarly analyzed, as follows:

Class	Retail Inventory 1st of month	Retail Inventory end of month	Retail Purchases During month
A	$600	$700	$300
B	700	650	500
C	400	450	200
Total	$1,700	$1,800	$1,000

Note: The above figures represent dollars, but the calculation would be the same if they were units.

Solution:

Formula[1]: Opening Inventory + Purchases − Closing Inventory = Sales.

A	$600 +	$300 −	$700 =	$200
B	700 +	500 −	650 =	550
C	400 +	200 −	450 =	150
Total	$1,700 +	$1,000 −	$1,800 =	$900

The sales figures derived actually include shortages. Thus, in class *A*, $900 worth was available of which $700 worth is left; $200 worth has moved out of stock, some of which may be attributable to shortages.

ASSIGNMENT 8:

In a certain classification, the inventory at the first of the month was $15,000 and at the end of the month, $14,600. The gross purchases during the month were $6,000 and the returns to vendors $400.

---

[1] This formula needs modification if markdowns are a factor in deriving sales in dollars. Markdowns as well as closing inventory would have to be subtracted.

Markdowns taken during the month totaled $400, $900 worth of goods was transferred to another classification in the department but $200 worth of goods was transferred into the classification; and $150 worth was returned by customers (all figures at retail). Find the gross and net sales figures.

DISCUSSION QUESTIONS:

1. What are the chief uses of derived sales information?
2. Is there any value to be gained by reducing derived sales by an estimate of shortage? Explain.

Managerial Decisions

1. In your branch store, it is not feasible to keep departmental sales records, since each sales person sells throughout the store. Nevertheless, departmental buyers located in the parent store are entitled to a commission on sales made in the branch. How can this remuneration policy be carried out without recording departmental sales in the branch?

2. Firms specializing in installing shortage control systems in department stores tend to make comparisons such as the following to justify the results of their efforts: "The average operating profit is only 2% of sales; therefore, every $100 we succeed in reducing shortages is equivalent to an increase in sales of $5,000." Would you as management's representative accept this conclusion? Explain.

ADDITIONAL ASSIGNMENTS

9. A store has an opening retail stock of $21,000; purchases at retail during the period of $7,000; gross sales, $13,000; returns from customers, $1,000; and allowances to customers, $400. What is the closing retail inventory?

10. The net sales for a year were $93,000. The book inventory, at retail, at the end of the year was $34,000; the physical inventory at retail was $30,000. What was the inventory shortage percentage?

11.

Opening inventory at cost	$28,000
Purchases at cost	49,000
Cost of sales from price tickets	45,200
Shortages estimated, 2% of cost of sales	

Find:

1. the value of the closing book inventory at original cost.
2. the value of the closing estimated physical inventory at billed cost.

11   How to Value Inventories by the Cost and the Retail Methods

The value placed on an inventory has a decided effect on profits. Accordingly, great care should be taken to determine, not necessarily the original cost, but the "cost or market value, whichever is lower." See the definitions below.

Today, the retail method is the commonly accepted method of taking and valuing an inventory, particularly in general merchandise and apparel stores. If properly used, the retail method depreciates the cost value of the inventory when prices are falling and tends to give original cost value when prices are rising. For accuracy, the following rules must be observed: (1) the store must be properly departmentalized and the retail method applied separately to each department; (2) markdowns must be taken promptly; and (3) all price changes must be properly classified and recorded.

Although the mathematical calculations involved are performed in the store office, rather than by the buyer or department manager, accuracy depends on the prompt taking of markdowns by the buyer and on his prompt reporting and accurate classifying of all price changes. Carelessness or manipulation on the buyer's part may result in (1) over- or under-valuation of the closing inventory, with its direct effect on profits, and (2) errors in the markdown and shortage figures.

DEFINITIONS

Inventory Valuation. A determination of the proper value of the inventory for profit-figuring purposes. The usual rule is "cost or market, whichever is lower." Thus, if an article in the inventory costs the store $1.00, but now has a replacement value of 90 cents, it is valued at 90 cents. If the replacement value is $1.10, however, it is valued at $1.00.

Original Cost Method of Inventory Valuation. Valuing an inventory at the original cost price billed to the store for the goods.

Cost or Market Method of Inventory Valuation. Valuing an inventory at the cost price of the items involved or at their current market value, whichever is lower. It is a threefold process, involving (1) taking physical inventory at billed-cost prices – determined from cost codes on price tickets or by reference to other cost records; (2) depreciating items that are not now worth what was paid for them; and (3) determining the approximate amount of transportation charges the store has incurred in transporting the inventory to the store – this is considered to be a part of the value of the inventory.

First-In-First-Out Method of Inventory Valuation (FIFO). A method of determining the value of an inventory, when costs of individual items in the inventory are not identified, that assumes that goods sell in the order in which received into stock; thus, the goods in the inventory are assumed to be the newest goods purchased and are assigned the cost value of the newest goods. Taking inventory at actual cost prices of each item in stock will usually give very similar totals, since goods actually sell in approximate order of their receipt; the retailer makes a real effort to sell the old merchandise first, before the new goods.

Last-In-First-Out Method of Inventory Valuation (LIFO). A method of determining the value of an inventory by assuming (1) that it is necessary to carry a fixed basic inventory assortment that has a fixed valuation and (2) that the sales made represent the newest goods purchased at prevailing prices. Thus, the so-called basic stock does not fluctuate with changes in the price level. During inflation, inventory is valued at a lower figure than under FIFO or when a determination of the actual cost prices of the goods in the inventory may be made.

Retail Method of Inventory. A method of determining the cost value of an inventory by determining the retail value of the stock (by means of a physical inventory or derivation from purchase and sales records) and reducing it to cost by multiplying it by the complement of the initial markup percentage on the total merchandise handled during the period. The validity of this method is based on the assumption that the average markup on the closing inventory is the same as the markup on the total merchandise handled.

Example:

	Cost	Retail	Comp. of markup
Opening inventory	$ 6,000	$ 9,900	
Purchases	24,000	40,100	
Total merchandise handled	$30,000	$50,000	60%
Closing retail inventory		12,000	
Closing cost inventory	7,200		
($12,000 X 60%)			

Additional Markup. An increase in price above the original retail price. Thus, if

100 articles originally retailed at $1 each are marked up to $1.09, the additional markup is $9 for the lot. The additional markups are added to the retail purchase figure in determining total merchandise handled, on which the so-called initial markup is based.

Markdown. A retail price reduction caused by a reduction in the value of the goods. Thus, if 100 articles retailing at $1 each became slow-selling and are reduced to 89 cents, the markdown is $11 for the lot. Markdowns are added to sales to obtain total retail deductions and do not reduce the total merchandise handled or the initial markup percentage.

Markdown Cancellation. An increase in price caused by marking goods back to (or toward) the original retail price. For example: If 100 articles originally retailing for $1 are marked down to 89 cents, and if subsequently 30 are marked back to $1, the gross markdown is $11; the cancellation $3.30; and the net markdown $7.70.

Revision of Retail Downward. A decrease in price that is subtracted from the retail purchase figure before the markup percentage is calculated. It includes *additional markup cancellations,* corrections of clerical errors in recording and pricing retail purchases, and retail price reductions growing out of a rebate (allowance) from the manufacturer. Markdowns are not included in revisions.

Additional Markup Cancellation. A decrease in retail price from a point above original retail to (or toward) original retail. Thus, if 100 articles were marked up from $1 each to $1.09 each and subsequently 30 were marked back to $1, the gross additional markup is $9; the additional markup cancellation, $2.70; and the net additional markup, $6.30.

Initial Markup Percentage. The difference between the total merchandise handled at retail and the total merchandise handled at cost, expressed as a percentage of the retail. Synonyms are cumulative initial markup percentage, cumulative markon percentage, and cumulative initial markon percentage. For example:

	Cost	Retail	Markup
Opening inventory	$ 5,900	$10,000	
Purchases	18,100	30,000	
Total merchandise handled	$24,000	$40,000	$16,000

Initial markup = $\frac{\$16,000}{\$40,000} = 40\%$

The complement of the initial markup is used to reduce the closing retail inventory to cost or market. For this purpose, purchases are usually accumulated over a period of a 6-month season or of a whole year. This means that the initial markup is not calculated for each month separately by adding purchases for the month to the month's opening inventory;

rather, purchases for the *season* are added to the opening inventory of the season.

A. EFFECT OF INVENTORY VALUATION ON PROFIT

1. Effect of errors in inventory valuation during one year.

● *Example:*

A buyer fails to recognize depreciation that has occured in his closing inventory and values his inventory at actual cost of $600 rather than the market value of $500. What is the effect on profits of this overstatement of $100?

Solution:

$$
\begin{aligned}
\text{Let } \$1,200 &= \text{Total merchandise handled} \\
\underline{600} &= \text{Closing inventory at cost} \\
\$\ \ 600 &= \text{Cost of merchandise sold} \\
\text{Let } \underline{\$1,100} &= \text{Net sales} \\
\therefore \ \$\ \ 500 &= \text{Gross margin}
\end{aligned}
$$

If closing inventory is really worth only $500:

$$
\begin{aligned}
\$1,200 &= \text{Total merchandise handled} \\
\underline{500} &= \text{Closing market inventory} \\
\$\ \ 700 &= \text{Cost of merchandise sold} \\
\underline{1,100} &= \text{Net sales} \\
\$\ \ 400 &= \text{Gross margin}
\end{aligned}
$$

Profits are overstated $100.

ASSIGNMENT 1:

1. If the market value of the opening inventory is overstated $200, what is the effect on profits?
2. If the market value of the opening inventory is understated $200, what is the effect on profits?
3. If both the opening and closing inventories are overstated $200, what is the effect on profits?
4. If the opening inventory is understated $200 and the closing inventory overstated $300, what is the effect on profits?

DISCUSSION QUESTIONS:

> Are a merchant's hired department managers more likely to overstate or to understate their inventories? Would the same be true of the merchant who owns the store? Why?

2. Effects of errors in inventory valuation over a 2-year period.

● *Example:*

> If the closing inventory is overstated $200 one year, what is the effect on profits the next year and for the 2 years combined, assuming no further error in valuation?

Solution:

> The closing inventory this year becomes the opening inventory next year. An overstatement of $200 in the opening inventory of the second year understates profits $200. (See assignment 1 (1) p. 118). With the inventory overstated $200 the first year and understated $200 the second year, the profits for the 2 years combined are correct.

ASSIGNMENT 2:

1. If the closing inventory is understated $200, what is the effect on profits the next year and for the 2 years combined?
2. If the closing inventory is overstated $200 this year and understated $300 the next, what is the effect on profits next year and for the two years combined?
3. If the closing inventory is understated $200 this year and is overstated $300 next year, what is the effect on profits next year and for the 2 years combined?

DISCUSSION QUESTION:

> Since a distortion of profits caused by an error in inventory valuation one year is offset by a compensating error in the reverse direction next year, why is it important to value inventories correctly?

Managerial Decision

What methods should a store's management introduce to ensure that inventories are properly valued?

B. COST METHODS OF INVENTORY VALUATION

3. FIFO method of inventory.

● *Example:*

A grocer has on hand as inventory of a commodity purchased pre-packed in individual bags. The prices had been fluctuating for the past few months. At inventory time, the merchant had 486 bags on hand. His most recent invoice showed 200 bags bought at 89 cents each. The previous invoice was for 200 bags at 95 cents each and the one before for 200 bags at $1.00 each. What value should be placed on the inventory, assuming no depreciation.

Solution:

```
200 bags at 89 cents. . . . . . . . . . . . . . . . . . . . . . . . . . . . .   $178.00
200 bags at 95 cents. . . . . . . . . . . . . . . . . . . . . . . . . . . . .    190.00
 86 bags at $1.00 . . . . . . . . . . . . . . . . . . . . . . . . . . . . .       86.00
    Total 486 bags . . . . . . . . . . . . . . . . . . . . . . . . . . . . .   $454.00
```

ASSIGNMENT 3:

A grocer has on hand as inventory 940 pounds of commodity in 5-pound packages. His most recent invoice for such goods showed the purchase of 50 pounds at 4 cents a pound and the previous invoice was for 400 pounds at 4½ cents and the one before for 600 pounds at 5 cents. What is the cost of the goods in the inventory?

DISCUSSION QUESTION:

For clothing, is it better to keep a record of the cost price of each specific item or to depend on FIFO?

4. Determining depreciation: market value vs. original cost

● *Example:*

For a 6-month period, the closing physical inventory at billed cost, as determined by cost codes on price tickets, is $80,000. Analysis of the items comprising the inventory reveals that most of the stock is still available at the billed prices paid, but that there is a lot of 150 articles for which $1.15 was paid, but which are now selling for 99 cents wholesale. Another lot of 1,000 items bought for $2.50 each now has a market value of $2.00. The cost purchases during the 6-month period were $300,000 and the transportation costs to the store on this merchandise were $1,000. Find the market value of the closing inventory.

Solution:

$$\text{Rate of transportation on purchases} = \frac{\$1,000}{\$300,000} = \frac{1}{3} \text{ of } 1\%$$

$\frac{1}{3}$ of 1% of $80,000 = $267, the share of the transportation charges to add to the value of the closing inventory.

Depreciation:
$$
\begin{array}{rl}
150 \times \$.16 = & \$\ \ 24.00 \\
1,000 \times \$.50 = & \underline{500.00} \\
\text{Total} & \$524.00^1
\end{array}
$$

Valuation of closing inventory:

Billed cost $80,000
Plus transportation 267
Minus depreciation 524
Market value $79,743

ASSIGNMENT 4:

Closing inventory at billed cost $26,000
Purchases — billed cost 50,000
Depreciation on closing inventory. 1,000
Transportation charges on purchases 500

Find market value of closing inventory.

DISCUSSION QUESTIONS:

For what types of goods would it be impracticable to check with manufacturers at inventory time to determine current market prices? Why?

5. Aging method of determining depreciation under cost method.

● *Example:*

In listing the inventory, a store records not only the billed cost in code

---

[1] If the two lots are not in perfect condition the depreciation figure should be increased.

from the price tickets, but also the date on which each item in stock was purchased. An analysis of the totals shows the following:

Goods less than 3 months old	$ 41,000
Goods 3–6 months old	24,000
Goods 6 months to 1 year old	21,000
Goods over 1 year old	14,000
Total physical inventory at billed cost	$100,000

From past experience, it is estimated that goods less than 3 months old are worth approximately what was paid for them, goods 3–6 months old depreciate 25%, goods 6–12 months old depreciate 50%, and goods over a year old depreciate 75%. The rate of transportation is 2% of purchases at billed cost. Find the market value of the inventory.

Solution:

Age Groups	Depreciation	Market Value
$ 41,000	00%	$41,000
24,000	25	18,000
21,000	50	10,500
14,000	75	3,500
$100,000		$73,000

Transportation in closing inventory	2,000
(2% of $100,000)	
Market value of closing inventory	$75,000

ASSIGNMENT 5:

The age analysis of a closing inventory at billed cost reveals:

Age Groups	Original Cost	Depreciation Rate
Less than 6 months	$79,000	10%
6–12 months	44,000	25
12–24 months	29,000	50
Over 2 years	3,000	100

Transportation charges are 1/3 of 1%. Find the market value of the inventory.

DISCUSSION QUESTIONS:

How is it possible to set depreciation rates that reflect probable losses in inventory value for various age groups? Are they only a guess?

6. Markdown approach to determine depreciation under the cost method.

● *Example:*

The cost code on a price ticket indicates that an article had a billed cost of $7.00. The retail price on the ticket is now $9.00, but the ticket indicates that the original retail was $12.00. Find the market value of the article.

Solution:

$$\$12 - \$7 = \$5, \text{the original markup.}$$

$$\frac{\$5}{\$12} = 41.7\%, \text{the original markup percentage.}$$

$9.00 (present retail) X 58.3%
(complement of markup) = $5.25, the market value of the article

or

Reductions in retail value $3, or 25% of $12. 25% reduction in cost value of $7 gives $5.25.

ASSIGNMENT 6:

Original retail, $5.00; billed cost, $3.00; current retail at inventory time, $3.98. Find the market value.

DISCUSSION QUESTION:

Is the concept of reducing the cost in proportion to reductions from original retail (owing to markdowns) a good one? Defend your answer.

Managerial Decisions

1. A store's accountant reports to the merchant that he has not included transportation charges in arriving at the value of the closing inventory. Would this exclusion have any material effect on the merchant's profit? Should the merchant insist that transportation be included? What disadvantages, if any, are there to including transportation in the value of inventory?

2. If you are merchandising women's ready-to-wear and are operating on the cost method of inventory, which of the methods of determining depreciation would you use? Why?

C. THE RETAIL METHOD OF INVENTORY

7. Retail method of determining value of physical inventory.

● *Example:*

	Cost	Retail
Opening inventory.	$ 5,114	$ 9,200
Purchases.	17,000	29,100
Closing retail inventory (physical).		6,100

Find the market value of closing inventory.

Solution:

	Cost	Retail
Opening inventory.	$ 5,114	$ 9,200
Purchases.	17,000	29,100
Total merchandise handled	$22,114	$38,300

Initial markup = $38,300 – $22,114 = $16,186 = 42%
Complement of initial markup = 100% - 42% = 58%
Closing inventory value at cost, $6,100 × 58% = $3,538

ASSIGNMENT 7:

The purchases during a period are $18,000 at cost and $33,000 at retail. The opening inventory is $10,000 at cost and $20,000 at retail. Closing inventory at retail is $9,000. Find the market value of the closing inventory.

DISCUSSION QUESTION:

Should the markup percentage on the closing inventory be the same as the markup percentage of the total merchandise handled? Why?

8. Retail method of obtaining market value of estimated physical inventory.

● *Example:*

	Cost	Retail
Inventory beginning.	$ 32,000	$ 53,000
Purchases.	118,000	171,000
Sales.		140,000
Markdowns		9,000
Estimated shortages.		6,000

1. What is the market value of closing inventory?
2. What is the percentage of markdowns?

Solution:

	Cost	Retail
Opening inventory....................	$ 32,000	$ 53,000
Purchases...........................	118,000	171,000
Total merchandise handled	$150,000	$224,000
Initial markup $224,000 - $150,000 = $74,000 = 33%		
Complement of initial markup = 67%		
Sales...............................		$140,000
Markdowns		9,000
Estimated shortages..................		6,000
Total retail deductions		$155,000
Estimated physical inventory at retail		
($224,000 - $155,000)		$ 69,000

(1) Market (cost) value of inventory ($69,000 X 67%) = $46,230

(2) Markdown % = $9,000 ÷ $140,000 = 6.4%

ASSIGNMENT 8:

Opening inventory at cost, $6,200 with a retail of $11,000; purchases, $10,000 at cost with a retail of $16,500; sales, $17,500; net markdowns, $3,800; estimated shortage, $550. Find the market value of the closing inventory.

DISCUSSION QUESTIONS:

The merchandise that was marked down has not been sold. What effect, if any, will this have on the market value? Which would be the soundest practice: to accumulate markup over 3 months, 6 months, or 1 year?

Managerial Decision

You are currently operating under the retail method of inventory in your clothing store but are bothered by the great amount of recordkeeping of all price changes that it requires. It is suggested that you determine depreciation by the markdown method (explained in problem 6 above). Would you make the suggested change? Why?

9. Effect of markdowns on market value of inventory under the retail method.

● *Example:*

Markup to date, 35%. Markdowns, $400 on retail stock of $7,500 before being marked down. How much is the cost value of the inventory reduced by the markdown, and what is the effect on profits?

Solution:

$400 × 0.65 = $260, the reduction in the cost value of the inventory. Profits are accordingly reduced $260.

Proof: Market value of stock before markdowns:

$$$7,500 × 0.65 = $4,875$$

Market value of stock after markdowns:

($7,500 – $400) × 0.65 = $7,100 × 0.65 = $4,615
Loss in value: $4,875 – $4,615 = $260

ASSIGNMENT 9:

The retail inventory at the end of a year is $75,000; the markup is 42%; and the net profit, $6,000. However, a great deal of the merchandise in stock is unsalable at the marked retail prices. The buyer has failed to take markdowns to bring the prices in line with current values. These reductions, which should have been taken but were not, amount to $6,500.

1. If the buyer took the markdowns before closing the books, what would be the operating profit?
2. What effect does the failure to take these markdowns have on the operating profit during the coming year, assuming that the goods will be properly priced at the end of that period?

DISCUSSION QUESTION:

Under the retail method, does a price reduction reduce profits immediately or only after the reduced goods have been sold?

10. Profit under the retail method — composite problem

● *Example:*

	Cost	*Retail*
Opening inventory.	$14,000	$22,000
Purchases — net, including transportation.	45,000	72,000
Net sales		65,000

	Cost	Retail
Price changes:		
Additional markups..............		1,000
Markdowns		4,500
Markdown cancellations...........		500
Revision of retail downward		150
Discounts to employees and customers		1,000
Shortages*....................		650
Cash discounts earned	1,894	
Alteration cost	1,150	
Expenses......................	14,050	

*Estimated shortages may be used for calculations between physical inventory dates.

Find the operating profit.

Solution:

	Cost	Retail	Initial Markup
Opening inventory...........	$14,000	$22,000	
Purchases................	45,000	72,000	
Net additional markups ($1,000 – $150)		850	
Total merchandise handled	$59,000	$94,850	37.8%
Net sales		65,000	
Net markdowns ($4,500 – $500) ..		4,000	
Discount to employees and customers		1,000	
Shortages.................		650	
Total retail deductions		$70,650	
Closing physical inventory at retail ($94,850 – $70,650).		24,200	
Closing physical inventory at cost or market ($24,200 × .622)	15,052		
Gross cost of merchandise sold. ...	$43,948		
Cash discounts earned	1,894		
Net cost of merchandise sold	$42,054		
Alteration costs	1,150		
Total cost of merchandise sold....	$43,204		
Net sales	65,000		
Total cost of merchandise sold....	43,204		
Gross margin	$21,796		
Expenses	14,050		
Operating profit	$ 7,746		

Alternative solution, using maintained markup:

	Cost
Maintained markup ($65,000 (sales) − 43,948)	$21,052
Cash discounts earned − add	1,894
	$22,946
Alteration costs − subtract	1,150
Gross margin	$21,796
Expenses	14,050
Operating profit	$ 7,746

ASSIGNMENT 10:

	Cost	Retail
Net sales		$33,000
Inventory, September 1	$15,000	20,000
Estimated shortages, 1% of sales.		330
Gross markdowns		2,500
Gross additional markups		800
Transportation charges (inward).	750	
Returns to vendors	1,300	1,800
Discounts to employees		650
Gross purchases.	20,000	30,000
Markdown cancellations		500
Expenses	7,900	
Cash discounts earned	750	
Additional markup cancellations		300

Find the estimated profit for the period.

DISCUSSION QUESTION:

If you were trying to figure a profit estimate from the above information, what would be the major reason preventing you from achieving a correct estimate?

Managerial Decision

In reporting price changes to the office, what system would you devise to distinguish among the four kinds of price changes?

11. Short-cut method of computing gross cost of merchandise sold and gross margin, where markup percentage is known.

Example:

Markup	39%
Net sales	$82,000
Net markdowns	3,500
Discounts to employees and customers	950
Estimated shortages	650
Cash discounts earned	1,800
Alteration costs	500

Find the gross cost of merchandise sold and the gross margin.

Solution:

Sales	$82,000
Markdowns	3,500
Discounts to employees	950
Shortages	650
	$87,100

Gross cost of merchandise sold = $87,100 × (100% − 39%) .	$53,131
Cash discounts earned	1,800
Net cost of merchandise sold	$51,331
Alteration costs	500
Total merchandise costs	$51,831
Gross margin ($82,000 − $51,831)	30,169

ASSIGNMENT 11:

Gross sales	$125,000
Gross markdowns	10,000
Alteration costs	900
Cash discounts earned	7,500
Markdown cancellations	3,000
Returns and allowances to customers	12,000
Expenses	34,000
Markup	41%
Discounts to employees	750
Shortages	1,200

Find the operating profit percentage.

DISCUSSION QUESTION:

Can a store have information concerning sales, retail reductions, and initial markup, and at the same time not have current inventory information and yet figure maintained markup? Defend your answer.

12. Effect on market value of inventory if high- and low- markup goods fail to sell in the same proportion in which they were purchased

● *Example:*

In a jewelry department, the total merchandise handled at retail (opening inventory plus purchases) is $120,000 and the retail closing inventory is $40,000. Two classes of jewelry are handled: costume jewelry, on which a markup of 30% is obtained, and "real" jewelry with a markup of 50%. During the year, two-thirds of the total merchandise handled at retail is in costume jewelry and only one-third in "real" jewelry, but at the end of the year the closing inventory is equally divided between the two classifications.

1. What is the market value of the inventory when the retail method is applied to the department as a whole?
2. How much does the retail method overstate or understate the market of the inventory?
3. How may such errors be avoided?

Solution:

(1) Application of average markup.

	Cost	Retail	Markup
Costume jewelry	$56,000	$ 80,000	30%
"Real" jewelry	20,000	40,000	50%
Total	$76,000	$120,000	36.7%
Closing inventory retail		40,000	
Closing inventory cost			
($40,000 X 0.633)	25,320		

(2) Analysis of closing inventory

	Retail	Markup
Costume jewelry	$ 20,000	30%
"Real" jewelry	20,000	50%
Total	$ 40,000	
Cost of costume jewelry ($20,000 X 0.70)	$ 14,000	
Cost of "real" jewelry ($20,000 X 0.50)	10,000	
Total	$ 24,000	
Value according to retail method	25,320	
Overstatement	$ 1,320	

    (3) (a) Make separate departments of each class.

        (b) Disregard error since situation will probably continue and a general overstatement in both opening and closing inventories will not distort profits; one error tends to offset the other.

ASSIGNMENT 12:

    A buyer has an opening inventory of $45,000 at cost and $70,000 at retail. Purchases of regular merchandise during the season are $100,000 at cost and $150,000 at retail. In addition, for a special sale, the buyer purchases goods for $30,000 at cost, which he retails at only $35,000. During the season, all of this special merchandise is sold and only regular goods, retailing at $30,000, remain in stock at the end of the season.

    Under the retail method, what is the market value of the closing inventory? How much is the market value overstated or understated?

DISCUSSION QUESTION:

    Since high- and low-markup goods often fail to sell in the proportions in which they were bought, is the retail method more likely to overstate or to understate the closing inventory? Why?

13. Avoiding recording markdowns by underpricing new invoices.

Example:

    A buyer wished to reduce the price of 1,500 yards of piece goods, retailing at $5.95 a yard, to $3.95 for a clearance sale. At the same time, he purchased in a job lot 1,500 yards of exceptionally fine material at a cost of only $1.75 a yard, even though the goods were readily salable at $5.95. Instead of reporting a markdown of $3,000, he marked the new goods at $5.95 a yard, but marked the retail price at $3.95 on the invoices. He thus avoided a markdown against his record and ran a successful sale. What is wrong with this procedure?

Solution:

    The closing book inventory at retail is not distorted by this practice, but the markup percentage is understated on the records. This leads to overstating the closing cost inventory and thus to overstating profits.

ASSIGNMENT 13:

    A buyer had 200 pairs of shoes on hand that retail at $18 a pair and that he reduced to $13. At the same time, he purchased 200 pairs of shoes at a cost of $12 a pair. He wishes to retail them at $18 a pair.

    To avoid the bother of recording a markdown on the old shoes, he

actually marks the new shoes $18 each, but passes the invoice through
with a retail price of $13 for each item. He figures that one transaction
will offset the other and that the value of his closing inventory at retail
will not be affected. His stock on hand, just before his transaction, is
$4,000 at cost and $6,000 at retail. Demonstrate specifically, by the
use of figures, whether the buyer is right in believing that the marking
of new goods higher than the corresponding invoices will offset the
unreported markdown.

DISCUSSION QUESTIONS:

If a buyer deliberately prices his incoming goods at higher prices than
he marks on his invoices to offset markdowns on old stock, what is the
effect on his initial markup? On his closing retail book inventory? On
his closing cost inventory? On his profits?

Managerial Decision

If you were a merchant employing a number of buyers, what rules would you set
for them to avoid distortion of cost inventory figures in connection with the
retail method of inventory?

14. **Handling transfers under the retail method when department sending the
goods must take a loss.**

Example:

A lot of goods retailing for $1,000 in Department A are to be
transferred to Department B, where they will be retailed for $750. The
markup to date in Department A is 40% and in Department B it is 30%.
(1) At what cost and retail value should the goods be transferred into
Department B? (2) At what cost and retail should they be transferred
out of Department A? (3) How much markdown should A take before
the transfer in order to avoid distorting its markup percentage?

Solution:

$750 ($B$ retail) × 70% (Complement of B markup) = $525 = Cost price for
transfer purposes.

$525 ÷ 60% (Complement of A markup) = $875, Retail for transfer
out

$1,000 − $875 = $125, the markdown

(1) $525 Cost and $750 Retail
(2) $525 Cost and $875 Retail
(3) $125

ASSIGNMENT 14:

The upstairs dress department of the Burke Company is merchandised separately from the bargain basement dress department. The downstairs buyer of dresses buys chiefly job lots and regular merchandise in low-price lines. On some occasions, however, he buys merchandise from the upstairs department, which the latter has found difficult to sell.

The upstairs buyer has 10 dresses, marked at $52.50 each, which he wants to sell to the basement buyer. The basement buyer says that he is well stocked with dresses of that particular type, but that he will take them at a price that will result in a normal markup for his department of 32%. He thinks he can sell them for $29.75. The initial markup in the upstairs department is 38%.

1. What is the cost at which the transfer should be made?
2. What is the markdown?
3. How much is the gross margin of the upstairs department affected by the markdown taken in connection with the transfer? Is the gross margin in the basement directly affected by the transfer?

DISCUSSION QUESTION:

Why not transfer the goods out of *A* at *B*'s buying and selling prices, with no markdown?

D. LIFO METHOD OF INVENTORY VALUATION

15. LIFO.

Example:

The following data are available for the first year of a LIFO operation:

	Cost	Retail	Initial Markup %	Net Markup* %
Opening inventory . . .		$200,000	38	36
Purchases	$256,000	420,000		
Sales		360,000		
Markdowns		20,000		

*Price reductions of last period are subtracted from the base period's purchases before this markup is calculated.

Retail prices have risen 10% during the year.

1. Find the cost of the closing inventory by means of the retail method.
2. Find the cost of the closing inventory by means of the LIFO method.

Solution:

1.

	Lifo Cost	Cost	Retail	
Opening inventory	$128,000	$124,000	$200,000	
Purchases		256,000	420,000	
Total merchandise handled		$380,000	$620,000	
% of markup				38.7%
Sales.			360,000	
Markdowns			20,000	
Total deductions.			$380,000	
Closing inventory at retail.			$240,000	
Closing inventory at cost under the retail method ($240,000 × 61.3%). . .	$147,120			

2.

Closing retail inventory,
   $240,000 ÷ 110% = $218,181, which is the first-of-year value of
                                          closing inventory.
Opening retail inven-
   tory   = 200,000
Increase in inventory
   – 1st-of-year prices = $18,181
$18,181 × 110% = $20,000, the current value of the increase in the
   inventory.
Net retail purchases, after markdowns:
   $420,000 – $20,000 = $400,000.
Net markup on purchases $400,000 – $256,000 = $144,000, or 36%
   of $400,000.
$20,000 × (100% – 36%) = $20,000 × 64% = $12,800, the cost of
   the increase in the inventory.

Cost of closing inventory:

LIFO cost beginning of year	$128,000
Increase.	12,800
Total	$140,800

Thus, *cost* under LIFO is $6,320 less than under the retail method.

ASSIGNMENT 15:

The following data are available for the first year of a LIFO operation:

	Cost	Retail	Initial Markup %	Net Markup %
Opening Inventory		$100,000	40	38
Purchases	$128,000	210,000		
Sales		180,000		
Markdowns		10,000		

Retail prices have risen 15% during the year.

1. Find the cost of the closing inventory by means of the LIFO method.

2. Find the cost of the closing inventory by means of the retail method.

DISCUSSION QUESTIONS:

Why is the LIFO method an advantage to the merchant during periods of rising prices? Is it of any value during declining price periods?

Managerial Decision

In view of the current trend of prices and tax rates, is this a good time to introduce the LIFO method?

ADDITIONAL ASSIGNMENTS

16.

(a) The opening inventory is overvalued $2,000 because of failure to take depreciation, and the closing inventory is similarly overvalued $1,300. What is the effect of the overvaluation on profits?

(b) If the opening inventory is overvalued $2,000 and the closing inventory is undervalued $1,300 (either by taking too much depreciation or failing to count all the stock), what is the effect on profits?

(c) If the opening inventory is overvalued $2,000 and the closing inventory is undervalued $1,300, what is the effect on profits?

(d) If the opening inventory is undervalued $2,000 and the closing inventory is overvalued $1,300, what is the effect on profits?

17. The following figures represent the operation of a ready-to-wear department during a year:

Gross sales during a year	$60,500
Gross markdowns	4,200
Gross purchases at cost	42,500
Expenses	15,325
Transfers in at cost	3,750
Cash discounts earned	2,950
Opening inventory, January 1, at cost	9,500
Transportation charges inward	3,850
Returns from customers	5,000
Transfers out at cost	2,100
Markdown cancellations	1,000
Gross purchases at retail	59,550
Returns to vendors at cost	3,000
Transfers in at retail	4,200
Alteration charges	850
Closing physical inventory, December 31, at retail	8,560
Allowances to customers	650
Opening inventory, January 1, at retail	13,500
Transfers out at retail	3,000
Additional markups	3,500
Returns to vendors at retail	6,500

1. Find the shortages.

2. Find the operating profit by using the usual method of reducing retail inventory to cost.

3. Find the operating profit by reducing total deductions to cost. (Gross cost of merchandise sold may be derived by applying the complement of the markup percentage to total deductions.)

18. A large metropolitan store has purchased tweed suits, made sales, and taken markdowns as follows:

Date of Pricing	Cost	Retail	Bought	Sold
January 2	$30.00	$52.00	92	83
January 15	26.00	38.00	75	70
February 15	18.95	26.50	425	350
April 5	15.95	19.95	156	140
Markdown prices at later dates		16.00		30
		12.00		25
		6.00		41

At each date on which new suits were priced, all unsold tweed suits in stock were reduced to the new lower retail price level. Finally, successive markdowns were taken on all suits and the last cleaned out at $6.

1. Find the initial markup percentage on these tweed suits.
2. Find the percentage of markdown.
3. Find the percentage of maintained markup.
4. If the last purchase of 156 suits had not been made, what would have been the maintained markup percentage?
5. Should the buyer have bought any suits at $15.95, in April?

12   How to Measure
Stock-Sales Relationships

It is important to make frequent comparisons of stock with sales in order to ensure adequate but not excessive stocks. Typical and goal stock-turn figures are available for most lines, so that a merchant may compare the turnover of his store with standards. A turnover may be too high or too low, but too low a turnover is more dangerous, for heavy stocks add to markdowns and expenses and reduce the return on investment in merchandise.

Capital turnover is a useful guide to the efficiency with which capital invested in merchandise is used in producing sales volume.

The stock-sales ratio is useful in planning the amount of the stock desired at the first of any month to realize a planned volume of business. Multiplying the planned sales by the ratio gives the planned stock.

Since stock-turn bears a causal relationship to profits, it is necessary to be able to calculate the effect on profits of changes deliberately made in stock-turn relationships and to know how to increase stock-turn without interfering with sales. Thus, stock-turn becomes an objective in profitable merchandising equal in importance to markup.

DEFINITIONS

Stock-Turn. The ratio between sales and average inventory. It is calculated in any one of the following ways:

1. Net sales ÷ average inventory at retail.
2. Gross cost of goods sold ÷ average inventory at cost.
3. Number of units sold ÷ average unit inventory.

Stock-Turn Rate. The stock-turn for a period of 1 year.

Average Stock (same as average inventory). An average of the stock on hand during the period. The general plan is to total the inventory figures at the first of each of the months of the year and the closing inventory and to divide by 13. Weekly inventories may be averaged. Sometimes only the opening and closing stocks for the year are averaged, but the latter figures are seldom representative of the season or year.

Capital Turnover. The ratio between net sales and the average inventory at cost. It is calculated: net sales ÷ average inventory at cost.

Stock-Sales Ratio. The ratio between the retail stock at the first (or end) of the month and sales for that month. The B.O.M. (beginning of the month) stock-sales ratio is the dollar stock on the first of the month divided by the sales for the month. The E.O.M. (end of the month) stock-sales ratio is the dollar stock at the end of the month divided by the sales for the month.

A. STOCK-TURN

1. Calculating stock-turn at retail and at cost.

● *Example:*

In a general store, inventory is taken only twice a year, at both cost and retail values. The figures are as follows:

	Cost	Retail
Beginning inventory (January 1st)	$13,000	$20,000
Mid-year inventory (July 1st)	11,000	16,500
Ending inventory (December 31)	10,750	17,500

Purchases during the year are $52,725 at cost and sales are $71,000. What is the stock-turn at both retail and cost?

Solution:

At Retail:

$$S.\ T. = \frac{\text{Net Sales}}{\text{Average Retail Stock}}$$

$$= \frac{\$71,000}{(\$20,000 + \$16,500 + \$17,500) \div 3} = \frac{\$71,000}{\$18,000} = 3.9$$

At Cost:

$$S.\ T. = \frac{\text{Cost of Merchandise Sold}}{\text{Average Cost of Stock}}$$

$$= \frac{\$13,000 + \$52,725 - \$10,750}{(\$13,000 + \$11,000 + \$10,750) \div 3}$$

$$= \frac{\$54,975.00}{\$11,583.33} = 4.7$$

ASSIGNMENT 1:

In a drug store, the sales for the year are $120,000. The stock at the beginning is $12,000 at cost and $24,000 at retail, and the stock at the end of the year is $9,500 at cost and $19,000 at retail. The purchases at cost during the year are $80,000. What is the stock-turn at retail? What is the stock-turn at cost?

DISCUSSION QUESTION:

How would you explain the difference in stock-turn figure at retail and stock-turn figure at cost to a prospective investor or creditor?

2. **Converting from stock-turn at retail to stock-turn at cost and vice versa.**

Example:

Store X computes its stock-turn on a retail basis to be 8. Store X wishes to compare its turn to that of its nearest competitor, store Y. Store Y has a stock-turn of 9 calculated at cost. The average markup on sales of store X is 34%, whereas the markup on inventory was 36% of retail. In store Y the markup on sales is 31% and 34% of retail on inventory.

1. Express the stock-turn of store X on a cost basis.
2. Express the stock-turn of store Y on a retail basis.

Solution:

(1) Let sales in store X = $80

$$\text{S. T. at retail} = \frac{\$80}{\$10} = 8$$

Cost of Merchandise Sold:
$80 × 66% = $52.80
Average Inventory at Cost: $10 × 64% = $6.40

$$\text{S. T. at Cost:} \frac{\$52.80}{\$6.40} = \$8.25$$

(2) Let cost of merchandise sold of store Y be $90

$$\text{S. T. at Cost} = \frac{\$90 \text{ (cost of sales)}}{\$10 \text{ (average cost stock)}} = 9$$

Sales: $90 ÷ 69% = $130.43
Average Retail Stock: $10 ÷ 66% = $15.15

$$\text{S. T. at retail:} \frac{\$130.43}{\$15.15} = 8.7$$

ASSIGNMENT 2:

The stock-turn of a men's store is 6 at retail. The store's markup on sales is 35% and its markup on stock is 37%. In the men's store across the street, the stock-turn is 7.5 on a cost basis. This store has markups on sales of 32% and on inventory of 35%.

1. What is the stock-turn of the first store at cost?
2. What is the stock-turn of the second store at retail?

DISCUSSION QUESTION:

Are turn-over ratios for most retail establishments expressed at cost or retail? Why? What is the advantage of showing turnover at retail? At cost?

3. Calculating stock-turn at retail from monthly data.

● *Example:*

Sales for the year are $100,000.
Stock figures are the year are as follows:

B.O.M.	Type of Inventory	Retail Stock
January	Physical Inventory	$ 17,000
February	Book Inventory	20,000
March	Book Inventory	23,000
April	Book Inventory	21,000
May	Book Inventory	20,750
June	Book Inventory	20,500
July	Physical Inventory	18,000
August	Book Inventory	19,500
September	Book Inventory	24,000
October	Book Inventory	21,000
November	Book Inventory	22,500
December	Book Inventory	25,000
January	Physical Inventory	21,000
Total of monthly stocks		$273,250

Find the stock-turn at retail for the year.

Solution:

$273,250 ÷ 13 = $21,019.23, the average inventory at retail

$$\text{S. T.} = \frac{\$100,000}{\$21,019.23} = 4.8$$

ASSIGNMENT 3:

The following figures are available.

	Retail Inventory	Retail Purchases	Net Sales	Markdowns
March — Beginning	$3,000	$2,500	$3,050	$ 75
April		1,800	2,000	25
May		1,950	1,850	30
June		2,185	1,550	100
July		2,000	1,875	85
August		2,350	1,450	50
Sept. — Mid-year	3,495	2,200	2,100	20
October		2,100	2,400	10
November		1,900	2,375	10
December		2,000	2,500	15
January		2,100	1,850	85
February		1,850	1,775	100
March — Ending	2,240			

Find the book inventory for the intervening months, and calculate the stock-turn for the year.

What is the shortage/overage percentage for each of the 6-month seasons?

DISCUSSION QUESTIONS:

What types of retail establishments calculate their stock-turn on a weekly basis? What kinds of retail stores would figure stock-turn quarterly, semi-annually, or annually? What are the major advantages and disadvantages of each of the above over a monthly calculation?

4. Monthly stock-turn and annual rate.

● *Example:*

The information below is a merchandise classification of a large department store.

	Sales	B.O.M. Stock at Retail
November	$25,000	$30,000
December	25,000	25,000
January	10,000	10,000
February		15,000

How much should stocks be reduced to turn the stock at an annual rate of 15 times?

Solution:

Stock-turn for one quarter

$$= \frac{\$60,000}{(\$30,000 + \$25,000 + \$10,000 + \$15,000) \div 4} = \frac{\$60,000}{\$20,000} = 3$$

S.T. = 3 times in 3 months or at the rate of 12 times a year.

The required stock-turn is 15. With the average monthly sales of $20,000 and a turnover rate of 15 or 15/12 monthly, the new average stock is 20,000 ÷ 5/4 = $16,000. This represents a reduction of $4,000 or 20% on the assumption that the rate of sale can be maintained for the rest of the year.

ASSIGNMENT 4:

If the annual stock-turn is 4, how much must stocks be reduced to achieve 6 turns a year?

DISCUSSION QUESTIONS:

In the first example a stock-turn of 3 was achieved for a 3-month period. Do you feel this is representative of what this department can achieve on a yearly basis? Why?

5. Averaging stock-turn.

● *Example:*

A drug store has six departments. The first department has a turnover rate of 4 and contributes 8% of the total sales. The second department's turnover is 5 and constitutes 20% of the sales volume. The third department has a turnover rate of 6 and accounts for 30% of the sales volume. The fourth department has a stock-turn of 2 and contributes 12% of the volume. The last two departments each have turnover rates of 5 but one department contributes 20% of the total volume.

1. What is the turnover for the entire store?
2. If 5 turns are needed for the entire store and the only opportunity to increase turnover is in the fourth department, what will the turnover have to be?

Solution:

Let Sales = $100

1.

Department	Sales		Turn		Average Stock
D_1	$ 8	÷	4	=	$ 2
D_2	20	÷	5	=	4
D_3	30	÷	6	=	5
D_4	12	÷	2	=	6
D_5	20	÷	5	=	4
D_6	10	÷	5	=	2
Total	$100				$23

Stock-turn = $100 ÷ $23 = 4.34

2.

Department	Sales		Turn		Average Stock
D_1	$ 8	÷	4	=	$ 2
D_2	20	÷	5	=	4
D_3	30	÷	6	=	5
D_4	12	÷	?	=	?
D_5	20	÷	5	=	4
D_6	10	÷	5	=	2
Total sales	$100	÷	5	=	Total Average stock of $20

Therefore, the stock for D_4 must be $3
Turnover for D_4 = $12 ÷ $3 = 4.

ASSIGNMENT 5:

There are six divisions of merchandise in a small retail store with sales and stock-turn distribution as follows:

	Sales	Stock-turn
A	10%	5
B	15%	10
C	16%	4
D	20%	3
E	22%	2
F	17%	3

1. What is the stock-turn in the store as a whole?
2. If 5.5 stock-turns are planned for the total store and the best opportunity to obtain a high stock-turn is in class E, what stock-turn would be necessary in E?

DISCUSSION QUESTION:

Is the stock-turn of a certain classification of merchandise representative of the stock-turn of the department?

Managerial Decision

You are hired upon graduation from college to be the head of a department in a medium-sized department store. Soon after your arrival on your new job, the merchandise manager discusses your new responsibilities. He tells you he is not satisfied with the past performance and expects you to increase the stock-turn. He tells you that you have 3 months to show results. After this statement he leaves. How will you go about analyzing the present stock-turn and making improvements?

B. CAPITAL TURNOVER

6. Computing capital turnover.

Example:

Net Sales	$500,000
Beginning inventory at cost	30,000
Closing inventory at cost	34,000

Find capital turnover for the period.

Solution:

$$\frac{\$500,000}{(\$34,000 + \$30,000) \div 2} = \frac{\$500,000}{\$32,000} = 15.6$$

ASSIGNMENT 6:

	Inventories at cost
July 1	$20,000
August 1	21,500
September 1	19,000
October 1	20,075
November 1	23,000
December 1	25,000
January 1	17,000

Net sales for the period are $80,000. What is the capital turnover for the six months under consideration?

DISCUSSION QUESTION:

What is the advantage of having capital turnover figures available as well as stock-turn figures?

7. Relationship between stock-turn and capital turnover.

Example:

The stock-turn in a store is 8 and the markup is 18%. Find the capital turnover.

Solution:

Let sales equal $160. The average retail stock is $160 ÷ 8 = $20. At cost, this is $16.40 ($20 × 82%).

$$\frac{\$160}{\$16.40} = 9.76, \text{ the capital turnover}$$

Short-cut solution:

$$\text{Stock-turn} = \text{capital turnover} \times (100\% - \text{markup } \%).$$

$$\text{Then, capital turnover} = \frac{\text{stock-turn}}{100\% - \text{markup } \%}$$

$$\text{Capital turnover} = \frac{8}{100\% - 18\%} = \frac{8}{82\%} = 9.76$$

ASSIGNMENT 7:

The stock-turn is 10 and the markup is 40%. What is the capital turnover?

8. Estimating stock-turn from capital turnover based on closing inventories.

Example:

Dun and Bradstreet reports 7 as the median ratio of net sales to closing cost inventory in a certain type of store. Inquiry in the trade reveals that closing inventories represent about 90% of the average inventory carried through the year. The typical markup is 40%. Estimate the stock-turn for the line.

Solution:

Let $1 equal the closing cost of stock. Therefore, $7.00 equals the sales. The average cost of stock equals:

$$\frac{\$1}{90\%} = \$1.11$$

$$\text{Average retail stock} = \frac{\$1.11}{100\% - 40\%} = \frac{\$1.11}{60\%} = \$1.85$$

$$\text{Stock-turn} = \frac{\$7.00}{\$1.85} = 3.78$$

ASSIGNMENT 8:

Estimate the stock-turn for the following:

	Initial Markup	Ratio of Net Sales to Closing Cost Inventory	Estimated Ratio of Closing Stock to Average Stock
A department store	39%	7.5	70%
A discount store	25%	12	85%
A drug store	35%	10	75%
An automotive store	25%	4	65%
A gift shop	45%	8	55%

DISCUSSION QUESTION:

Does a 10% reduction in inventory at cost result in a 10% increase in capital turnover? Demonstrate.

C. STOCK-SALES RATIOS

9. Computing stock-sales ratios.

● *Example:*

In a grocery store the sales and B.O.M. stocks at retail are as follows:

	Sales	B.O.M. Stocks
January	$30,000	$39,000
February	32,000	35,000
March	31,000	36,000
April	---	34,000

1. Find the beginning of the month stock-sales ratios for January, February, and March.
2. What are the end of the month stock-sales ratios for the same months?

Solution:

(1) January . . . . $39,000 ÷ $30,000 = 1.30

February . . . .   35,000 ÷ 32,000 = 1.09

March . . . .   36,000 ÷ 31,000 = 1.16

(2) January . . . . $35,000 ÷ $30,000 = 1.17

February . . . .   36,000 ÷ 32,000 = 1.12

March . . . .   34,000 ÷ 31,000 = 1.10

ASSIGNMENT 9:

Sales for June, $10,000. Retail stock first of June, $42,000 and end of June, $38,000. Find both the beginning and end of the month stock-sales ratios for June.

DISCUSSION QUESTION:

What additional information do you have in the stock-sales ratio that you do not have when given a stock-turn figure?

10. Computing stocks from stock-sales ratios.

● *Example:*

A B.O.M. stock-sales ratio for May of 2.5 is typical for a certain line of goods. If sales of $15,000 are expected in May, how much stock should be on hand on May 1?

Solution:

$$\text{Since stock-sales ratio} = \frac{\text{Stock at beginning of month}}{\text{Sales for month}}$$

Stock at beginning of month = 2.5 X $15,000 = $37,500

ASSIGNMENT 10:

The E.O.M. stock-sales ratio planned for April in the millinery department is 0.8 and sales of $20,000 are planned. What is the amount of the stock to be carried at the end of April?

DISCUSSION QUESTION:

Is the reciprocal of stock-turn equal to the stock-sales ratio?

Managerial Decision

If you are given the choice of capital turnover figures or stock-sales ratios monthly, which would be the more valuable — first, if you are the manager of a department, then, if you are the president of the store?

D. INCREASING STOCK-TURN

11. How to achieve a higher stock-turn.

● *Example:*

In taking over an apparel department, the buyer finds sales of $100,000 and stocks averaging $40,000 at retail. The gross margin is 33-1/3%. The stock is distributed over 4 classifications, with an average of 4 price lines in each, an average of 10 styles in each price line, 5 sizes in each style, and 5 colors in each size. The average unit in stock is $4.00.

The merchandise manager insists that the stock-turn be increased to 3 times a year. The buyer considers two different solutions: (1) increase sales to $120,000 and (2) reduce the stock to $33,333.34.

The buyer estimates that to gain the additional $20,000 in sales will require $5,000 promotional expenses. Increased handling expenses are 5% of additional sales.

If the stock reduction method is chosen, markdowns will be reduced by 1% and a 6% reduction in carrying charges can be seen against the average cost of merchandise.

1. Which alternative should the buyer take and how much more profitable than the other will it be?
2. On the average, how many units of each different size and color in a style number are currently carried in stock?
3. How can the stock be cut most judiciously without interfering with sales?

Solution:

1. (a) Increasing sales: At 33-1/3% gross margin, $20,000 more in sales will provide $6,667 more gross margin at an expense of $5,000 for promotion and $1,000 for handling. The additional sales will contribute about $667 additional profit.

(b) Decreasing stock: A $6,667 smaller retail inventory is about $4,444 lower at cost, 6% of which is $267. Furthermore, a 1% cut in markdowns should increase gross margin by the cost of the markdowns[1] avoided or by about 2/3 of 1% on sales of $100,000, or $667. Thus the total profit gain is $667 + $267 = $934.

2. The total current stock in units is $40,000/$4.00, or 10,000 units. This consists of 4,000 different units. (4 × 4 × 10 × 5 × 5). With 10,000 units there must be an average of 2.5 units of each different item.

3. The following simplification may be considered:

Number of classifications	4
Number of price lines	4
Number of styles – average	8½
Number of sizes	4
Number of colors	4
Average stock of each	4
Total units, 8,704	

Total dollar stock $4.00 × 8,704 = $34,816 or close to the $33,333 goal.

ASSIGNMENT 11:

In order to increase stock-turn from 4 to 5, by what percentage should stock be reduced with sales constant?

DISCUSSION QUESTION:

If one of the keys to maintaining a good stock-turn is controlling inventories, why do many merchants not do an effective job of inventory control?

12. Increased turnover and profit.

Example:

An apparel retailer has a turnover of 8 times a year; an initial markup of 38%; markdowns of 15%; shortages of 0.4%; alteration cost of 0.8%; cash discounts of 5%; and expenses of 30%.
The goal turnover established by the merchant is 10 times. The markdowns vary with the amount of stock carried.

1. What percentage must present stock be reduced to achieve 10 turns?

---

[1] See problem 9, section XI, for an explanation of the cost of the markdown concept.

2. What is the present profit percentage?
3. If the estimates of the effect of stock-turn are correct, how much
   will profit be increased?

Solution:

1. Assume sales of $80

$$\frac{\$80}{8} = \$10, \text{ the average stock}$$

$$\frac{\$80}{10} = \underline{\$8}, \text{ the goal average stock}$$

$$\phantom{\frac{\$80}{10} = } \$2, \text{ the reduction of average stock}$$

$$2/10 = 20\%, \text{ the percentage reduction in stock}$$

Short method: $\dfrac{\text{Goal turn} - \text{Actual turn}}{\text{Goal turn}} = \dfrac{10 - 8}{10} = 20\%$

2. To find present profit:

Profit = Gross margin − Expenses

Gross Margin = Maintained markup + Cash discounts − Alteration cost

Maintained markup = Initial markup − Reductions × (1 − Initial Markup)

$$\text{M. M.} = 0.38 - (0.15 + 0.004) \times (1 - 0.38)$$
$$= 0.38 - (0.154 \times 0.62)$$
$$= 0.38 - 0.0955 = 0.2845 \text{ or } 28.45\%$$
$$\text{G. M.} = 0.2845 + 0.05 - 0.008$$
$$= 0.3345 - 0.008 = 0.3265 \text{ or } 32.65\%$$
$$\text{Profit} = 0.3265 - 0.30 = 0.0265 \text{ or } 2.65\%$$

3. Estimating Future Profit:
   With stock reduced 20% there should perhaps be a 20% reduction
   in markdowns from 15% to 12%.

$$\therefore \text{M. M.} = 0.38 - (0.12 + 0.004) \times (1 - 0.38)$$
$$= 0.38 - (0.124 \times 0.62)$$
$$= 0.38 - 0.07688$$
$$\text{M. M.} = 0.30312 \text{ or } 30.3\%$$
$$\text{G. M.} = 0.303 + 0.05 - 0.008 = 0.345 \text{ or } 34.5\%$$
$$\text{Profit} = 0.345 - 0.30 = 4.5\%$$

The above stock reduction and new profit projection does not account
for any reduction in interest, insurance, occupancy, or selling expenses

that might be realized. Of these expenses, 20% might also be saved by the department; however, the saving in markdowns may be overstated.

ASSIGNMENT 12:

A furniture department has a turnover of 3.5, with an initial markup of 42%; markdowns of 4.2%; shortages of 0.6%; alteration cost of 2%; cash discounts of 1.5%; and expenses of 36%. Occupancy expenses are 10% and selling salaries, 5%. Interest and insurance on merchandise total 8% of the average cost of investment.

The goal turnover is 4 times. It is estimated that markdowns vary directly with stock investment, that occupancy could be reduced 12%, and that selling payroll could be reduced 5% if the goal turnover is reached without reducing sales.

1. What percentage must stocks be reduced to achieve 4 turnovers?
2. How much will profits be increased with a turnover of 4?

DISCUSSION QUESTION:

What are some of the problems that may arise if a stock reduction plan is undertaken?

Managerial Decision

After instituting a stock reduction to increase turnover, you realize that some of the older salesmen are telling customers what you don't carry any more, rather than selling what is available. How should you handle this problem?

ADDITIONAL ASSIGNMENTS

13. From the following data, find the stock-turn for the season.

Month	Inventory at Retail First of Month	Gross Sales	Returns
August	$10,000	$2,500	$350
September	14,000	3,000	225
October	12,000	3,600	150
November	11,000	3,900	125
December	13,000	4,500	275
January	10,100	2,800	375
February	9,500		

14. The following data are for one month:

Beginning inventory at retail	$ 20,000
Beginning inventory at cost	14,000
Closing inventory at retail	16,000
Closing inventory at cost	12,000
Net sales	100,000
Cost of merchandise sold	80,000

Find the following:

1. S. T. at retail
2. S. T. at cost
3. Express S. T. at retail and cost at annual rates
4. Capital turnover per month
5. B.O.M. stock-sales ratio
6. E.O.M. stock-sales ratio.

15. A store having two departments had a $250,000 sales volume in Department X, and $200,000 in Department Z. The stock-turn for X was 4 and for Z was 2. What is the stock-turn for the store?

16. In a young men's shop 90% of the yearly sales are made in 5 months. The stock-turn for the year is 10 times. In the 5-month period the turnover is 8 times.

(a) What is the turnover for the remaining 7 months?

(b) Express the turnover for the 7 months as an annual rate.

17. The stock at the beginning of the year was $10,000 at retail. At the end of each month, the buyer reordered the quantity sold during the month and reorders were received within a few days when the old stock was virtually sold out. The average monthly sales were $9,000. What is the annual turnover?

18. The net sales in a store are $50,000 and the average retail stock is $20,000. The initial markup is 35% and the maintained markup 30%. Compute the stock turnover at cost.

19. The sales for December were $10,000; the stock B.O.M. at retail, $26,000; the stock E.O.M. was $30,000.

(a) What was stock-sales ratio December 1st?

(b) What was the stock-turn for the month?

20. If the stock-sales ratio at the B.O.M. was 6, and at the E.O.M. 4, what was the stock-turn for the month?

13   How to Measure Return on the Investment in Merchandise and in Space

Annual profits are commonly compared both with the sales and with the investment required to generate the profits. In virtually all stores, return on the investment is higher than the return on the sales, since annual sales generally exceed the value of the investment in a retail business.

For purposes of merchandising, it is more useful to compare profits with the *merchandise investment* alone rather than with the entire investment, since the merchandising executives exercise control only over the investment in merchandise for resale. A common goal is to aim at an increase in the ratio of profit to the average cost of the merchandise investment even when there is little opportunity to increase the profits relative to the sales.

The merchandise inventory is not the only scarce economic resource that the merchandiser must attempt to use to best advantage. He is equally concerned with the space required to stock and display the merchandise assortment required to achieve his sales goal. Thus, the sales and the profit earned per square foot of space occupied become major elements in inventory management.

DEFINITIONS

The Return on the Average Investment in Merchandise. The return may be measured at the gross margin level, the controllable margin level, or the operating profit level. The profit margin, at the level selected, is divided by the average inventory at cost and may be expressed as an index rather than as a percentage. The percentage may be found by multiplying the capital-turn by the profit return expressed as a percentage of sales. On the gross margin level, the return is generally called the gross margin per dollar of cost investment in merchandise.

Net Worth. The owner's equity in the store. The difference between the assets and liabilities. Profits are commonly expressed both as a percentage of net worth and as a percentage of net sales. (Profits may also be expressed as a percentage of the total investment, including both owned and borrowed capital.)

A. RETURN ON THE MERCHANDISE INVESTMENT

1. Return on the merchandise investment (gross margin level).

● *Example:*

> The gross margin on a certain line is 36%, the initial markup 40%, and the stock-turn is 4 times a year. Express the margin as a percentage of the merchandise investment.

Solution:

> Let $100 equal the retail sales. The margin, then, is $36, and the average retail inventory is $25. The average cost inventory, then, is 60% of $25 or $15. The return on the merchandise is $36/$15 or 240%. This may be expressed as an index of 240 or as $2.40 for every dollar of merchandise investment (at cost).

ASSIGNMENT 1:

> What gross margin will yield 180% on the average merchandise investment if the stock-turn at cost is 3?

DISCUSSION QUESTION:

> What is the significance of a "return on investment" measurement as compared to margin as a percentage of sales?

2. Return on the merchandise investment (operating profit and controllable margin levels).

● *Example:*

> In a hosiery operation, the stock-turn is 6 times a year; the initial markup is 40%; and the operating profit is 5% of sales.
>
> 1. What is the operating profit as a percentage of the merchandise investment?
> 2. If a return index of 75 is desired, what operating profit on sales would be necessary at the same markup?

Solution:

> 1. Let sales = $100 and operating profit $5. Since turnover is 6, the average retail stock is $100/$6 = $16.67. Since markup is 40%, the cost of stock is 60% of $16.67 or $10.00; $5 (profit) ÷ $10 = 50% return as a percentage of the merchandise investment.

2. Average stock at cost = $10.00 per $100 sales; 75% of $10.00 = $7.50; $7.50 ÷ $100 = 7.5%, the necessary percentage of operating profit on sales.

ASSIGNMENT 2:

In a camera department, the initial markup is 45%, the controllable margin, 18%, and the stock-turn, 4. What is the return index at the controllable margin level?

3. Return on the investment and gross margin relationships.

● *Example:*

Management has set an annual gross margin goal of $2.10 for every dollar of cost inventory carried in a certain department. The capital-turn in this department is estimated to be 6 (sales divided by the average cost inventory).
What gross margin must the department achieve to realize this goal?

Solution:

Formula: Return on the investment = capital-turn × profit margin. On the gross margin level, then,

$$\$2.10 = 6 \times \text{gross margin}$$
$$\text{gross margin} = \frac{\$2.10}{6} = 0.35 \text{ or } 35\%$$

ASSIGNMENT 3:

1. With the goal for return on the investment at the gross margin level set at $1.82 per dollar of merchandise investment and the gross margin expectancy 36.4%, what capital-turn will have to be achieved?
2. If the expectancy for price reductions in the situation above is 6%, what stock-turn should be achieved?

DISCUSSION QUESTION:

To achieve a particular profit return at the gross margin level, which factor can be more readily manipulated: the gross margin percentage on sales or the capital-turn?

4. Return on net worth.

● *Example:*

In tie shops the average net profit on sales is 4% and the net sales are 5 times the net worth. Find the profit as a percentage of net worth.

Solution:

Let $100 = net worth and $500 = sales.
Profit is 4% of $500 or $20, which is 20% of net worth.

ASSIGNMENT 4:

If an installment furniture store earns a profit of 10% on its sales and its sales are 3 times its net worth, what is its profit on net worth? What is the relationship of this problem to capital turnover?

DISCUSSION QUESTION:

If you were the manager of a store, which of the following is more meaningful: profit as a percentage of sales or as a percentage of net worth? What outside factors might influence your decision about which measurement to use?

Managerial Decision:

If you were the new owner of a department store with thirty departments, would you have a "return on investment" calculated on each department? Why?

B. RETURN ON SPACE OCCUPIED

5. Space allocation

● *Example:*

Two adjacent departments have space, sales, and sales per square foot as follows:

	Square feet	Annual sales	Sales per square foot
Department *A*	900	$ 63,000	$70
Department *B*	1,000	50,000	50
Total	1,900	$113,000	$59.47

Department *A* is in urgent need of 200 square feet of additional space to provide adequate display and storage space for a line that is enjoying an upward trend in popularity. There is considerable evidence that a good deal of potential business is being lost because of the inadequate space. The manager is convinced that he can generate $70 a square foot from the additional space requested.

The only practical way to do this is to take away 200 square feet from Department *B* where space does not seem to have been used to best advantage and where volume is barely holding its own. Better layout planning should increase the average sales per square foot in *B* to $55. But dollar sales, nevertheless, will be reduced considerably in *B*, to which the manager of that department objects.

1. If management decides to make the proposed change, how much may total sales of the two departments combined be increased?
2. What will be the increase in sales per square foot for the total area?

Solution:

	Square feet	Sales per square foot	Sales
Department *A*	1,100	$70.00	$ 77,000
Department *B*	800	55.00	44,000
Total	1,900	$63.68 ($121,000/1,900)	$121,000

Sales are currently $113,000, so total sales would hopefully be increased $8,000, but at the expense of a $6,000 loss in Department *B*. Sales per square foot will increase from $59.47 to $63.68.

ASSIGNMENT 5:

Management, in connection with the situation above, wants to achieve a goal of $65 a square foot for the 1,900 square feet occupied by the two departments in question, and the manager of Department *A* feels he will need a little more than the additional 200 square feet to be provided in order to have an adequate layout in view of potential sales. It is estimated that an additional adjustment will not effect the sales per square foot forecast for *A* ($70) but sales volume in *B* would be further curtailed.

1. What should be the space allocation between *A* and *B* to produce sales per square foot of $65 for the combined space? ·
2. Should the effect on the morale of the manager of Department *B* be an important factor in a decision about whether to make the move suggested by the solution above?

DISCUSSION QUESTION:

In practice, is it possible to estimate sales per square foot with sufficient accuracy to yield realistic sales forecasts?

ADDITIONAL ASSIGNMENTS

6. The merchandise manager is demanding a controllable margin of $1.75 for every dollar of merchandise investment in a certain department. The stock-turn goal is 4 and the initial markup expectancy is 40%.

(a) As a percentage of sales, what controllable margin should the department manager attempt to achieve?

(b) Last year's reductions were 10% and last year's direct expenses were 12%, with cash discounts earned 3% of sales. How might the buyer adjust these elements to achieve the controllable margin goal in (a)? Assume no change in initial markup and stock-turn goals.

7. The following figures are available:

Net profit	14% of sales
Net worth	50% of sales
Cost inventory	20% of sales
Initial markup	30% of retail

If the turnover increases from the present rate of 5 times to an anticipated rate of 6 times:

(a) How much will the percentage of profit be increased because of a lower interest charge on the reduced stocks? (Compute at 8%.)

(b) What other expenses and cost factors are likely to be favorably affected by the lower inventory?

(c) Express the percentage of profit in (a) as a percentage of net worth.

8. The following figures are available for the men's departments:

	Initial Markup %	S. T.	Profit as % of Sales	% of Store Sales
Men's clothing	44%	2.5	4	3
Men's furnishings	42%	4	10	4
Boys' wear	41%	3	7	1.5
Men's and boys' shoes	41.5%	2	6	1

(a) Find the capital-turn for each of the departments.

(b) Find the index of return on merchandise investment in each department.

(c) Find the relative dollars of profit for each of the departments.

(d) What are your conclusions about the relative importance of these departments to the store?

9. A lingerie department has a markup of 44%. It makes an operating profit of 15% on its sales and has a stock-turn of 4.5. The dress department in the same store has a 40% markup, makes 10% profit, and has 10 stock-turns.

(a) Compare the profits of the two departments in relation to the merchandise investment in each.

(b) The dress department is 40% larger in sales than the lingerie department. How do the dollar profits of the two departments compare?

(c) What is your conclusion about the relative "efficiency" of the two departments?

(1) In which would it be more profitable to increase stock investment?

(2) Assuming that in both departments an expenditure of a certain amount for advertising will result in the same increase in sales, in which would it be more profitable to promote?

Part IV   DOLLAR PLANNING AND CONTROL

14   How to Analyze
Dollar Sales and Stocks

A store's data on sales and stocks must be broken down into departmental and classification figures in order to determine whether a proper balance between sales and stocks is being maintained and whether markups and markdowns are being kept at desirable levels. Such analyses usually reveal the weak spots in merchandising operations and should lead to corrective action.

DEFINITIONS

Dollar Control. The analysis and planning of sales and stocks in terms of dollar value.

Unit Control. The analysis and planning of sales and stocks in terms of pieces of merchandise.

Selling Department. A physical division of a store, containing related merchandise grouped for purposes of (1) determining the profit for each grouping, (2) controlling buying and pricing more exactly, and (3) promoting sales more effectively.

Classification (or Dissection). A subdivision of a store or a selling department for which separate merchandising records are kept but to which expenses are not charged and for which operating profit is not determined.

Classification Control. The analysis and planning of sales and stocks in terms of dollar value within each merchandise classification.

Perpetual Inventory Method of Classification Control. The determination of the dollar book inventories within each classification from daily sales and purchase records.

Periodic Inventory Method of Classification Control. The determination of sales data within each merchandise classification from periodic counts of the inventory on hand.

162

A. INVENTORY ANALYSIS BY CLASSIFICATION

1. Stock distribution by classification or price line.

● *Example:*

There are three classifications in a department and sales of $20,000 are distributed as follows:

Classification	Sales
A	65%
B	20
C	15
Total	100%

The stock-turn desired is· 5 for the period. Plan stocks for each classification assuming that all three require assortments that include price lines, sizes, and colors.

Solution:

The percentages should be adjusted to yield a larger than average turnover in *A* because a larger than average stock-turn is usually possible in a classification in which sales are larger than average. Also adjust the percentage to yield a smaller than average stock-turn in *C.*

Classification	Stocks	
A	60%	$2,400
B	20	800
C	20	800
	100%	$4,000

These are arbitrary adjustments, not based on a formula, but they reflect a principle.

ASSIGNMENT 1:

There are four price lines in a certain classification with sales distribution as follows:

Price Line	Percentage of $ Sales
$ 8.15	30%
10.25	28
11.50	22
12.60	20

The stock-turn planned for the classification is 10 times a year and the sales are planned at $90,000. Plan average stocks by price line to allow for a more rapid turnover in the best-selling price lines.

DISCUSSION QUESTION:

Discuss the feasibility of changing the price lines in the problem above.

2. Classification control based on periodic inventories.

● *Example:*

In a certain classification of goods in a department, the stock at the beginning of a 6-month period was $20,000 at retail with a markup of 35%. The purchases for this classification during the period were $29,000 at cost and $46,000 at retail. The markdowns taken during the period were $2,500 and the inventory at the end of the period was $15,000 at retail. Shortages for the department averaged 1% of net sales.
Find the net sales, stock-turn, and maintained markup for the classification.

Solution:

	Cost	Retail	Markup
Opening inventory	$13,000	$20,000	
Purchases	29,900	46,000	
Total merchandise handled	$42,900	$66,000	35%
Closing inventory	9,750	15,000	
Total retail deductions		$51,000	
Cost of goods sold	$33,150		
Markdowns		2,500	
Sales plus shortages		$48,500	
Net sales ($48,500 ÷ 101%)		48,022	

$$\text{Stockturn} = \frac{\$48,022 \text{ (net sales)}}{\$17,500 \text{ (average inventory at retail)}} = 2.7$$

Maintained markup = sales ($48,022) - cost of goods sold ($33,150) = $14,872

ASSIGNMENT 2:

A men's shirt department is divided into 5 classifications. Records of inventories, purchases, and markdowns are kept by classification, but not records of sales. The following figures represent the operations:

Classification	Inventory Jan. 31 Cost	Inventory Jan. 31 Retail	Inventory July 31 Retail	Purchases Feb. 1–July 31 Cost	Purchases Feb. 1–July 31 Retail	Markdowns Feb. 1– July 31 Retail
1.	$ 2,500	$ 3,800	$ 1,000	$ 2,400	$ 3,700	$ 900
2.	6,000	9,500	3,500	12,000	16,200	500
3.	1,400	2,000	1,800	6,500	8,100	500
4.	2,200	3,200	2,500	8,000	9,300	600
5.	1,700	2,900	2,000	6,000	8,800	500
Total	$13,800	$21,400	$10,800	$34,900	$46,100	$3,000

Shortages for the whole department for the period are $1\frac{1}{2}\%$ of net sales.

1. Find the sales, turnover, and gross margin in each of the above classifications and for the department as a whole.
2. What is the markdown percentage in each classification and in the department as a whole?
3. What percentage of total sales is in each classification?

DISCUSSION QUESTIONS:

Should the inventory in any of the 5 classifications be increased or decreased? Why?

B. PLANNING MARKUP BY CLASSIFICATION

3. Profit differences by classification caused by differences in expenses.

Example:

In a selling department, the expenses are 30%, the operating profit is 5%, and the average price of the items sold is $2. In the case of the expenses of 60 cents chargeable to this average sale item, one third are fixed (per item) and two-thirds are variable but maintain a constant percentage relationship to sales.

1. With a 35% gross margin, what profit in dollars and in percentage would be realized on an item retailing at 50 cents; at $5.00?
2. What markup should be obtained on each of the items in question to yield 4% profit on each (assume no markdowns)?

Solution:

1. Profit

50-cent item:

Gross margin, 35%.	$.175
Fixed expense per item	.20
Variable expense, 20%	.10
Total expense	.30

Operating loss = $.125 = 25%

$5 item:

Gross margin, 35%	$1.75
Fixed expenses per item	.20
Variable expenses, 20%	1.00
Total expense	1.20

Operating profit: $.55 or 11.0%

2. Markup

50-cent item:

Total expenses = $	.30
Profit of 4% =	.02
Markup	$ .32 = 64% markup

$5 item:

Total expense = $1.20
Profit of 4%	.20
Markup	$1.40 = 28%

ASSIGNMENT 3:

The following information is available in regard to the operation of a department with 3 classifications:

Class	Average Retail Transaction	Sales	Annual Stock-turn
A	$50	$150,000	6
B	30	60,000	3
C	15	45,000	3

Department Expenses

Selling and recording expenses depending on transactions	$32,000
Charges for space depending on average stock measured in transaction units	24,000
Other expenses depending on sales volume	17,000

To determine the profitability of each classification, it is decided to allocate the first group of expenses according to the number of transactions handled in each; the second group according to the average unit (not dollars) stock; and the third group according to dollar sales.

1. If a 28% markup is planned in each class, what is the net profit for the department and for each classification?
2. If a 4% net profit is desired in each classification, plan the initial markup for each and for the department as a whole.

DISCUSSION QUESTION:

If the expenses incurred in purchasing and selling a $100 suit are only a little more in dollars than those of handling a $70 suit, would you take a higher than average markup on the lower-priced suit and a lower than average markup on the higher-priced suit? Defend your answer.

Managerial Decisions

1. You maintain records that show weekly sales volume and stock figures for each type of goods. What supplementary data should you keep so that you can interpret these figures correctly in planning future sales and stocks?

2. Your sales volume in dollars is the same for $2.50 ties as for $5.00 ties. Should you strive for the same stock investment at each price? Why?

4. Profit differences by classification caused by differences in reductions.

Example:

The planned sales and reductions in a department are as follows:

Classification	Sales	Reductions
A	$10,000	$ 200
B	5,000	600
C	2,000	100
D	3,000	300
	$20,000	$1,200

The expenses of the department are estimated at $6,400 and are distributed to the classifications in proportion to the sales. A 5% profit is deemed a reasonable goal.

1. Plan the initial markup percentage for the department and for each classification.
2. What is the advantage of planning a separate markup for each classification?

Solution:

1.

Classification	Sales	Reductions	Expenses Prorated According to Sales	5% Profit	I.M.U.
A	$10,000	$ 200	$3,200	$ 500	38.2%
B	5,000	600	1,600	250	43.7
C	2,000	100	640	100	40.0
D	3,000	300	960	150	42.7
Total	$20,000	$1,200	$6,400	$1,000	40.6%

This problem can also be solved by using percentages of reductions, of expenses, and of profits, as explained in section 4B.

2. In planning an initial markup for each classification, the merchant recognizes that reductions are not the same for each. Such planning helps to assure a profit and helps the merchant to assure that each classification is contributing to profit.

ASSIGNMENT 4:

In each of two classifications of a department, the merchant obtains a markup of 40%, but in class *A* markdowns are 10% and only 2% in class *B*; 70% of the sales are in class *A* and 30%, in class *B*. How much do the maintained markups differ in each classification? Plan separate markups for each, so that both will have the maintained markup percentage that is realized in the department as a whole.[1]

---

[1] See section 4B for the formulas for calculating the initial and the maintained markup.

DISCUSSION QUESTIONS:

Is it more important to aim at equality in maintained markup than equality in initial markup? Why?

Managerial Decision

In planning the initial markup percentage for your store, should the profit be the planned or the resultant figure?

5. Markup on additional volume.

Example:

A household appliance merchant operates on a 30% initial markup and anticipates sales of $300,000 on the lines he now carries. His markdowns average 5% of expected sales and his expenses 25%. He is considering the addition of television sets, which will probably add $48,000 to his sales but provide an initial markup of only 25% and markdowns of 8%. He expects no increase in his occupancy and buying expenses but servicing, advertising, and selling might increase expenses and costs $4,800. How much profit may the merchant expect without television? With television?

Solution:

Estimated maintained markup on normal volume:

$$30\% - 5\% \times (100\% - 30\%) = 30\% - 3.5\% = 26.5\%$$
$$26.5\% \text{ of } \$300,000 = \$79.500$$

Estimated expenses on normal volume:

$$25\% \text{ of } \$300,000 \text{ or } \$75,000$$

Estimated operating profit on normal volume:

$$\$79,500 - \$75,000 = \$4,500$$

Estimated maintained markup on television sales:

$$25\% - 8\% \times (100\% - 25\%) = 25\% - 6\% = 19\%$$

19% of $48,000	$9,120
Estimated additional expenses	4,800
Estimated addition to profit	$4,320

Thus, without television sets, the merchant can expect to earn $4,500, but with television, $8,820.

ASSIGNMENT 5:

A merchant is contemplating the addition of a new line that should increase his sales volume 10%. But it will provide an initial markup of only 30% whereas his normal markup is 45%. His reductions have averaged 10% but on the new line they should not be more than 5%. His normal expense rate is 35%, but the new volume should increase his dollar expenses no more than 5%. What is the merchant's profit likely to be without and with the addition of the new line? Express the answer both as change in dollar profit and change in percentage of profit.

Note: Assume normal sales of $200,000.

DISCUSSION QUESTION:

What is the danger of adding low-markup goods, even when there is evidence that they will augment profit?

6. Markup on high-priced merchandise.

Example:

A merchant's average sale price of women's suits is $100.00 with an initial markup of 42%, markdowns of 7%, and direct expenses (before overhead) of 20%. He experiences some demand for a high-grade branded suit that costs $140.00, but he doubts if he could sell an appreciable number at a price higher than $200.00. The actual expenses of handling and selling a $200 suit will be about the same as those for a $100.00 suit, but markdowns will probably reduce the average sale on the expensive suits to $180.00. Also, net alteration costs, which average $4.00 on the $100.00 suits, will probably be $6.00 on the better line. The cash discount rates on the two lines are both 8% of cost.

How will the profit on the $200 suit compare with the profit on the average unit of sale?

Solution:

Maintained markup on average sale of $100:

$$42\% - 7\% \times (100\% - 42\%) = 42\% - 4.1\% = 37.9\% = \$37.90$$

The average cost, then, is $62.10.

Gross margin = maintained markup + cash discounts – alteration costs.
Gross margin = $37.90 + 8% of $62.10 – $4 = $38.87

Expenses (20% of $100). 20.00

Controllable profit 18.87

Controllable profit = $\dfrac{\$18.87}{\$100.00}$ =   18.87%

Maintained markup on $200 suit:

$180 (final sale price) – $140 (cost)	$40.00 (22.2%)
Gross margin = $40.00 + 8% of $140 – $6	45.20
Direct expenses (same as average)	20.00
Controllable profit	25.20
Controllable profit = $\dfrac{\$25.20}{\$180.00}$ =	14%

Although the controllable profit in dollars would be higher on the $200 suits, the profit in percentage would be smaller. Since some expenses of handling the $200 line may turn out to be higher than estimated (such as advertising), the markup may not be adequate to make a significant contribution to profits.

ASSIGNMENT 6:

A specialty store sells most of its women's sports coats in a classification with prices from $25 to $100, averaging $50. Its initial markup is 42%; reductions, 10%; net alteration cost, 2%; cash discounts, 5%; and expenses 35%.

The store is considering the introduction of a higher-priced zone, $100 to $250, averaging $150. The reductions here are likely to be 15%; the alteration costs, 3%; the cash discounts, 5%; and the expenses per transaction 50% higher in dollars than the expenses per transaction in its popularly priced classification.

What markup percentage would be necessary if the higher-priced merchandise is to yield the same percentage of profit as now realized on the popularly priced goods?

DISCUSSION QUESTION:

Would the markup in assignment 6 be a satisfactory one at which to introduce the higher-priced line? Defend your answer.

Managerial Decision

Since a low markup on additional volume tends to increase profit (because many expenses are fixed and because others increase only with the units sold, not with their value), would you adopt a policy to take a lower than average markup to secure added sales volume? Defend your answer.

C. AVERAGING MARKUP BY CLASSIFICATION

7. Averaging markups on different classifications — total unknown.

Example:

One-half your retail stock has a markup of 40%; one-third of the stock, a markup of 38%; the balance of the stock, a markup of 36%. What is the average markup on the entire inventory?

Solution:

Weights		*Markup %*		*Weighted Markup %*
1/2	X	40	=	20
1/3	X	38	=	12-2/3
1/6	X	36	=	6

38-2/3, the average
markup % on
the total

Alternate solution:

6	X	40	=	240
4	X	38	=	152
2	X	36	=	72
12				464 ÷ 12 = 38-2/3%,

the average
markup % on
the total

ASSIGNMENT 7:

The markup on 35% of retail purchases is 35%; on 40% of retail purchases, 40%; on 20% of retail purchases, 20%; and on 5%, 5%. What is the markup on the purchases in the four classes combined?

DISCUSSION QUESTION:

In assignment 7 do you think it wise to carry goods that because of competition will sell at only a 5% markup and fail to carry their share of expense? Discuss.

8. Averaging markup in different classifications — total known.

Example:

In a certain store there are 5 classifications; sales are distributed as follows: *A*, 40%; *B*, 15%; *C*, 10%; *D*, 7%; and *E*, 28%. The markup on *A* averages 12%; on *C*, 10%; on *D*, 15%; and on *E*, 22%. What markup should be obtained on *B* in order to average 20% in the store as a whole? If a markup of 25% is all that is obtainable for *B*, what would be the average markup in the store?

Solution:

	$ Sales		Markup %	$ Markup
1. Let total sales equal	200	X	20	40.00
Class A	80	X	12	9.60
Class C	20	X	10	2.00
Class D	14	X	15	2.10
Class E	56	X	22	12.32
Total of all but				
Class B	170			26.02
Class B	30		(46.6)	13.98

$13.98 \div $30 = 46.6\%$, the markup needed for Class B

2. $30 \times 25\% = 7.50, the dollar markup for Class B
This, added to the dollar markup for the other classifications
(see table above), gives $33.52 or 16.7% for the store as a
whole.

ASSIGNMENT 8:

In an infants' wear store, one-third of the sales are in play clothes,
one-half in furnishings, and one-sixth in dress clothes. A markup of 39%
is obtainable on dress clothes but only 24% on the play clothes. What
markup must be obtained on furnishings in order to average 38% in the
store?

DISCUSSION QUESTION:

In practice, would the buyer have more flexibility in pricing his
furnishings than his play clothes and his dress clothes? Discuss.

Managerial Decision

You need an average markup of 40% in your store. On all lines, except one, you
can obtain a markup higher than the average. On the one line (if the sales are not
in excess of 10% of total sales), a markup of only 20% will permit you to attain
the storewide average of 40%. Should you take a markup of only 20% on this
line, even though there is the possibility that very large sales at this markup may
reduce the planned average of 40%? Defend your answer.

ADDITIONAL ASSIGNMENTS

9. *Classification Plans:* Before this year a men's shirt department kept
records of sales and stocks only for the department as a whole. The spring of last
year had shown an increase in sales volume of 12% compared with the preceding
year, but in the fall the volume decreased by 6.8%. The gross margin in the
department was 28%, and the markdowns were $1\frac{1}{2}\%$. These compared with
outside comparative standards of 30.5% for gross margin and of 3% for

markdowns. Classification records of sales and stocks were introduced to locate
the difficulty. By the end of the first month, the following facts were obtained:

Classifications	Sales Feb. 1– March 1 This Year	Stock on Hand March 1	End of Month Stock-Sales Ratio
1	$12,080	$25,850	2.1
2	26,650	40,000	1.5
3	10,525	23,995	2.4
4	9,900	8,652	0.9
Total	$59,155	$98,497	1.66

A detailed examination revealed that sales were being lost in classification 4
because of the incompleteness of the stocks. Frequent small orders were being
placed, the average order being only one-third as large as that in the hosiery
department. The cost of handling many small orders and shipments was adding
considerably to the expenses of the department.

A survey of customer demand for shirts in the community was also made.
Market reports indicated a 19% current increase in volume of classification 2
type shirts over last year, but a decline of 11% in classification 3, and a 6%
decline in classification 1 shirts. An examination of competitor's stocks showed
greater assortments in classification 2 shirts than this store carried.

In each classification there are many price lines. For example, there are 10 in
classification 3. A study of purchases at each price showed that the best-selling
price lines were as follows:

Class. 1	. . . .	$6.00 and $7.50
Class. 2	. . . .	5.95 and 6.75
Class. 3	. . . .	9.95 and 12.50
Class. 4	. . . .	5.00 and 6.00

On the basis of this analysis, early in March sales for the entire spring season
were planned at $528,000. Annual stock-turn was planned at 8.2 times with a
slightly lower than average turn for the spring season.

A separate season turn was planned for each of the 4 classifications.

1. Distribute the planned season's sales by classification, assuming that
stocks will be promptly adjusted in view of the findings.

2. Plan desirable average retail stocks for each classification. Should the
stock-turn be the same in each?

3. Suggest a control system to keep stocks balanced to sales by
classification.

10. A department with 3 classifications exhibited the following condition
for a year:

Class	Sales	Markdowns	Direct Expense	Cash Discounts
A	$150,000	$ 7,500	$15,000	$1,500
B	90,000	6,000	20,000	1,200
C	140,000	9,000	24,000	2,500
Total	$380,000	$22,500	$59,000	$5,200

The indirect expenses charged the department were $56,000 and the operating profit was $12,000, after crediting the department with the cash discounts. Shortages were $5,000. The stock-turn was 4 times.

For next year, a sales increase of 12% is expected, distributed in the same proportion as this year. The same markdowns as last year are planned and the same shortage percentage. Direct expenses and cash discounts will probably increase in proportion to sales increase, but overhead (indirect expense) is expected to remain the same.

As for planned profits, the merchandise manager feels that this department should make as large a percentage return on average retail stock as is made by the store as a whole. In the store as a whole, operating profits are 4% of sales and the stock-turn is 6 times a year. The planned turnover for this department is 5 times and cannot be increased further if stock assortments are to be maintained.

This year the same initial markup was obtained in each classification, but for next year the merchandise manager decides to plan a separate mark-up for each, one that will reflect the different direct expenses and markdowns.

1. What was the initial markup this year?
2. What was the net profit this year in each classification (overhead and shortages prorated according to sales)?
3. What initial markup should be planned next year for the department and for each classification?

11. *Men's Clothing Department Survey:* A large promotional men's wear store of the discount type exchanges expense data with six other stores that have similar policies and carry similar lines of merchandise.

The men's clothing department showed a loss 2 years ago and a very small profit last year. Accordingly, a careful analysis was made under the follwing heads:

(a) Merchandise and operating statements;
(b) Sales by months;
(c) Classification analysis;
(d) Markdown analysis;
(e) Age-of-stock analysis;
(f) Advertising analysis.

(a) Merchandising and Operating Statements. See table 1.

TABLE I
MERCHANDISING AND OPERATING STATEMENT

Merchandise Statement	Amount	% of Markup	Group Average (% of Markup)	Best Showing (% of Markup)
Retail stock beginning of year	$128,436	38.3		
Retail purchases	624,615	37.5		
Total	$753,051	37.9	37.7	39.2
Retail stock end of year	117,737	37.9		
Total deductions	$635,314			

	Amount	% of Sales	% of Sales	% of Sales
Markdowns	$ 51,833	9.1	9.1	6.2
Employees' discounts	10,345	1.8	2.3	0.7
Shortages	5,094	0.9	0.6	-0.7
Total reductions	$ 67,267	11.8	12.0	
Net sales	$568,045	100.0	($689,000)	($1,113,000)
Gross cost of merchandise sold	394,530	69.4	69.3	
Cash discounts earned	33,119	5.8	5.7	6.2
Net cost of merchandise sold .	$361,411	63.6	63.6	
Alteration costs	26,297	4.6	4.4	4.0
Total merchandise cost	$387,708	68.2	68.0	
Gross margin	180,337	31.8	32.0	35.6

Expenses	Amount	% of Sales	Group Average % of Sales	Best Showing % of Sales
Administrative	$ 8,959	1.6	1.5	1.5
Occupancy	30,400	5.3	5.4	5.1
Publicity	57,490	10.1	9.9	9.5
Buying	27,999	4.9	5.2	4.6
Selling	53,531	9.5	9.6	9.0
Total expenses	$178,379	31.4	31.6	29.7
Operating profit or loss	1,958	0.4	-0.1	3.4

Additional Data	Amount	% of Sales	Group Average % of Sales	Best Showing % of Sales
Number of transactions	21,598			
Returns	$ 46,002	7.6*	10.8*	
Average retail stock	$149,262			
Stock-turn			3.8	2.8
Selling cost (% of direct selling salaries to net sales)			5.18	5.40
Selling salaries per transaction	1.80		$ 1.53	
Sales per square foot	$61.50		$60.50	

*Of gross sales.

(b) Sales by months. See table 2.

TABLE 2
SALES BY MONTHS

	Annual Sales	Group Average	% of Increase or Decrease Over Last Year	Group Average
February	6.7	6.8	9.0	-8.4
March	7.0	7.0	-6.5	-12.8
April	12.0	9.6	40.6	6.3
May	7.6	7.6	9.0	-6.7
June	10.8	10.9	1.0	-13.8
July	6.9	5.9	12.2	-6.9
August	3.7	7.1	-17.6	-19.6
September	4.8	5.6	-9.5	-15.2
October	8.8	9.8	-18.3	-10.1
November	11.9	9.7	-20.2	-19.6
December	10.2	8.8	2.8	-11.4
January	9.6	11.2	12.5	-9.5
Total	100.0	100.0	2.4*	

*Average.

(c) Classification analysis.

The men's clothing department is subdivided into 10 classifications. Six of these account for 90% of the volume. Sales and stocks both in terms of dollars and of units were recorded for each classification every month, as were markdowns. See table 3.

TABLE 3
SALES, STOCKS, AND MARKDOWNS BY CLASSIFICATION

Spring Season

Classifications	$ Sales	Average $ Stocks	Unit Sales	Average Unit Stocks	Markdowns	Initial M.U.%
1	21,580	22,549	449	452	5,038	36.8
2	126,575	43,000	3,227	1,614	7,528	36.5
3	42,375	23,740	1,354	827	3,652	36.8
4	6,210	6,226	152	154	870	36.4
5	12,019	17,540	298	429	196	40.5
6	36,604	19,093	1,052	628	2,845	39.8

Fall Season

1	19,852	22,612	465	490	5,138	36.3
2	113,215	50,030	3,214	1,682	9,098	37.1
3	4,612	6,997	94	182	1,438	38.2
4	8,192	4,700	176	115	467	37.2
5	96,650	35,120	2,488	946	9,370	39.1
6	11,752	18,563	345	476	854	40.2

(d) Markdown Analysis.

It is a rule of the department that the buyer indicate the reason for each markdown on the markdown form. The amount of markdowns classified by reason is totaled each month. Markdowns are also analyzed each month by classification. See table 4.

TABLE 4
MARKDOWN CAUSES

Reasons for Markdowns	Amount
Special sales from stock	$36,195.48
Broken assortments	19,963.77
Competitive reductions	3,419.05
Wrong materials purchased	885.00
Allowances to customers	65.15
Job lots	80.60
No reason listed	1,152.10
Gross markdowns	$61,761.15
Markdown cancellations	9,927.70
Net markdowns	$51,833.45

(e) Age of stock analysis.

At each 6-month inventory, the season letter of each item is included in the listing and a report is prepared by age of stock. The age of merchandise and the percentage of total stock in each age group is determined for each classification. See table 5.

TABLE 5
INVENTORY ANALYSIS BY CLASSIFICATION
END OF FALL SEASON THIS YEAR

Classification	Less Than 6 Mos. Old	6 to 12 Mos. Old	12 to 18 Mos. Old	Over 18 Mos. Old	Total
1	$ 7,598.50	$ 8,456.50	$ 412.00	----	$ 16,467.00
2	35,286.12	5,675.00	2,192.00	----	43,153.12
3	3,408.50	4,046.00	652.46	----	8,106.96
4	380.25	1,392.88	173.12	----	1,946.25
5	17,745.50	488.62	596.00	----	18,830.12
6	10,355.00	4,157.60	932.00	----	15,444.60
7-10.	7,776.27	3,902.70	2,110.00	----	13,788.97
Total	$82,550.14	$28,119.30	$7,067.58		$117,737.02
% of total stock. . .	70.1	23.8	6.1	0	100.0
Group average.	61.06	24.12	13.80	1.02	100.0

(f) Advertising analysis.

Advertisements of men's clothing are classified under two heads: (1) promotion of regular merchandise at regular prices and (2) promotion of sales merchandise. The expenditures for each type this year were as follows:

Cost of advertising regular merchandise	$ 9,543.10	50.2%
Cost of advertising sale merchandise	9,454.10	49.8
	$18,997.20	100.0%

The advertising of regular merchandise, as distinct from lower-priced promotional merchandise, analyzed by classification and price line, appears in table 6.

TABLE 6
ADVERTISING OF REGULAR MERCHANDISE
BY CLASSIFICATION AND PRICE LINE

Classification	Price Lines Advertised	No. of Times Advertised
1	$50.00	10
	60.00	2
2	75.00	22
	85.00	3
3	45.00	2
	35.00	1
4	50.00	2
5	37.50	2
	50.00	5
	75.00	6
6	37.50	8
	50.00	7
	75.00	10
		80

1. Which sales distribution by months seems preferable, that of the department under consideration or that of the group of 7 departments?

2. Compare the stock-turn in each classification. In which should it be increased? In which decreased?

3. Is the advertising by price line satisfactory in view of the actual sales?

4. Does the analysis of reasons for markdowns and for advertising expenditures suggest the desirability of any change in policy?

5. Is the department doing a good job in controlling slow-selling merchandise?

6. In what respect is the department particularly strong? Particularly weak?

7. Is the department's general showing better or worse than average?

8. What specific recommendations may be made to improve the showing?

15   How to Plan Sales

Forecasting sales is the first step in all merchandising planning. Stocks, markdowns, and expenses are planned with a view to the most probable volume. Dollar sales volume depends on two variables: the trend of the number of transactions and the trend in the size of the average sale. The number of transactions, in turn, depend on (1) the long-term or secular trend, (2) the seasonal variations, (3) the changes in outside conditions, and (4) the changes in conditions within the store or department. The size of the average sale depends on price changes, changes in the price-line emphasis, changes in the number of items of merchandise per transaction, changes in relative demand for different classes of goods (merchandise mix), and changes in markup.

The sales planner should be able to use index numbers in order to compare his sales data with those of others and in order to differentiate between dollar changes and changes in transactions.

A. SALES TRENDS

1. Sales trends calculated in dollars (or in units) for a short time ahead.

● *Example:*

In a men's shoe operation, the following figures are available:

Month	Last Year	This Year
October	$4,000	$4,500
November	5,600	6,500
December	7,300	

What are the probable sales for December this year, assuming a continuation of the current trend?

Solution:

October increase $500 ÷ $4,000 = 12.5%

November increase $900 ÷ $5,600 = 16%

Since the recent November sales may reflect future conditions better than do the older October figures, it would be reasonable to plan about a 16% increase in December over the year before: $7,300 × 1.16 = $8,468.

ASSIGNMENT 1:

The following sales figures for a quarter are available by weeks in the case of the $10 price line in a men's shirt department:

	Unit Sales	
	Last Year	This Year
1st week of season	40	43
2nd week of season	48	52
3rd week of season	62	62
4th week of season	59	65
5th week of season	68	72
6th week of season	73	70
7th week of season	48	
8th week of season	59	
9th week of season	64	
10th week of season	69	
11th week of season	83	
12th week of season	77	
13th week of season	68	

Plan sales, by weeks, for the balance of the season. (Apply average percentage increase to date to each of the remaining weeks.)

DISCUSSION QUESTION:

Because of the many factors that can affect weekly sales figures, would it be better to use aggregate figures in planning sales?

2. Sales trends calculated in seasonal percentages.

● *Example:*

An analysis of sales for the past several years reveals the following seasonal distribution:

July 10%
August 14
September 14
October 20
November 12
December 30

The sales in July this year were $3,000 and in August, $3,200. Estimate the sales for the remaining 4 months.

Solution:

Sales in July and August are normally 24% of season's total.
24% of season's total = $3,000 + $3,200 = $6,200
100% = $6,200 ÷ 24% = $25,833
September, 14% of $25,833 = $3,617
October, 20% of $25,833 = $5,167
November, 12% of $25,833 = $3,100
December, 30% of $25,833 = $7,750

ASSIGNMENT 2:

In a mail-order store, the analysis of the sales of one article revealed that sales during the life of the preceding spring and summer catalog were distributed as follows, during the first half of the period:

	Cumulative Sales
1st week	2%
2nd week	8
3rd week	12
4th week	13
5th week	18
6th week	27
7th week	36
8th week	38
9th week	44
10th week	48
11th week	49
12th week	56
13th week	61
. . . .	
26th week	100

Sales of this article during the first 5 weeks of the current corresponding period were 1,500 units. Estimate the probable sales in units for the next 5 weeks and for the season as a whole.

DISCUSSION QUESTIONS:

Is this method of planning better for dollar or for unit planning? Why?

3. Determining trend for next year or season.

● *Example:*

The spring season sales in a hosiery line over a 6-year period were as follows:

Year	Season's Sales in Round Numbers	Year	Season's Sales in Round Numbers
1st	$20,000	4th	$26,000
2nd	22,000	5th	28,300
3rd	24,500	6th	30,100

Assuming a continuation of the average rate of growth, with no change in outside conditions or in conditions within the department, what sales volume would be forecast for next year?

Solution:

Sales by Years	$ Increase	% Increase
$20,000		
22,000	$2,000	10.0%
24,500	2,500	11.4
26,000	1,500	6.1
28,300	2,300	8.8
30,100	1,800	6.4
Median increase	$2,000	8.8%

$30,100 + $2,000 = $32,100 (median dollar increase used)
$30,100 + 8.8% of $30,100 = $32,749 (median percentage increase used)

Percentage increase is likely to be the more reliable if dollar increments are increasing each year. (This is not the case in this problem.) A plan of $32,100 is reasonable in view of the premise that outside and inside conditions are not expected to change the trend.[1]

ASSIGNMENT 3:

Beginning with a depressed economic period, annual sales have been as follows:

Sales

$110,000
112,500
113,600
115,720
117,200

Assuming that economic conditions will continue favorable during the coming year, plan sales for next year on both a dollar and a percentage basis.

DISCUSSION QUESTIONS:

1. How important are sales forecasts, and are they really necessary? Why?
2. Is it wise to base sales forecasts on past sales trends alone? Why?

---

[1] This method is faulty, since it assumes that the sales for last year in the series are on the trend line. If last year had been unusually good, the forecast for the coming year would probably be too large. If last year had been unusually bad, the forecast for the coming year might be too small. The "line of least squares" is statistically superior:

Sales in $1,000	Half-Year Periods	Sales X Periods	Periods Squared
20	−5	−100	25
22	−3	−66	9
24.5	−1	−24.5	1
26	+1	+26	1
28.3	+3	+84.9	9
30.1	+5	+150.5	25
Total: 150.9		+70.9	+70

150.9 ÷ 6 = 25.2, the point on the trend for the base, the middle of the series that is half-way between the 3rd and 4th year. Thus the 3rd year is one-half year period earlier than the base and the 4th year is one-half year period later than the base. Next, + 70.9 ÷ 70 =1.01, the semi-annual increment. Since the coming year is + 7, 1.01 X 7 = 7.07, the increment from the base. 25.2 + 7.1 = 32.3, that is, $32,300.

Note: Although the above is a sound method for determining a long-time or secular trend, in practice this method may be of little value in forecasting sales for a coming year. Over a short run, cyclical forces and inside store conditions are likely to have much more influence than the trend – especially over a portion of a business cycle.

B. SALES PLANNING BY MONTHS

4. Planning for the months of a season.

● *Example:*

Sales of $280,000 have been forecast for a 6-month fall season. Last year this season's sales were distributed as follows: August 11%, September 15%, October 18%, November 19%, December 24%, January 13%. But there is one less selling day in October and one more in November this year than last. Last year there were 27 selling days in October and 24 in November. Promotion plans this year are similar to those of last. Plan monthly sales for this year.

Solution:

$$\text{October} = \frac{26}{27} \times 18\% = 17.3\%$$

$$\text{November} = \frac{25}{24} \times 19\% = 19.7\%$$

August = 11% of $280,000	=	$ 30,800
September = 15% of 280,000	=	42,000
October = 17.3% of 280,000	=	48,440
November = 19.7% of 280,000	=	55,160
December = 24% of 280,000	=	67,200
Januray = 13% of 280,000	=	36,400
Total.		$280,000

ASSIGNMENT 4:

Last year, June, with 24 selling days, accounted for 18% of the spring season's sales of $50,000. A sales increase of 6.5% for the season is planned this year, and there are 25 selling days in June. Plan sales for June this year.

DISCUSSION QUESTION:

What are the most important reasons for using sales planning by months?

5. Adjustment for Easter.

● *Example:*

This sales in a dress department over a 4-year period for March and April were as follows:

Year	March	April	Date of Easter
1st	$16,100	$14,200	April 8
2nd.	18,000	13,700	March 31
3rd	17,450	16,950	April 20
4th	19,000	15,600	April 5
5th			March 25

The fourth year was one of business recession and no marked improvement was anticipated during the first half of the fifth year. An increase much greater than that realized last year over the year before does not seem likely. Plan sales for both March and April of next year, in view of· the date of Easter.

Solution:

Year	Combined Sales March and April	Increase
1st	$30,300	
2nd	31,700	$1,400
3rd	34,400	2,700
4th	34,600	200
5th		

The following facts: (1) under more normal conditions the department had shown a strong upward trend, and (2) the fifth year was expected to show a gradual recovery, may justify a plan of $35,000, an increase of $400.

In the second year, with Easter on March 31, about 56.8 of the volume was realized in March and 43.2 in April. Since Easter is even earlier in the fifth year, 57% for March and 43% for April are reasonable. This gives a plan for March of about $20,000 and of $15,000 for April.

ASSIGNMENT 5: .

The outlook for the spring season of this year is a sales increase of 12% over last year. Sales last year in March were $18,500 and in April, $17,100. Easter falls this year on April 17. Ten years ago Easter fell on the same date. In that year, the department's sales were $15,800 in March and $15,300 in April. Plan sales for both March and April this year.

DISCUSSION QUESTIONS:

If the influence of Easter is largely limited to March and April, should the 2-month period be considered as a single period rather than as two separate monthly periods? Why?

6. Index of physical volume.

Example:

The Federal Reserve Board has issued the following sales indexes, corrected for seasonal variations, for a 6-month period and a private statistical bureau has issued the following price index for the same months:

	Sales Index	Price Index
January...............	101	94.2
February..............	103	94.5
March................	103	94.8
April................	104	95.5
May	105	96.3
June	104	97.7

Prepare an index of physical volume.

Solution:

Since

$$\text{Sales} = \text{Price} \times \text{Physical volume}$$

$$\text{Physical volume} = \frac{\text{Sales}}{\text{Price}}$$

Dividing the sales index each month by the price index for that month gives:

January................	107
February..............	109
March.................	109
April.................	109
May	109
June	106

ASSIGNMENT 6:

In one store, the sales index for May of this year, based on the average daily sales 5 years ago, was 118 and the price index, 99.6. The index of seasonal variation for May was 102. In June, the sales index was 180 and the price index, 136. The index of seasonal variation for June was 147. Adjust the sales indexes for the 2 months for seasonal variation; then, adjust the resultant figures to provide an index of physical volume indicative of the secular trend.

DISCUSSION QUESTIONS:

1. Discuss the importance of using the sales indexes in planning sales.
2. Is an index of physical volume the same as an index of transaction change?

7. Forecasting sales in terms of transactions.

● *Example:*

The following data are available covering the spring season's sales for the past 5 years, starting with a depression year:

Sales	Average Sale	Price Index
$45,600	$2.50	100
52,100	2.70	105
65,800	2.80	107
73,000	3.10	110
78,300	3.20	112

1. The forecast for the spring of this year for the department in question:

    (a) No further rise in prices; stabilization at last year's prices.

    (b) Demand for slightly better quality goods; this is expected to increase the average sale 1%.

    (c) No change in markup.

    (d) A 1% increase in amount of merchandise per transaction.

    (e) No change in relative demand for goods in different classifications of the department.

    (f) Continued improvement in business, but cyclical trend probably near peak.

    Plan transactions and dollar sales for the spring of this year, using the data given.

2. (a) Average seasonal variation in dollar sales in the past 5 years:

February	10%
March	15
April.	20
May	25
June	22
July	8
	100%

(b) Easter this year is on March 28. Some years ago, when it fell on March 27, dollar sales in March equaled those in April.

(c) June was relatively more important in the last 2 years than in the former 2.

(d) Special February promotion planned to increase February business 15% above normal.

(e) One less selling day in May than normally.

Solution:

1. Since much of the sales increase has been caused by price increases and since prices are stabilizing, it will be wise to plan in terms of transactions.

Sales		Average Sale		Number of Transactions	Increase in Transactions
$45,600	÷	$2.50	=	18,240	
52,100	÷	2.70	=	19,262	1,022
63,800	÷	2.80	=	22,785	3,523
73,000	÷	3.10	=	23,548	763
78,300	÷	3.20	=	24,468	920

A conservative forecast would be for 25,000 transactions. Since there is no change in the price level, in the initial markups, or in the relative demand for goods in different classifications, the only factors that will increase the size of the average sale are the demand for slightly better quality goods (1%) and the increase in the amount of merchandise per transaction (1%).

2% increase over $3.20 = $3.26.

The probable dollar sales then are:

25,000 (transactions) × $3.26 = $81,500

2. The estimated seasonal variation for this year and the resultant dollar sales are:

	%	$
February	11.5%	$ 9,372.50
March	17.0	13,855.00
April	17.5	14,262.50
May	24.0	19,560.00
June	22.5	18,337.50
July	7.5	6,112.50
Total		$81,500.00

ASSIGNMENT 7:

The following figures for a store are available for a series of years:

	Gross Transactions	Gross Average Sale	Net Sales	Retail Price Index
1st year	(data not available)			
2nd year	100,000	$.49	$47,000	88
3rd year	110,000	.54	56,800	96
4th year	115,000	.50	55,000	101
5th year	120,000	.60	69,500	102
6th year	130,000	.65	81,800	103
7th year	131,000	.65	82,150	106

Certain adverse inside conditions kept the seventh year's transactions virtually at the sixth-year level, but the trend over a period of years is expected to express itself in the eighth year. Prices are expected to rise 5% but the physical amount of merchandise included in the average transaction is expected to decline 2%. No change is foreseen in the relative demand for goods in different merchandise classifications in the department. No change in price line emphasis is planned. Forecast the gross transactions for the eighth year, the gross average sale, the gross dollar sales, the returns and allowances percentage, and net sales.

DISCUSSION QUESTION:

What are the advantages in making a sales forecast using transaction figures rather than depending wholly on dollar figures?

Managerial Decision

A small merchant forecasts his sales for a season of 6 months and uses this in setting a purchase limit for the season, but he makes no attempt to break down his sales and purchase plans into months. Do you concur in his procedure?

C. TRAFFIC PRODUCTIVITY

8. Traffic productivity ratio.

An analysis of the relationship between the number of potential customers entering a store (or contacted in a department) and the sales (as measured either in units of merchandise or in transactions) broadens the basis for decision-making. In the past, sales results have been compared primarily with the cost of achieving these sales.

Example:

Traffic for 1 week entering a department 800
Units of merchandise sold a week 200
Transactions a week 150
Sales a week $20,000
Gross margin on sales 25%
Size of sales force 20
Planned unit sales a week 300

Find:

1. Traffic productivity ratio
2. Percentage of traffic sold
3. Percentage of walk-outs
4. Units sold per customer
5. Traffic-to-sales-force weekly ratio
6. Profit margin per unit of traffic
7. Planned traffic
8. Size of sales force needed for planned unit sales

Solution:

(1) $$\text{TPR} = \frac{\text{Units sold}}{\text{Traffic}} = \frac{200}{800} = 0.25$$

(2) $$\%\text{ of traffic sold} = \frac{\text{Transaction}}{\text{Traffic}} = \frac{150}{800} = 18.8\%$$

(3) $$\%\text{ of walkouts} = \frac{\text{Traffic} - \text{Transactions}}{\text{Traffic}}$$
$$= \frac{800 - 150}{800} = 81.2$$

(4) $$\text{Units sold per customer} = \frac{\text{Units sold}}{\text{Transactions}} = \frac{200}{150} = 1.3$$

(5) $$\text{Traffic-to-sales-force ratio} = \frac{\text{Traffic}}{\text{Sales force}} = \frac{800}{20 \times 5} = 8$$

Note: It is assumed that salespeople work 5 days a week.

(6)   Margin per unit of traffic = TPR $\times$ Gross Margin % $\times \dfrac{\text{Sales}}{\text{Units sold}}$

$$= 0.25 \times 0.25 \times \frac{\$20,000}{200} = \$6.25$$

(7)   Planned traffic $= \dfrac{\text{Planned unit sales}}{\text{TPR}} = \dfrac{300}{0.25} = 1{,}200$

(8)   Size of sales force needed $= \dfrac{\text{Planned traffic}}{\text{Traffic ratio} \times \text{days}}$

$$= \frac{1{,}200}{8 \times 5} = 30 \text{ (on a full-time basis)}$$

ASSIGNMENT 8:

	Typical Day
Traffic	200
Transactions	40
Units sold	75
Number of salesmen	10
Gross margin	60%
Daily wages per salesman	$15
Sales	$2,750

Find:

1. TPR
2. Percentage of traffic sold
3. Percentage of walk-outs
4. Units sold per customer
5. Traffic-to-sales-force ratio
6. Profit per unit of traffic
7. Selling cost percentage

DISCUSSION QUESTION:

Discuss the benefits of knowing your store's traffic productivity ratio.

9. Using the traffic productivity ratio.

Example:

The following data for a typical week are available about the performance of two salespeople, Mr. Jones and Mr. Smith.

	Mr. Jones	Mr. Smith
Sales	$1,000	$1,000
Customers contacted (traffic)	110	60
Transactions completed	45	40
Units sold	50	50
Average unit of sale	$20	$20
Wages	$100	$100
Selling Cost	10%	10%

Which is the better (more valuable) salesperson? How should refresher training for the two men differ?

Solution:

Both Mr. Jones and Mr. Smith have sold the same amount of merchandise in both dollars and in units. Both have the same wages and the same selling cost. But Mr. Jones flits quickly from customer to customer; he is something of a sales-snatcher. He loses interest if the customer does not quickly decide to buy. Thus, his TPR is only 45.5 and his walk-out ratio, about 59%. Mr. Smith, on the other hand, sells 50 units to every 60 contacts and his walk-out ratio is only 1/3%. Although he contacts fewer customers than Mr. Jones, he does give satisfaction to those he meets and sells them 1.25 units per transaction to Mr. Jones' 1.11. Mr. Smith is the more valuable salesperson, building good will and repeat trade.

Nevertheless, Mr. Smith should be taught how to speed up his contacts and how to prevail upon customers to come to a favorable decision a little faster. Mr. Jones needs to be slowed down and given fundamental retraining in the technique of handling the undecided customer and the "looker."

ASSIGNMENT 9:

In view of the TPR and walk-out ratios in example 8 above, (1) should the department in question enlarge its outside promotional activities so as to attract more customers or (2) should it increase its inside selling activities and concentrate on improving its merchandise assortment? Defend your answer.

DISCUSSION QUESTION:

How much effect do you think advertising has on your traffic productivity ratio?

ADDITIONAL ASSIGNMENTS

10. Last year your sales amounted to $120,000. For the coming year you plan an increase of 10% in the average sale and a decline in the number of transactions of 12%. What sales volume should you plan for next year?

11.

(a) If sales last year were $200,000 and consumer prices were expected to increase 2% next year and transactions were expected to decrease 5% because of a new competitor in the area, determine the expected sales for next year.

(b) If sales were $110,000 last year and consumer prices were expected to decrease 2% because of the recessionary period and transactions were expected to rise by 8% because of a new industrial plant opening in the store's trade territory, plan the estimated sales.

12. In planning the sales volume for the month of February, you take into consideration the fact that this year there are 24 selling days compared with 23 selling days last year. You also estimate an increase in sales volume of 12%. If last February your volume of business was $7,000, what sales volume should you plan this year?

13. During five years, sales were as follows:

1st year	$ 5,640,000
2nd year	8,400,000
3rd year	7,102,000
4th year	10,030,000
5th year	12,875,000

During these years, retail prices were fairly constant and the increase in sales closely approximated the increase in physical volume. Early this year it seemed probable that, by the end of the year, retail prices would be 15% below the level prevailing in former years. (The average decline for the year, then, would be about 7½%.) It was estimated that the trend in physical volume of business would continue as before. What sales plan should be made for this year?

14. In a shirt department, the dollar sales and the price lead had moved as follows:

	Sales Volume	Approximate Price Index
1st year	$ 934,000	75
2nd year	998,000	78
3rd year	958,000	80
4th year	1,200,000	89
5th year	1,600,000	95
6th year	1,500,000	90

It was estimated that the price of shirts would increase 12% in the seventh year. Forecast the sales for that year.

15. The manager of an accessories department reported a marked increase in the number of transactions and in the number of units sold. Transactions are currently 1,000, a week and units sold 1,500, resulting in 1.5 units per customer, which is an unusually high ratio. A traffic count reveals that 3,000 potential customers enter the department during a typical week.

What is the TPR ratio? The transactions-to-sales ratio? The walk-out ratio? If an analysis of walk-outs reveals most to be women under 25 years of age, what action would be called for?

16. Through the fall season, a sales force of eighteen regular salespeople consumated daily sales of $4,800 representing 1,000 units. The salespeople earned $20 a day each.

During the Christmas season, the force was increased to 25 and daily sales increased to $5,760 representing 1300 units. Traffic in the store increased from the fall normal of 2800 to 5100. Find:

    1. The selling cost during the pre-Christmas season and during the Christmas season.

    2. The TPR during the pre-Christmas season and during the Christmas season.

    3. What has happened to the average sale?

    4. Was the Christmas force too large or too small?

17. Monthly sales in a merchandise line of a fairly large store for the past five years were as follows:

NET SALES ($ in 100's)

	19xx (last year)	19xx	19xx	19xx	19xx (5 years ago)
February	$ 71.8	$ 78.4	$ 84.2	$ 77.0	$ 62.3
March	69.9	94.1	86.7	78.8	79.6
April	54.0	55.9	53.6	52.3	52.2
May	61.7	63.1	68.2	88.8	64.7
June	68.9	75.1	73.9	64.7	70.0
July	66.6	58.9	57.0	44.0	57.9
August	157.0	97.9	124.4	97.8	101.8
September	119.6	96.1	99.4	89.5	87.9
October	67.9	66.1	71.7	64.3	76.0
November	74.1	78.7	76.7	65.4	83.0
December	73.9	79.0	68.9	84.0	63.4
January	56.2	70.6	62.4	69.2	49.9
Total	$941.6	$913.9	$927.1	$875.8	$848.7

You are now put in as manager of this line and need to plan the sales budget for the next spring period. Using a statistical approach, (1) plot the sales figures for the past 5 years; (2) draw in your lines showing trend of sales; (3) develop a seasonal index or a percentage of yearly sales for each month; (4) project the planned sales figures for the spring season of the next year.

Stocks are planned with three ends in view: first, to realize a desired annual stock-turn; second, to maintain adequate assortments at all times; and third, to keep a balanced relationship between sales and stocks as the season progresses.

It is seldom wise to plan the same rate of stock-turn for each month. In general, monthly stock fluctuations should not be as extreme as monthly sales fluctuations; that is, a larger turn should be planned in the months of larger volume than in the months of small volume.

Stock plans that grow out of predetermined turnover ratios may be thought of as controllers' plans, in contrast to buyers' stock plans that are likely to be based primarily on assortment needs. A desirable method of planning stocks for the first of each month or week is for both controller and buyer to make independent plans that may then be compared and brought together. For example, the controller may aim at 6 turns a year or an average of one-half turn a month; with sales of $5,000 in a normal month he may plan a first-of-the month stock of $10,000. The buyer, working independently and considering his physical stock requirements by such factors as classifications, price lines, brands, colors, and sizes, may arrive at a figure of $11,000. In conference, the buyer would then be required to justify the need of a stock $1,000 in excess of the controller's figure. The final retail plan may be a compromise.

The formal methods of setting retail stocks may be classified as follows:

1. Basic stock method, suitable for merchandise having a stockturn of 6 times a year or less. The B.O.M. stock is set by adding a basic stock figure to the planned sales for the month. The basic stock, for this purpose, is defined as the difference between the average stock at retail and the average monthly sales. This method provides for the mainte-nance of at least a basic stock at all times. Thus, the formula is:

B.O.M. stock at retail = Sales for month +
(Average stock at retail – Average monthly sales)

2. Percentage deviation method, suitable for all stock-turns, whether high or low. The stock fluctuations from the average stock are 50% of the sales fluctuations from the average monthly sales. For example, if sales in December are 50% higher than the average monthly sales for the year, the stock on December 1st is set 25% higher than the average retail stock for the year (that is, annual sales divided by planned annual stockturn). As a formula:

$$\text{B.O.M. stock at retail} = \text{Average stock at retail} \times \tfrac{1}{2} \left(1 + \frac{\text{Sales for month}}{\text{Average monthly sales}} \right)$$

3. Weeks' supply method. The stock is planned in terms of a predetermined number of weeks' supply based on a turnover goal. For example, if 6½ stock-turns are desired in a 6-month season (26 weeks), the number of weeks' supply to be carried is 26 divided by 6½, or 4. The sales for the 4 weeks ahead are then forecast to determine the amount of stock needed at the beginning.

4. Stock-sales ratio method. Each month's sales are multiplied by its planned B.O.M. stock-sales ratio to determine the B.O.M. stock at retail.

A. FORMULAS BASED ON STOCK-TURN GOALS

1. **Annual stock-turn rate 6 or less; annual (or seasonal) sales and sales for calendar month known.**

● *Example:*

Planned annual stock-turn, 5; planned annual sales, $90,000; planned sales for April, $7,800. Find stock at retail for the first of April.

Solution:

Formula 1:

$$\text{Stock at retail, April 1} = \$7,800 + \left(\frac{\$90,000}{5} - \frac{\$90,000}{12} \right)$$
$$= \$7,800 + (\$18,000 - \$7,500) = \$7,800$$
$$+ \$10,500 = \$18,300$$

ASSIGNMENT 1:

Planned spring season (6 months) stock-turn 4; planned season sales, $42,000; planned sales in May, $12,000. Find stock at retail for the first of May.

DISCUSSION QUESTION:

Why would this method be less satisfactory for annual stock-turn rates higher than 6?

2. **Annual stock-turn rate 6 or less, annual (or seasonal) sales and sales for a 4-week (or 5-week) period known.**

● *Example:*

Planned turn for 6-month season, 2½; planned season sales, $76,875; planned sales for a 4-week control period in May, $9,400. What should stock be on May 1 at retail?

Solution:

There are 6.5 periods of 4 weeks each in a 26-week season, so the average 4-week sales are $76,875 ÷ 6.5, or $11,825. Applying formula 1:

$$\text{Stock at retail May 1} = \$9,400 + \left(\frac{\$76,875}{2\frac{1}{2}} - \$11,825 \right)$$
$$= \$9,400 + (\$30,750 - \$11,825) = \$9,400 + \$18,925 = \$28,325.$$

ASSIGNMENT 2:

The planned annual stock-turn, 3.6; planned annual sales, $72,000; planned sales for June (a 5-week month), $5,500 and for July (a 4-week month), $3,600. Find stock for the first of June and for the first of July.

Note: To find the average sales for a 5-week period, divide the annual sales by 10.4.

DISCUSSION QUESTION:

What purpose does the 4-week control period, as opposed to a calendar month, serve?

3. **Annual stock-turn rate 6 or more; annual (or seasonal) sales and sales for one month (1/12 of year) known.**

● *Example:*

Planned annual stock-turn, 8; planned annual sales, $184,000; planned sales for June, $12,275. Find stock at retail for June 1.

Solution:

Formula 2:

$$\text{Stock June 1} = \frac{\$184,000}{8} \times \frac{1}{2}\left(1 + \frac{\$12,275}{\$184,000 \div 12}\right)$$
$$= \$23,000 \times \frac{1}{2}(1.8) = \$23,000 \times 0.9 = \$20,700$$

ASSIGNMENT 3.

Planned 6-month season stock-turn, 5; planned sales for 6-month season, $300,000; planned sales for September, $45,000. Find stock for September 1.

DISCUSSION QUESTION:

Why is it wise to plan stock fluctuations from average at only 50% of the sales fluctuations from average monthly sales?

4. **Annual stock-turn 6 or more; sales for a 4-week period (or 5-week period) known.**

● *Example:*

Planned annual stock-turn, 10; planned annual sales, $68,800; planned sales for a 4-week control period in September, $6,000. Find stock for the first of September by an appropriate formula.

Solution:

Formula 2:

$$\text{Stock at retail September 1} = \frac{\$68,800}{10} \times \frac{1}{2}$$
$$\left(1 + \frac{\$6,000}{\$68,800 \div 13}\right) = \$6,880 \times \frac{1}{2}\left(1 + \frac{\$6,000}{\$5,292}\right)$$
$$= \$6,880 \times \frac{1}{2}(2.13) = \$7,327$$

ASSIGNMENT 4:

Planned 6-month season-turn, 2½ but much higher in the fall season; planned season sales, $36,000; planned sales for June (a 5-week month), $5,500, and for July (a 4-week month), $3,600. Find stock for the first of June and first of July by two formulas.

DISCUSSION QUESTION:

What necessary assumptions are implicit in the example solved above?

5. Adjusting formulas if there is a forecastable seasonal variation in the value of the average sale.

● *Example:*

The planned 6-month season sales are $60,000; the planned season-turn is 3; the average sale for the season is $6, but the average sale in March (early in the season) is $10 and the average sale in June (late in the season) is $5. The planned sales for each of these months (March and June) are $10,000. Find the stocks for March 1 and June 1.

Solution:

The application of either formula 1 or 2 without adjustment would result in the same dollar stocks for both months. But with the average sale in June half that of March, the unit sales in June would be double those of March and the unit stocks on June 1 would be double those on March 1. This represents too great an increase in stock in June over March. Actually, March 1 stocks would be too small in units and June 1 stocks too large in units. To avoid the difficulty, the formulas may be applied to the units of sales and stocks rather than to the dollars:

$60,000 ÷ $6 = 10,000, the planned transactions for the season

$10,000 ÷ $10 = 1,000, the planned transactions for March

$10,000 ÷ $5 = 2,000, the planned transactions for June

10,000 transactions ÷ 3 (the turn) = 3,333, the average stock in units

10,000 transactions ÷ 6 (no. of months) = 1,667, the average monthly sales in units

Applying formula 1:

Unit stock first of March = 1,000 (transactions) + (3,333 − 1,667)
= 1,000 + 1,667 = 2,667; 2,667 × $10 = $26,667, the dollar stock for March 1

Unit stock first of June = 2,000 (transactions) + (3,333 − 1,667)
= 3,667; 3,667 × $5 = $18,335, the dollar stock for June 1

Applying formula 2:

Unit stock March 1 = 3,333 (units) × ½ (1 + 1,000/1,667)
= 3,333 × 2,667/3,333 = 2,667.

The answer is the same as with formula 1, since at 6 turns a year (3 a season), the two give the same result.

Unit stock 1st of June = 3,333 (units) × ½ (1 + 2,000/1,667)
= 3,333 × 3,667/333 = 3,667;
3,667 × $5 = $18,335, the dollar stock on June 1.

ASSIGNMENT 5:

The planned stock-turn for a dress department is 12 times a year or 6 for a season. The planned sales for the fall season are $240,000, and the planned average sale is $20. The estimated sales and average sales for each of the months are: August, $35,000 and $25; September, $40,000 and $22; October, $50,000 and $20; November, $45,000 and $18; December, $40,000 and $25; January, $30,000 and $14. Find the stocks for the first of each month in units and in dollars. (Assume that the months are of equal length.)

DISCUSSION QUESTION:

Why are the transactions often a better guide for planning stock than are the dollar sales?

6. Planning stocks in terms of weeks' supply; average weekly rate of sale known.

● *Example:*

During a 2-month busy season, sales average $1,200 a week and during a 4-month dull season, $600. The rate of stock-turn (on an annual basis) wanted during the busy season is 8 and during the dull season, 6. How much stock should be carried each season?

Solution:

$$\frac{\text{Sales (in weeks)}}{\text{Stock-turn}} = \text{Stock (in weeks' supply)}$$

$$\frac{52}{8} = 6.5, \text{ and } \frac{52}{6} = 8\ 2/3$$

$1,200 × 6.5 = $7,800, the stock to carry during busy season.
$600 × 8 2/3 = $5,200, the stock to carry during dull season.

ASSIGNMENT 6:

Sales planned at $8,000 a week for the coming 6 month season; stock-turn rate (annual) desired, 6. Find amount of stock to carry.

DISCUSSION QUESTION:

What are the implications of a constant relationship of inventory to sales as indicated in the example above?

7. Planning stocks in terms of weeks' supply; sales for each week ahead planned.

● *Example:*

Weeks of Season	Sales Last Year	Sales This Year
1	$1,900	$2,100
2	1,750	1,850
3	1,650	1,950
4	1,600	
5	1,650	
6	1,800	
7	1,900	
8	2,400	
9	2,300	
10	2,250	
11	2,100	
12	2,100	
13	1,900	

Planned annual stockturn rate, 10.4. Find the amount of stock to have on hand at the beginning of the fourth week this year, assuming a continuation of the past trend.

Solution:

Sales first 3 weeks last year $5,300
Sales first 3 weeks this year $5,900
Ahead . . . . . . $ 600

$$\frac{\$600}{\$5,300} = 11.3\%; \quad \frac{52}{10.4} = 5 \text{ weeks' supply necessary.}$$

Sales next 5 weeks (fourth through eighth week) last year, $9,350. $9,350 + 11.3% of $9,350 = $10,407, the amount of stock to have on hand at beginning of the fourth week.

ASSIGNMENT 7:

A millinery department had sales last year as follows:

Week Ending	Sales	Week Ending	Sales
April 3	$1,500	May 1	$1,700
April 10	1,600	May 8	1,500
April 17	1,650	May 15	1,300
April 24	1,800	May 22	1,000
		May 29	900

Sales in March this year were 4% ahead of last year and the forecast is for even more favorable outside and inside conditions during the coming few months. A stock-turn of approximately 17 times a year is desired. How much stock should the department have on hand early in April? Early in May?

DISCUSSION QUESTION:

If 5-weeks' supply in stock is necessary for a stock-turn of 10.4, should this 5-weeks' supply be maintained throughout the year? Justify your answer.

B. THE APPLICATION OF STOCK-SALES RATIOS

8. Stock-sales ratios and sales given; find stocks.

● *Example:*

First-of-the-month stock-sales ratio at retail for March, 3.2; for April, 3.8. Planned sales for March, $12,000; for April, $16,000.

1. Find stock for March 1 and April 1.
2. Find stock-turn for March and express it on an annual basis.

Solution:

(1) $12,000 × 3.2 = $38,400, March 1 stock at retail
     $16,000 × 3.8 = 60,800, April 1 stock at retail

(2) Stock-turn for March = $\dfrac{\$12,000}{\frac{1}{2}\,(\$38,400 + \$60,800)} = \dfrac{\$12,000}{\$49,600}$

= 0.24; 0.24 × 12 = 2.88 = Annual rate of stock-turn

ASSIGNMENT 8:

First-of-the-month stock-sales ratio for December, 3.6; for January, 4.5; planned sales for December, $6,400; for January, $3,800.

1. Find stocks for December 1 and January 1.
2. Find stock-turn for December and express it on an annual basis.

DISCUSSION QUESTION:

Why are stock-to-sales ratios helpful in planning future purchases?

9. First- and end-of-the-month ratios.

● *Example:*

The October first-of-the-month stock-sales ratio is 5.4 and the October end-of-the-month ratio, 5.8. Find the stock-turn for October and express it on an annual basis.

Solution:

For every $1 of sales in October, the stock on the 1st is $5.40 and at the end, $5.80. The average stock, then, is $\dfrac{\$5.40 + \$5.80}{2} = \$5.60$. The stock-turn for the month is $\dfrac{\$1}{\$5.60} = 0.18$. On an annual basis, it is 0.18×12, or 2.16.

ASSIGNMENT 9:

A department has a first-of-the-month stock-sales ratio of 2.1 and an end-of-the-month ratio of 1.8. Find the stock-turn for the month.

DISCUSSION QUESTION:

Given a stock-turn figure, can you work back to the beginning and ending stock-sales ratios?

10. Adjusting stock-sales ratios.

● *Example:*

The planned sales volume in a glove department for the spring season and the corresponding "standard" stock-sales ratios are as follows:

	Feb.	March	April	May	June	July
Planned sales	$26,000	$35,000	$48,000	$22,000	$12,000	$6,000
Stock-sales ratios B.O.M.	4.65	3.60	2.40	4.72	7.51	14.0

The buyer believes that in view of his nearness to the glove market, his careful method of stock control, and the popular prices carried, he can get 1.8 turns during the period. What adjustments should he make in the standard stock-sales ratios to obtain 1.8 stockturns during the 6-month period, and still keep his stock balanced?

Solution:

	Sales	"Standard" B.O.M.S.S.R.	B.O.M. stock
February	$26,000	4.65	$120,900
March	35,000	3.60	126,000
April	48,000	2.40	115,200
May	22,000	4.72	103,840
June	12,000	7.51	90,120
July	6,000	14.0	84,000
Total sales	$149,000		6)640,060
Average stock			$106,676

$$\text{Stock-turn} = \frac{\$149,000}{\$106,676} = \text{approximately } 1.40$$

$$\frac{1.4 \text{ (stock-turn)}}{1.8 \text{ (stock-turn wanted)}} = 77\% \text{ (approximately)}$$

The stock-turn is only 77% of the desired rate. To increase the stock-turn 23%, the stock-sales ratios must be cut 23%.

Month	"Standard" B.O.M. S.S.R.	Adjusted S.S.R.	B.O.M. Adjusted Stock
February	4.65	3.58	$93,080
March	3.60	2.77	96,950
April	2.40	1.85	88,800
May	4.72	3.64	80,080
June	7.51	5.79	69,480
July	14.00	10.78	64,680
			6)493,070
Average stock			$82,180

$$\text{Proof:} \quad \frac{\$149,000}{\$82,180} = 1.8, \text{ adjusted stock-turn (approximately)}$$

ASSIGNMENT 10:

A hosiery department, by applying a standard stock-sales ratio, obtains a resultant stock-turn for the spring season of 2 times, but because of its nearness to the market and limited assortment policy, the manager feels that he can obtain 3 turns during the 6-month season. The standard stock-sales ratio for October 1 is 2.85. Adjust this ratio in view of the higher stock-turn desired.

DISCUSSION QUESTIONS:

Even though published standard stock-sales ratios can be adjusted to yield a higher or lower stock-turn than they presently do, does this fact make them suitable for the guidance of a store in stock planning? Why?

11. Computing stock-sales ratios.

Example:

For a certain catagory of merchandise, ten stores report the following sales and stocks for June:

Store	Sales	Stocks First of Month
1	$82,000	$123,000
2	62,000	111,600
3	46,000	147,200
4	26,000	104,000
5	37,000	66,600
6	36,000	90,000
7	54,000	97,200
8	81,000	97,200
9	36,000	75,600
10	23,000	62,100

1. Compute the stock-sales ratio for each store, the average ratio, and the "goal" ratio.
2. Plot the sales and ratios with the ratios along the Y-axis and draw by inspection the straight line or curve that best fits them. Read off stock-sales ratio values along the curve for value-intervals of $10,000 each between $20,000 and $80,000. (Note that the larger the volume, the lower the stock-sales ratio.)

Solution:

1. The stock-sales ratios are as follows:

Store	Ratio	Store	Ratio
1	1.5	6	2.5
2	1.8	7	1.8
3	3.2	8	1.2
4	4.0	9	2.1
5	1.8	10	2.7

Arranging these from smallest to largest: 1.2; 1.5; 1.8; 1.8; 1.8; 2.1; 2.5; 2.7; 3.2; 4.0. The mode or point of concentration is 1.8, and the median, between 1.8 and 2.1, is 1.95. Because of the concentration at 1.8, 1.9 may be taken as the typical stock-sales ratio.

The "goal" ratio may be set at the average of the 25% to 33-1/3% of the stores having the best ratios. The three best (lowest) are 1.2, 1.5, and 1.8. The average is 1.5. This may be taken as the goal. (Note: Since so few figures are available, it may be wise to take the third best, or 1.8, as the "goal.")

2. Because of the variations in volume, this goal ratio may be too low for the smaller stores in the group. Applying the method of least squares to the logarithms of the sales and of the corresponding stock-sales ratios yields these values:

Sales Volume Intervals	Ratios
20,000	3.1
30,000	2.8
40,000	2.5
50,000	2.2
60,000	1.9
70,000	1.6
80,000	1.3

ASSIGNMENT 11:

Thirty-eight infants' wear departments exchanged the stock-sales ratios for the month of May with the following results:

Store	Sales for Month	Stock-Sales Ratios
1	$46,000	2.3
2	62,500	2.2
3	26,000	2.8
4	23,000	3.6
5	49,000	3.4
6	8,000	2.4
7	20,000	6.0
8	25,000	4.4
9	29,000	4.3
10	12,000	3.4
11	14,000	3.4
12	17,000	4.6
13	10,000	5.5
14	2,000	9.0
15	12,000	4.8
16	14,000	4.6

Store	Sales for Month	Stock-Sales Ratios
17	3,000	8.0
18	500	4.2
19	2,000	3.8
20	4,000	3.7
21	5,000	3.8
22	7,000	7.6
23	1,500	6.9
24	2,000	4.0
25	1,000	8.2
26	2,000	6.1
27	3,000	4.0
28	3,500	6.8
29	3,000	6.6
30	2,500	4.3
31	2,500	4.5
32	5,000	5.8
33	2,000	5.4
34	3,000	5.9
35	2,500	5.9
36	2,000	5.0
37	2,500	5.1
38	2,000	7.4

1. Compute the average and "goal" stock-sales ratios.
2. Plot these ratios and draw by inspection the curve that best fits them. Since the range of sales is so great, a straight line will not be suitable, but above the $20,000 point the curve will approach a straight line. (If plotted on double log paper, a straight line rather than a curve may best fit the entire data.)
3. What are the "standard" stock-sales ratios for May sales volumes from $1,000 to $70,000? (Use $1,000 intervals to $10,000 and then $5,000 intervals.)

DISCUSSION QUESTION:

In view of the shape of the stock-sales ratio curve when plotted against the sales volume, is it the small or the large department that shows the greater improvement in stock-turn as sales increase?

Managerial Decisions

1. After planning sales by months, you are confronted with the need to decide how large a stock to plan for the first of each month. Is it better to set a stock-turn goal for the purpose of determining the resultant stock, or to set a stock goal independent of stock-turn, and have the stock-turn be the resultant figure?

2. In March, as well as in June, you plan to have the same dollar sales volume. Under what conditions should the stock in dollars be lower on June 1 than on March 1?

ADDITIONAL ASSIGNMENTS

12. Planned sales of $30,000 for the year are distributed as follows:

January	$1,800		July	$2,070
February	1,980		August	2,160
March	2,280		September	2,310
April	2,610		October	2,490
May	2,400		November	2,430
June	2,370		December	5,100
Total	$13,440			$16,560

The planned annual turnover is 4½.

(a) Find the stock for the first of each month by the basic stock method. Assume that months are of equal length.

(b) If March, June, September, and December represent periods of 5 full weeks and the other 8 months periods of 4 full weeks, calculate the stocks for the first of each month.

13. With the same monthly sales as in problem 12, with (b) subsection, assume the planned annual turnover to be 12. Calculate the stocks for the first of each month by the percentage deviation method.

14. Planned sales:

February (4 weeks)	$ 6,000
March (5 weeks)	9,000
April (4 weeks)	8,000
May (4 weeks)	8,500
June (5 weeks)	10,000
July (4 weeks)	6,500
	$48,000

Planned season stock-turn, 4. Plan stocks for the first of each month by an appropriate method.

17

How to Plan Purchases
and Set Open-to-Buy

The chief function of purchase planning and control is to adjust the flow of purchases so as to maintain stocks at a desired level in relation to sales.

Planned purchases are resultant figures growing out of planned sales and planned stocks. Markdowns and shortages may also enter into the calculation. Adjustments growing out of developments not contemplated when original plans were made must also be provided for.

A. THE OPEN-TO-BUY

1. Calculating planned purchases and open-to-buy.

● *Example:*

On the basis of past sales, a buyer estimates that his sales will be $30,000 in December of this year. His retail stock on December 1st is $25,000 and he wants to reduce it to $15,000 by the end of the month.

1. How much should he buy at retail for December delivery?
2. If he has already ordered $5,000 at retail, for December delivery, what is his open-to-buy?

Solution:

(*a*)   Formulae: Planned retail purcheses = Planned closing stock
at retail + Planned sales[1] − Opening stock at retail

or

Planned retail purchases = Planned sales[1] + Planned
Increase in stock or − Planned decrease in stock

Application: Planned retail purchases = $15,000 + $30,000 −
$25,000 = $20,000 *or* Planned retail purchases =
$30,000 − ($25,000 − $15,000) = $20,000

(*b*)   Formula: O.T.B. = Planned purchases −
Commitments for period to date

Application: $20,000 − $5,000 = $15,000

---

[1] When markdowns, discounts to customers and employees, and shortages are planned, they are added in at this point.

ASSIGNMENT 1:

> Sales of $3,600 are expected in January and the buyer had a retail stock of $6,000 for January 1st and is aiming at $5,000 for January 31st. During the first week in January, he received stock of $1,000 at retail and at the end of the week has $600 at retail on order for delivery during January. What are his planned purchases for the month? What is his open-to-buy for the balance of the month?

DISCUSSION QUESTION:

> If in connection with assignment 1 the buyer adhered exactly to his open-to-buy but also took markdowns of $500 that month, what would be the effect on his O. T. B. for February?

2. Adjusting purchase plans for markdowns.

Formula: Planned purchases at retail = Planned closing stock at Retail + Planned sales + Planned markdowns – Opening stock at retail.

● *Example:*

Stock at retail, March 1	$10,000
Planned sales, March	11,000
Planned stock at retail, April 1	8,000
Goods received to date at retail (March 1–15)	1,500
Markdowns planned for month	400
Goods on order for March delivery at retail	2,500

Find the planned purchases for the month and the O. T. B. for the balance of the month.

Solution:

Planned sales, March		$11,000
Markdowns planned		400
Stock, March 1	$10,000	
Planned stock, April 1	8,000	
Planned decrease in stock		−2,000
Planned purchases, March		$ 9,400
Goods received to date	$ 1,500	
Goods on order	2,500	
Total commitments		4,000
Open-to-buy at retail		$ 5,400

ASSIGNMENT 2:

> On April 15, a buyer wishes to determine how much he should purchase during the balance of his spring season (January through June in this store). At present he has a retail stock of $28,700 and wishes to reduce it to $23,000 by June 30. He anticipates sales of $4,500 for the balance of April, $8,000 for May, and $7,000 for June. He plans to take no markdowns during the remainder of April, but expects markdowns of about $600 during May and $900 during June. He has outstanding orders for delivery during the season of $10,300 at retail. Find the amount the buyer is open-to-buy at retail for the remainder of the season.

3. Planning markdowns for a period.

● *Example:*

> Last year, during a 6-month fall and winter season, the department's sales were $50,000 and its markdowns 8%. This year the buyer is planning a sales increase of 5%. Prices are rising somewhat and the department has on hand less low-selling stock than it had a year ago. Last year, half of the season's markdowns were deferred until January, the last month of the season. Practically none were taken in August and September. The result was a large accumulation of old stock in January, some of which, in spite of markdowns, was carried over to the spring season. Plan the markdowns for each month of the fall season.

Solution:

> A plan of 7% of sales for markdowns is reasonable in view of the facts stated. For the season, 7% of $52,500 = $3,675, the planned markdowns. Planned distribution: August 10%; September 10%; October 15%; November 20%; December 25%; January 20%. In dollars, before desirable rounding out:

August	$ 367.50
September	367.50
October	551.25
November	735.00
December	918.75
January	735.00
Total	$3,675.00

ASSIGNMENT 3:

> In one department, the markdowns for the spring season were 8%. The

Controller's Congress typical figure for this department was 6.3%. Only 65% of the department's stock was less than 6 months old, whereas the Controllers Congress figure is 80%. In November, when the plans for the next spring season were being made, the department had not improved its stock condition and prices were tending downward. Normally, 18% of the spring season's markdowns are taken in April. During the coming season, Easter will fall late in April, 2 weeks later than normal. Planned spring season sales are $85,000. Plan markdowns for April.

DISCUSSION QUESTION:

If you have a set markdown figure for the month, will this defer or lead to unnecessary markdowns?

4. Planned purchases and O.T.B. with sales adjustment.

● *Example:*

Originally planned sales, May (a 5-week period)	$22,000
Actual sales, May 1–14 (2 weeks)	12,000
Planned markdowns, May	1,000
Actual markdowns, May 1–14	400
Actual retail stock, May 14	60,000
Planned retail stock, end of 5-week period	54,000
Outstanding orders at retail for delivery during balance of the month	7,800

It is expected that sales will be evenly distributed over the month, so the planned sales for the remaining 3 weeks will have to be revised. Find the planned purchases for the balance of the month and the O.T.B.

Solution:

Stock, May 14	$60,000
Planned stock, end of period	54,000
Planned decrease in stock	-$ 6,000
Planned sales, balance of period $\left(\dfrac{\$12,000}{2} \times 3\right)$	18,000
(current weekly rate of $6,000 × 3)	
Planned markdowns for balance of month	600
($1,000 – $400)	
Planned purchases	$12,600
Commitments	7,800
O.T.B.	$ 4,800

ASSIGNMENT 4:

```
Originally planned sales, March ...................  $ 42,000
Actual sales, March 1–10 .......................      15,000
Planned markdowns, March ......................       1,800
Actual markdowns, March 1–10 ..................          400
Actual retail stock, March 10 ...................    118,000
Planned retail stock, April 1 ...................    100,000
Outstanding orders at retail, March 10, for delivery during
   balance of March ........................          6,500
```

In view of sales to March 10th, it is estimated that the total sales for the month will exceed the original plan by at least $5,000 because the last part of the month is much more active than the first part.

Find the open-to-buy for the balance of March.

5. Markdowns omitted from original plan.

Example:

A store uses the following formula to compute planned purchases at the first of each month:

$$\frac{\text{Planned}}{\text{purchases}} = last\ year's\ \text{sales} \left\{ \begin{array}{c} + \text{increase} \\ - \text{decrease} \end{array} \right\} \begin{array}{c} \text{in stock planned} \\ \text{this year} \end{array}$$

This planned purchase figure is increased or decreased weekly by the the difference between last year's sales to date and this year's sales to date. All markdowns taken increase the planned purchases at the end of each week in which they are taken.

In one department, it takes at least 3 weeks to get delivery after orders are placed. The planned purchase figure, adjusted on the first of the month, is $16,000. The sales during the first week were $3,200 against corresponding sales a year ago of $3,000. No markdowns were taken during the first week. At the end of the month, the actual sales were $14,600, against last year's figure of $13,900. Also, total markdowns for the month were $250. If the buyer adhered in his ordering exactly to his plan, how much would his stock be under or over his plan at the end of the month?

Solution:

```
Original planned purchases ......................    $16,000
Excess of sales over plan ......................         200
Revised plan, end of 1st week ..................     $16,200
```

Excess of sales over plan for balance of month
($700 – $.200) 500
Markdowns taken balance of month 250
Revised planned purchases to end of month $16,950

Since it takes fully 3 weeks for delivery, the difference of $750 between $16,950 and $16,200 will not arrive by the end of the month even though ordered promptly. Accordingly, the stock at the end of the month will be $750 below plan.

In this instance it may be wise to base original purchase plans on estimated sales and markdowns.

ASSIGNMENT 5:

The following sales and stock plans were made for the first half of the spring season in a small leather goods department:

	February	March	April
Planned sales	$ 7,000	$ 9,000	$10,500
Planned stock at retail, B.O.M.	30,000	35,000	34,000

The actual sales in February were exactly equal to plan, $7,000; the sales, March 1–6, were $1,600 and the sales plan for March as a whole is now revised to $8,000. The average stock carried through February and on hand March 6 was about $28,000. The stock is largely new merchandise, reasonably complete and well assorted, even though much less in quantity than was indicated by the plan. No markdowns were taken during the season to date.

Planned initial markup was 39%, and actual markup for the season to date, 41%. Gross margin last year was 35% for the season. The outstanding orders on March 6 for March delivery were $3,600 at retail.

1. Find the open-to-buy at retail for the balance of March. (In this store markdowns increase the open-to-buy only when taken.)
2. What action should the buyer take in regard to his open-to-buy and general showing in view of the facts that there were at the time no unusual market offerings available and that two recent advertisements had not brought in satisfactory volume? If the action has any effect on the markup, indicate the effect in detail.

DISCUSSION QUESTION:

What weaknesses are shown by an analysis of this merchandising plan?

B. THE OPEN-TO-ORDER

6. Open-to-order control.

● *Example:*

Planned sales and markdowns, April	$ 46,000
Planned sales and markdowns, May	50,000
Planned stock, May 1	140,000
Actual stock, April 1	130,000
Outstanding orders for April delivery, April 1	15,000
Outstanding orders for delivery after April 30, April 1	8,000
Planned outstanding orders, May 1	25,000

Find:

1. The open-to-buy for April

2. The open-to-order for April

Solution:

1. Planned sales and markdowns for April ...... $ 46,000
   Planned stock, May 1 140,000
   Total required $186,000
   Stock, April 1 130,000
   Planned purchases for April 56,000
   Outstanding orders for April delivery 15,000
   O.T.B. for April delivery .... $ 41,000

2. Planned sales and markdowns for April ...... $ 46,000
   Planned stock, May 1 140,000
   Planned outstanding orders as of May 1 25,000
   Total required $211,000
   Stock, April 1 .... $130,000
   Outstanding orders, April 1, for
     both current and future delivery   23,000 $153,000
   O.T.O. April 1 58,000

Note: This indicates that in addition to $41,000 that may be ordered for April delivery, $17,000 more may be ordered in April for delivery *after* April 30.

ASSIGNMENT 6:

Planned sales and markdowns for December	$120,000
Planned outstanding orders as of January 1	30,000
Actual outstanding orders, December 1	25,000
Actual stock, December 1	250,000
Planned stock, January 1	180,000

Find the O.T.O. for December

DISCUSSION QUESTION:

How can the buyer decide how much of his planned orders for December should be placed for December delivery and how much placed for delivery after the first of the year?

C. THE BUDGETING GAME

Using the 5 years of data that are given in Table 1, and the form given in Figure 2, you are to plan a 6-month budget, first for the spring season, and then for the fall season in the Menswear Department. These are actual figures taken from a store in a midwestern city and you have just been appointed as the new buyer for the department.

The spring season will be used as a practice period for training since the student will be working only with 1 month at a time in his beginning planning experience.

As each month's decision is completed for the spring season the student will submit his decision to the instructor. He may either be requested to punch his own decision on an IBM card or submit his answers on the necessary budget form provided (Figure 1). It is possible for all of his answer to be placed on one IBM data card using the following format: (All figures will be right verified within the field designated.)

Field 1–10-the month (February will be considered month 1)
Field 11–20-B.O.M. inventory (add cents)
Field 21–30-Purchases at retail (add cents)
Field 31–40-Advertising (add cents)
Field 41–50-Markdowns (add cents)
Field 51–60-Payroll in hours
(All figures will be entered without decimals)
Field 64–80-Student's Name

Each decision is then completed and run and a printout is obtained that will be discussed later in the steps of the game.

Step 1. Sales Forecast

Sales should be planned using some statistical method if the student has been exposed to one, perhaps a typical time series analysis. This would involve the student's plotting the data on graph paper and then using some method for developing a trend line through this data. This could be done with the moving

TABLE 1
MENSWEAR DEPARTMENT

	Sales (net)	BOM Retail Inventory	Total Advertising	Transactions Per Hour: 1.55 No. Transactions (net)	Av. Sales Check
19__ February	10,800	77,710			
March	16,400	92,300			
April	14,800	100,000			
May	23,900	105,500	97		
June	34,500	110,000	459		
July	12,500	80,100	589		
August	24,900	104,000	116	1750	14.23
September	24,700	117,400	1269	1771	13.95
October	25,700	139,800	1224	1406	18.28
November	33,000	154,000	1110	1560	21.15
December	59,800	123,800	1744	3916	15.27
January	12,000	86,000	974		
19__ February	10,600	89,400	977		
March	15,900	111,600	876		
April	19,500	146,000	1321		
May	22,600	123,800	3906		
June	48,000	113,000	2923		
July	19,800	101,800	178		
August	20,000	100,500	1102	1825	10.96
September	23,100	133,400	2733	1395	16.56
October	23,200	160,200	2539	1203	19.29
November	25,000	160,500	939	1342	18.63
December	47,900	141,700	1196	3064	15.63
January	11,400	92,700	639	773	14.75
19__ February	9,500	86,500	605	776	11.60
March	15,600	93,900	776	1288	12.11
April	17,200	104,600	1468	1576	10.91
May	25,000	114,100	2072	2420	10.33
June	40,800	104,900	2811	4645	8.78
July	12,200	80,100	575	1725	7.07
August	13,100	70,600	457	1430	9.16
September	24,300	109,600	1209	1878	12.94
October	18,600	117,900	1190	1175	15.83
November	22,100	117,100	701	1375	16.07
December	47,600	98,600	1807	3362	14.16
January	8,400	71,400	153	732	11.48
19__ February	10,400	68,200	1,259	839	12.40
March	13,800	76,600	844	1380	9.34
April	14,400	81,800	496	1541	9.34
May	19,700	117,000	746	2181	9.03
June	34,400	110,800	1070	4113	8.36
July	13,100	86,700	195	1772	7.39
August	18,300	78,500	171	1996	9.16
September	21,300	81,500	1918	2169	9.82
October	21,200	97,100	1211	1508	14.06
November	26,300	113,200	1328	1746	15.06
December	48,000	112,600	566	3685	13.03
January	11,700	72,800	606	1069	10.94
19__ February	9,600	62,500	310	902	10.64
March	15,100	86,400	930	1290	11.71
April	23,900	102,000	1475	1937	12.34
May	25,100	122,100	848	2494	10.06
June	41,100	119,800	1856	3903	10.53
July	19,900	105,800	210	2365	8.41
August	21,800	101,400			
September	21,300	101,900			
October	23,600	116,800			
November	23,800	106,800			
December	59,500	98,600			
January	10,000				

SIX-MONTH MERCHANDISE PLAN

_____ Season   Department Menswear

		Aug.	Sept.	Oct.	Nov.	Dec.	Jan.	Total
Sales	Last Year							
	Plan							
	Adjusted							
	Actual							
B.O.M. Inven-tory	Last Year							
	Plan							
	Adjusted							
	Actual							
Retail Pur-chases	Last Year							
	Plan							
	Adjusted							
	Actual							
Cost Pur-chases	Last Year							
	Plan							
	Adjusted							
	Actual							
Gross Margin	Last Year							
	Plan							
	Adjusted							
	Actual							
Adver-tising	Last Year							
	Plan							
	Adjusted							
	Actual							
Payroll	Last Year							
	Plan							
	Adjusted							
	Actual							
Mark-down	Last Year							
	Plan							
	Adjusted							
	Actual							

		Gross Marg. %	Aver. Stock	Turnover	Shortages
Season Totals	Last Year				
	Plan				
	Actual				
IMU	41.5%				

FIGURE 1

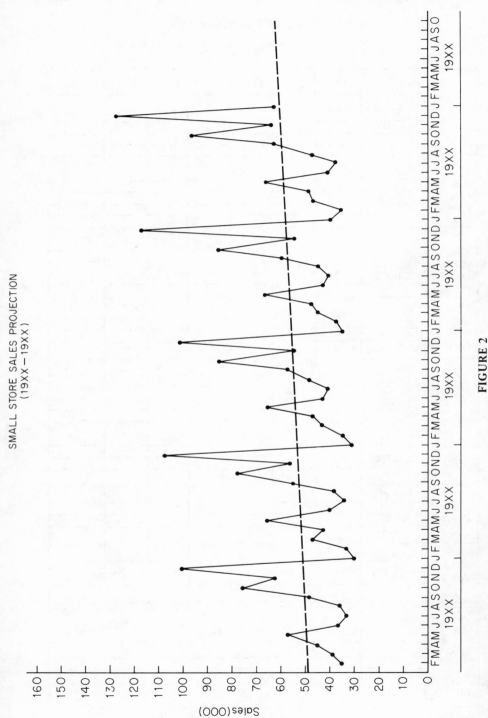

SMALL STORE SALES PROJECTION
(19XX – 19XX)

FIGURE 2

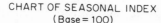

CHART OF SEASONAL INDEX
(Base = 100)

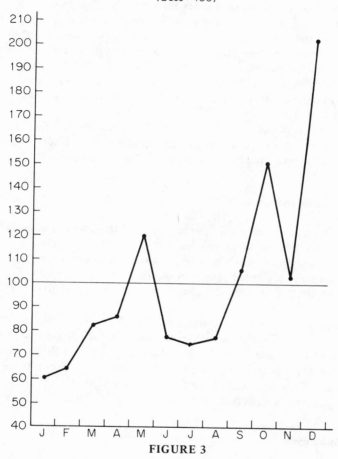

FIGURE 3

average method, the least squares method, etc. For those not trained in statistics, a free-hand line could be used if the person using it is careful to balance the data above and below the line and if they would at all times remember that a trend line is a smooth, free-flowing line.

Once the trend line has been computed through the historical data given in Figure 1, then a forecast for 6 months or a year should be made as a forecast for the game period. This forecast would be rounded to the nearest $100 in value.

A good method of forecasting sales is to use the least squares method (illustrated in Figure 2, but with data that is not related to the "game"). Sales are plotted and the trend line plotted. Next, an index of seasonal variation is determined by calculating the percentage variation of each month's sales from the trend line for that month. Following this, the average variation or index (called the seasonal index) is computed by taking all the individual monthly seasonal indexes for 1 month, say February, and averaging them. This average would then represent the seasonal index for February. A graph of these averages may then be drawn as in Figure 3 (again the illustration is of other figures than figures used in the "game"). The percentage or seasonal index for each month can then be applied to the trend line at a specific point for that particular month. For example, as in Figure 2, suppose that the point on the projected trend for next June is $62,000 and the seasonal index for June is 77, as illustrated in Figure 3. The planned sales for next June would then be $62,000 × 0.77, or $47,740.

A refinement in planning would be to project transactions rather than dollar sales in the same fashion as above, and then multiply the planned transactions for each month as estimated by the average sale for that month.

Step 2. Merchandise Inventory

The merchandise inventory for the beginning of the month may be developed through (1) the use of stock-to-sales ratios, or (2) a correlations chart of inventories as they are related to sales, or (3) planned stock-turn figures using one of the formulas presented in section 16. The ratios mentioned in method (1) above can be developed from the past 5 years of historical data furnished in Table 1.

Of course, in planning, the ending inventory for the month would be the beginning inventory for the following month. In actual play of the game the student is required to use the ending inventory figure given in the printout as the figure to use for the next month's beginning inventory. Normally all figures will be rounded to the nearest $100 for budget planning. (If the inventory decision is punched on IBM data cards, then this figure will include the cents.)

Step 3. Markdowns

The planning of markdowns may be done through the use of the M.O.R. (Merchandise Operating Results) Report of the National Retail Merchants Association. The Association figures, if they are available and are used, should be accepted as averages from many diverse stores. If they are not available, similar figures are available in *Menswear Magazine* or can be furnished by any good department or men's specialty store.

If only an annual markdown percentage figure is available, it could be applied to the projected sales figure planned for the year ahead and then the resultant dollar figure could be distributed over the months, based on an estimate of the probable amount required as the season progresses. (Again, if these figures are punched on IBM data cards, they would include the cents, even though they may have been rounded to the nearest $50.)

Step 4. Shortages

Shortages in the game are a constant figure, currently at 1½% of sales for each month. (Again, if these figures are punched, they will contain the cents figures.)

Step 5. Planned Purchases at Retail

The planned purchase figure in this game is identical to the open-to-buy, since any on-order merchandise is omitted. It is assumed all merchandise will be delivered the month that it is purchased. The typical formula then will be: Planned sales + Markdowns + Shortages + E.O.M. inventory – B.O.M. inventory = Planned purchases at retail. All figures are planned to the nearest $100. This figure is used in the computer program at retail and is automatically multiplied times the cost complement (58.5%). (If this figure is to be IBM punched, it will contain the cents.)

Step 6. Payroll

The plan for developing the payroll is through the use of the following formulas, using the past historical figures provided in Figure 1.

$$\text{Average sales check} = \frac{\text{Total value of average monthly sales checks available}}{\text{Number of sales checks available}}$$

(Average sales checks were only available for part of the monthly periods)

$$\text{Number of transactions} = \frac{\text{Planned sales for the month}}{\text{Average sales check for the month}}$$

$$\text{Number of hours of work} = \frac{\text{Number of transactions}}{\text{Average transactions per hour}\,(1.55)}$$

(The average transaction per hour figure was one computed in this particular department over a period of time as part of a time and motion study project. This figure is also given in Table 1.)

This decision is left in *number of hours.* If a computer is used, it is automatically programmed to multiply the average wage times the number of hours. If a computer is not used, the instructor will provide the average wage factor.

The game is computerized to adjust the number of hours needed depending on the weather, advertising, and inventory purchases. If weather is exceedingly good, sales could be above expectations and then the computer would automatically hire the extra help to make the sales. If the right combination of advertising, weather, and inventory were available, the same situation could exist and more help would be necessary and would be hired. However, this additional help is brought in at a less efficient rate of production, thereby increasing the cost to the business. If adequate help is available, no change or adjustment occurs in the planned number of hours of employment, even if sales decrease because of inclement weather, because these people are available and normally would be retained unless they were on a part-time basis.

Step 7. Advertising

The advertising decision for the appropriate month could be computed by developing an advertising-to-sales correlation chart based on the 5 years of past historical data given in Figure 1. The regression line that would emerge is somewhat representative of what is sometimes called the "normal advertising curve." If the student will plot the data in such a chart, it can be seen that a minimum amount of advertising has to be used for all small sales figures just to "maintain your position in the market." Then, as the advertising dollars are increased, they become more effective. Finally, the expenditures reach a point of diminishing return and the effectiveness of the advertising becomes less and less until it reaches a point at which almost no additional sales are realized by expending more dollars.

Another method of determining the advertising expenditures might be to take a planned percentage of annual sales and then distribute this amount of money over each month based on the need or objective to be accomplished. A suggested source to help the student in this analysis might be the current National Retail Merchants Association publication, *Sales Promotion Calendar*, or a local business firm may have some suggestions.

Step 8. Planned Gross Margin

The figure for gross margin can now be developed since all figures are now available:

```
Sales (From Step 1) ....................................... XX
Cost of goods sold
    Beginning inventory (Step 2 X Cost complement – 58.5%) ..... XX
    Purchases at retail (Step 5 X Cost complement – 58.5%) ...... XX
        Total goods available ........................ XX
Less ending inventory (Step 2 X Cost complement – 58.5%) ..... XX
        Net cost of goods sold ............................... XX
                GROSS MARGIN ............................ XX
```

For simplicity, cash discounts earned and alteration costs are omitted.

Step 9. The Variables

The most important variable that is used in this game is in the form of "possible hours of sunshine". Many variables were tested but this particular variable had a very high correlation to sales; therefore, it was used. Data for 10 years were gathered from the weather bureau in the area of this store. Norms of possible hours of sunshine were then established for each month of the year and the standard deviations for each month were developed. When a random card is drawn from a random deck of possible sigmas away from norm, it is then placed in the game deck and the following reactions occur: (1) If fairly normal weather is drawn — any sigma close to zero position — it will have little effect on sales and sales will be approximately normal for that month. (2) If a -2.5 sigma card is drawn, representing very bad weather, sales would be cut drastically. (3) The opposite would be true if a $+2.5$, or very good weather, is drawn. Sales would be far above plan, extra help would have to be hired (known as unplanned selling expense in the game), but profits would probably rise because of fixed expenses.

If sales fall, there is a direct effect on planned inventory, for it will not decrease as fast as planned and more will be left than planned for the beginning of the next month. This would call for a cut back in purchases. Now if sales were to increase above normal, inventories would fall below planned for the next month, which would necessitate additional purchases.

Any card from a random deck of standard deviation cards can be drawn to develop the weather. Most random decks of sigma cards might contain at least 200 to 250 possible variations of weather. All of these change the sales, the inventory, and everything else that was planned. It is through this learning to adjust that the student gets his practical experience in making changes necessary to cope with such conditions that actually happen in the "real world."

Other variables that can and do affect the sales when inventory is too low. Normal inventories for each of the months have previously been computed as a mean and the standard deviation of this mean also has been computed. If the inventory gets too small, this will reduce sales. It is one of the weighted variables put into the normal equation to solve for sales.

If the inventory is excessive, the student soon finds that his profit has been depleted by the unnecessary interest that he had to absorb at 5% on all inventory. If he had not had inventory in excess of what was needed to supply the normal sales figure, he would not have had this additional expense.

Excessive advertising, if it is at the top of the advertising curve where it begins to flatten out, becoming very ineffective, does not create sales. Too little advertising will have the effect of not creating sales either, so it behooves the student to develop his figures carefully to put together the right mix of personnel, advertising, and inventory in order that he might obtain the highest sales, lowest cost, and highest profit.

Details of how to handle these variables appear in the Teachers' Guide.

The Printout from the program

For the final analysis the student will receive a printout (if a computer is used) giving him the following information:

1. Actual sales for the month
2. The ending inventory
3. The average sales check used in the computations
4. The gross margin
5. Planned selling expense
6. Unplanned selling expense
7. Total selling expense (the sum of 5 + 6)
8. Planned advertising
9. Other variable expenses
10. Operating profit
11. Then at the end a listing is furnished the student of the decisions he made so that he can be sure no decision was incorrectly entered.

Summary

The game is not a complex game but coordinates the student's learning in statistics, accounting, and marketing, and at the same time basically covers all the major points in planning a budget in any store.

If the student will work the first 6-month figures as a learning or practice experience, he will then be ready to put together the entire fall 6-month budget normally developed in most successful stores.

ADDITIONAL ASSIGNMENTS

7. Planned inventory on March 1, $149,500; planned sales for March, $42,500; ending inventory planned for March 31, $161,500. What is the planned purchase figure for the month of March? If outstanding orders for March on March 1 are $28,000, what is the open-to-buy?

8. Planned retail inventory for July 1 is $150,000 and for July 31, $130,000. Planned sales for July are $35,000. Planned markdowns for the same period are expected to maintain the same ratio as last year: 1.8% of sales; shortages are similarly estimated at 1% of sales. On June 1, outstanding orders for July delivery had already been placed, totaling $100,000 retail. Find the open-to-buy still available for July delivery.

9. Retail inventory on May 3 is $161,300; merchandise received at retail from May 3 to 10 was $17,000; planned sales for May (starting with May 3) is $30,800 and actual sales May 3 to 10, $11,500; planned markdowns for the May period are 1.7% of sales and actual markdowns May 3 to 10, 1.6% of sales to date. Planned stock for May 31 is $167,000 and outstanding orders at retail on May 10 are $15,000. Sales and markdowns for the rest of the month are expected to be sufficient to bring both figures to the plans by the end of the month. Find the open-to-buy on May 10.

10. The following information is available:

	Planned Sales	Planned Stock (Retail) 1st of Month	Planned Markdowns
November	$30,000	$55,000	$1,000
December	40,000	60,000	1,000
January...........	25,000	45,000	5,000

Actual stock at retail, November 10	$57,000
Actual sales, November 1-10....................	8,100
Actual markdowns, November 1-10	300
Outstanding orders at retail on November 10 for delivery during November	15,600
Outstanding orders for December delivery	4,200

The first third of November normally accounts for 30% of November volume. In view of the sales showing to date, it is necessary to revise downward the planned sales for the entire month of November, but no change is contemplated in the December plans. Find the open-to-buy for the balance of November and for December.

11. In a dress department, the purchases and sales during the first 7 months of a fiscal year were as follows:

Month	Retail Purchases	Sales
February	$14,000	$ 5,500
March	14,500	8,600
April	10,100	9,200
May	24,700	13,400
June	5,300	10,800
July	1,500	7,200
August	8,800	5,200

An inventory taken in September revealed that 76% of the stock was unseasonable. Stock-turn is planned at 4 times a season and 8 times a year.

An analysis of sales by price lines showed that the leading five lines, in order of importance, were $29.50, $25.00, $16.50, $49.50, and $89.50. But the buyer's buying plan called for ten times as large a dollar investment in $89.50 dresses as in $16.50 dresses. The second largest investment, according to the buying plan, was in $49.50 dresses.

1. What was the cause of the poor assortment in September?
2. Revise the purchases for each month to bring them into line with the sales.
3. Suggest a method of control to keep purchases adjusted to sales both by month and by price line.

18

How to Plan and Control Expenses

This section on expenses has been introduced at this point because of the impact of expenses on the merchandise plan discussed in section 17.[1] Proper control of expenses is quite possibly the single most important detail to be taken into consideration when setting up the systems of the store or stores to be compared. The first major step of control is to plan a classification of the expenses according to a standard arrangement so that specific trends in the various elements making up expenses may be observed and fair comparisons made. Expense classification, however, involves much more than setting down standard headings for expenses, such as payroll and repairs. It involves the problem of determining what to include and what to exclude from the figures under each heading. For example, the payroll of an alteration is not an expense at all, but a part of the cost of merchandise, and depreciation on fixed assets is an expense, even though it is not paid out. Likewise, an unincorporated merchant should include — for managerial, but not tax, purposes — a reasonably imputed salary for himself in the expenses, even though he does not draw it out, in order to determine whether the business is earning anything above the value of his personal services.

As indicated earlier, expenses may be classified as direct and indirect. The former can be directly assigned to the selling departments or workrooms, but the latter may be distributed to the selling departments and workrooms on some arbitrary but equitable basis. Although some stores do distribute indirect expenses to departments, determining a net operating profit for each, others do not. If not, the departmental "profit" is the departmental contribution to the store's profit.

There are a great many possible methods for distributing expenses. For indirect expenses, the most common method is in proportion to the sales volume in dollars of each department. Although this method is sound for some expenses, the majority can be more fairly allocated on other bases. The expense of sales

---

[1] This section may be deferred until sections 19 and 20 on Unit Planning and Control have been covered.

auditing, for example, depends on the number of saleschecks handled, not the amount of sales, and should be distributed accordingly. The expense involved in setting up a large number of bases of allocation for different expenses has led many stores to adopt fewer methods than strict departmental cost accounting would suggest.

There are two ways to approach the expense planning problem. One is to set an overall expense goal that will insure a profit and the other is to plan each item of expense at a point at which the services received from the outlay are believed to contribute to long-run profits in greater measure than the cost of the expense. Since it is hard to estimate expense-income relationships in detail, overall expense goals are necessary even when careful, detailed planning is done.

DEFINITIONS

Expenses. The costs of operating a business, other than the costs of merchandise, that are properly chargeable to an accounting period.

Expenditures. The outlays made during an accounting period. Some are for expenses, some for merchandise, and some for the purchase of other assets.

Expense Classification. The grouping of expense accounts according to a standard plan.

Natural Divisions of Expense. An expense classification based on the nature of the service realized from the outlay rather than on the function of the business for which the outlay is made.

The commonly recognized natural divisions are as follows:

> Title
> Payroll
> Fringe benefits
> Advertising (media costs)
> Taxes
> Supplies
> Services purchased
> Unclassified
> Traveling
> Communications
> Pensions
> Insurance
> Depreciation
> Professional services
> Donations

Losses from bad debts

Equipment rentals

Real property rentals

Expense Center. A grouping of the expenses having to do with the performance of a specific function. For department stores, a minimum of nine such centers are recommended.

Fixed and policy expenses[2]

Control and accounting

Accounts receivable and credit

Sales promotion

Superintendency and building operation

Personnel and employee benefits

Material handling (including delivery)

Direct and general selling

Merchandising

For large stores, these are fanned out into as many as seventy-one expense centers.

Expense Distribution. A general term to describe all types of assignment of expenses to selling departments. Some are charged directly to the departments; some are allocated on an appropriate basis and some are prorated.

Direct Expenses. Expenses that can be assigned to departments directly and immediately without the intervention of any element of judgment.

Allocated Expenses. Expenses, other than direct, for which good and appropriate bases of expense distribution exist, so that the assignment of expense represents a reasonable estimate of the true expense incurred by each department.

Prorated Expenses. Joint expenses that cannot be charged directly to selling departments nor allocated to them on a basis that measures the service each has received. They are assigned to selling departments in proportion to dollar sales volume. *Note:* Some stores neither allocate nor prorate expenses to selling departments, charging them only for direct expenses and obtaining for each a controllable margin or department contribution, as it is often called.

Open-to-Spend. The difference between an expense budget for a period and the amount spent to date, when the former is the larger.

---

[2] Fixed and policy expense included general management; real estate costs; furniture, fixture and equipment costs; and other fixed and policy expenses. Each of these four may be treated as a separate expense center.

Requisition System of Expense Control. A system of authorizing expenditures for expense items only after an outlay has been requested in writing and has been checked against the budgeted figure for that type of outlay.

Work Load. The gross number of units of work performed or to be performed in an expense center during a period.

Relative Work Load. The amount of work load incident to $100 of total sales. It is found by dividing the work load by the sales in units of $100. Thus, sales of $100,000 are expressed as 1,000 units of $100 each. Also called work load factor.

Man-hours. The summation of all the productive hours worked by all employees in a work center during a period. It includes the scheduled hours worked by supervisors.

Productivity. The output of the work load per man-hour. It is found by dividing the work load by the number of man-hours required to handle the load.

Effective Pay Rate. The average rate of pay per hour for a work center. It is found by dividing the total payroll for the center by the total number of man-hours worked.

Payroll Expense Percentage. The total payroll for the work center expressed as a percentage of the total net sales. The sales are the store sales when the center services the store but when the selling department is regarded as a work center; the sales are the department sales.

A. EXPENSE CLASSIFICATION AND DISTRIBUTION

1. Standard expense classification.

Example:

A department store with sales of $1,000,000 keeps the following accounts.

Accounts
Rent paid
Salaries of employees
Delivery supplies
Advertising
Coal
Salaries of officers
Display supplies
Legal fees
Selling supplies
Cost of new fixtures (life 10 years)
Telephone

Electricity (purchased)
Express on incoming merchandise
Insurance
Water
Cost of altering building (lease has 5 years to run)
Buying office fee
Janitor
Taxes (other than income)
Club memberships
Retirement allowances
Losses from bad debts
Equipment rentals
Donations
Medical insurance

Classify these expenses according to the natural divisions.

Solution:

1.

Payroll:
    Salaries of employees
    Salaries of officers
    Salaries of janitor
Fringe benefits (medical insurance)
Advertising
Taxes
Supplies
    Delivery
    Display
    Selling
    Water
    Coal
Services purchases
    Electricity
    Buying office fee
Unclassified
    Club memberships
Traveling

> Communication
>> Telephone
> Pensions
>> Retirement allowances
> Insurance
> Depreciation
>> Fixtures
>> Alterations
> Professional services
>> Legal fees
> Donations
> Losses from bad debts
> Equipment rentals
> Real estate rentals
>> Rent paid

Note: Express on incoming goods is to be charged to cost of purchases.

ASSIGNMENT 1:

Classify the above expense accounts into the nine basic expense centers. Note that some accounts have to be broken down into subdivisions. For example, salaries of employees will appear in all the nine centers.

2. Expense distribution.

Example:

During a 6-month period, a selling department with sales of $400,000 and a gross margin of 33% incurs direct expenses as follows: buying, $20,000; selling, $24,000; advertising media, $16,000. During the same period, the store as a whole incurred the following expenses, part of which are to be borne by the department in question.

Delivery	$ 40,000
Real estate and equipment costs	150,000
Accounting and credit office	65,000
Executive offices	75,000
Personnel office	15,000
Interest,[3] insurance, taxes on merchandise	50,000
Miscellaneous expense	115,000
	$510,000

[3] Interest may properly be treated as a deduction from "other income" rather than as an expense; but in this store each department's expense account is charged with interest on its average investment in merchandise inventory as well as insurance and taxes levied on the inventory.

The following information is available to help in the allocation and proration of these expenses to the department in question: store sales, $3,000,000; store transactions, 1,600,000; department transactions, 16,000; number of employees in the store, 500; in the department, 40; number of store deliveries, 900,000; in the department, 31,500; total selling area of store, 100,000 square feet; area of department, 2,000 square feet; average stock investment in store, $1,000,000; in department, $25,000.

1. Find the controllable margin, treating delivery and merchandise charges as direct expenses.
2. Calculate the total expenses to be allocated to the department and those to be prorated.
3. Find the operating profit.

Solution:

(a) Gross margin = 33% of $400,000, which is $132,000
     Direct expenses
          Buying $20,000
          Selling   24,000
          Advertising   16,000
          Delivery[4]   1,400
          Merchandise charges[5]   1,250   62,650
     Controllable margin $69,350

(b) Real estate:

$$2,000 \div 100,000 = 2\%$$
$$2\% \text{ of } \$150,000 =$$ $ 3,000

     Accounting:

$$16,000 \div 1,600,000 = 1\%$$
$$1\% \text{ of } \$65,000 =$$ 650

     Personnel:

$$40 \div 500 = 8\%$$
$$8\% \text{ of } \$15,000 =$$ 1,200

                    Total allocated $ 4,850
          Executive and miscellaneous (prorated)

$$\$400,000 \div \$3,000,000 = 13.3\%$$
$$13.3\% \text{ of } \$190,000 = \$25,270$$ 25,270

                    Total indirect $30,120
          Controllable margin   69,350
          Operating profit $39,230

[4] $31,500 \div 900,000 = 3\text{-}1/2\%$ $3\text{-}1/2\% \text{ of } \$40,000 = \$1,400$
[5] $\$25,000 \div \$1,000,000 = 2.5\%$ $2.5\% \text{ of } \$50,000 = \$1,250$

ASSIGNMENT 2:

As many expense items as possible are charged directly to each selling department in a store with three departments; for example: sales and buyers' salaries as well as direct advertising. However, many expense items are joint costs and must be distributed to each of the three departments in an equitable manner.

Executive offices	$ 9,500
Accounts receivable	4,000
Accounts payable	1,500
Sales audit	3,000
Personnel office	4,000
Insurance and taxes on merchandise	8,000
Real estate and equipment costs	25,000
Janitorial services	6,000
Light, heat, power	3,000
Advertising office and general advertising	3,500
Window display	1,800
Merchandise office	3,500
Receiving and marking	1,700
Delivery	6,000
General selling (customer service)	10,000
Total indirect expenses	$90,500

Additional Data:

Department	Sales	Number of Total Sales Transactions	Number of Credit Transactions	Average Retail Inventory	Cost Purchases	Average Number of Employees
A	$135,000	50,000	35,000	$70,000	$ 76,000	12
B	108,000	9,000	6,000	40,000	72,000	9
C	200,000	125,000	45,000	60,500	100,000	15

	Packages Delivered and Returned	Number of Invoices
A	20,000	750
B	9,000	400
C	11,000	1,100

Department	Square Feet Space Occupied	Weighted Value of Space Occupied	Newspaper Lineage	Pt. Value of Window Space Used	Direct Expenses
A	4,000	12,000	2,800	1,200	20,000
B	6,000	12,000	3,100	600	16,000
C	7,000	10,500	1,800	700	25,000

	Initial Markup	Gross Margin
A	40%	35%
B	33%	30%
C	35%	30%

Instructions:

1. Distribute the indirect expenses to each department. Use the most appropriate method of distributing each expense item, pointing out the base used.
2. Find the operating profit for each department.

DISCUSSION QUESTIONS:

Should indirect expenses be distributed to departments? Why or why not?

B. EXPENSE CONTROL

3. Setting the expense control figure.

Example:

A store contemplates sales for next year of $125,000 at a gross margin of 30%. It wishes to realize an operating profit of at least $5,000. What should be the maximum allowed for operating expenses?

Solution:

        30% of $125,000 = $37,500
        less   5,000
        Balance $32,500 expenses

ASSIGNMENT 3:

Last year a retailer had expenses of $50,000, which were 25% of sales. Maintained markup was 29%; cash discounts earned, 3%; alteration costs, 1%.

This year he expects an 18% increase in sales. He aims to increase his dollar operating profit 50% over last year's figure. The percentages for alteration costs, discounts earned, and maintained markup should remain the same as last year. In planning for this year's operations, determine how much can be allowed for operating expenses (in both dollars and percentage). What is the logic in aiming at an expense figure that is lower in percentage than last year's figure?

DISCUSSION QUESTION:

In practice, would it be generally feasible to make profit the planned figure and expense the resultant one? Defend your answer.

4. Planning the advertising outlay.

Example:

A store with sales of $100,000 and gross margin of 35% is spending 1% for advertising and 32% for other expenses. Of these expenses of $32,000, $16,000 are fixed and $16,000 are directly variable with sales. It is estimated that $500 more spent for advertising should bring in $5,000 more sales, but that a second $500 increase would bring in only $3,000; a third $500, only $2,000; and a fourth $500, only $1,000. Determine the most profitable advertising outlay.

Solution:

Sales	Gross Margin at 35%	Adver- tising	Variable Expense	Fixed Expense	Total Expense	Operating Profit
$100,000	$35,000	$1,000	$16,000	$16,000	$33,000	$2,000
105,000	36,750	1,500	16,800	16,000	34,300	2,450
108,000	37,800	2,000	17,280	16,000	35,280	2,520
110,000	38,500	2,500	17,600	16,000	36,100	2,400
111,000	38,850	3,000	17,760	16,000	36,760	2,090

An advertising outlay of $2,000, or 1.9% of sales, would seem to be the most profitable.

ASSIGNMENT 4:

A store with sales of $200,000 is now spending 2% of it for advertising. Fixed expenses are 15%; variable expenses, including advertising, 20%; and gross margin, 40%. It is estimated that additional advertising will increase sales as follows:

Added Advertising	Added Sales
1st $1,000	$8,000
2nd 1,000	5,000
3rd 1,000	3,000
4th 1,000	2,000
5th 1,000	1,000

What is the most profitable advertising outlay and percentage?

DISCUSSION QUESTION:

How can such estimates be made intelligently?

5. Payroll planning.

Example:

A men's furnishings merchant has three salespeople who can handle as many as 300 transactions a week apiece. He himself in busy seasons can devote time to make about 100 sales. He estimates his sales for the first 3 weeks before Christmas as follows:

1st week in December $4,500
2nd week in December   5,100
3rd week in December   6,000

The average sale is about $3 at this time. Extras can handle only about 150 transactions each and also cut down the effectiveness of the regular force about 10%.
How many extras should he hire each of the 3 weeks?

Solution:

	$ Sales	Trans- actions	Regulars and Self (normal)	Less 10%	Transac- tions by Extras	Number of Extras
1st week . . .	4,500	1,500	1,000	900	600	4
2nd week . . .	5,100	1,700	1,000	900	800	5-1/3
3rd week . . .	6,000	2,000	1,000	900	1,100	7-1/3

The need for a fractional extra may be handled by a part-time worker, but the delay in selling caused by confusion of extras and congestion in the third week may make eight full-time extras desirable to avoid losing business.

ASSIGNMENT 5:

A clothing merchant relates clerk-hours to weekly transactions with the following results:

Transactions a Week	Clerk-Hours	Transactions a Week	Clerk-Hours
1,000	350	1,600	510
1,200	395	1,800	560
1,400	455	2,000	850

Each clerk works 35 hours a week.

1. Draw a chart showing the correlation between Transactions and Clerk-Hours. Plot the transactions on the X-axis and the clerk-hours on the Y-axis. Draw the straight line that best approximates these points.

2. How many full-time clerks would be required for transactions of 1,500 a week? Of 2,500 a week?

3. If the average sale is $15 and the average clerk's salary $100, what would be the normal selling-cost percentage with transactions of 1,000 a week? Of 2,000 a week?

DISCUSSION QUESTIONS:

At busy seasons, such as Christmas, would clerk-hours increase relatively faster or slower than the increase in transactions? In other words, is a straight-line trend not to be expected?

6. Productivity analysis.

Example:

In the accounts receivable office, the number of gross credit sales transactions handled in November were 40,000; the number of man-hours worked, 800; and the department payroll, $1,600. The store-wide sales during the month were $500,000.

1. Find the productivity, the effective pay rate, and the payroll cost per unit.

2. Express the payroll expense in terms of the work load, productivity, and effective pay rate.

3. Find the relative work load and express the payroll expense percentage in terms of the relative work load, productivity, and effective pay rate.

4. What are the possible ways of reducing the expense percentage?

Solution:

(1)   Productivity = Transactions ÷ Man-hours
            = 40,000 ÷ 800 = 50 (transactions per hour)
    Effective pay rate = Payroll expenses ÷ Man-hours
            = $1,600 ÷ 800 = $2.00 (per hour)
    Payroll cost per unit = Payroll ÷ Transactions
            = $1,600 ÷ 40,000 = $.04

(2) $\dfrac{\text{Work load}}{\text{Productivity}} \times$ Effective pay rate = Payroll expenses

$$\dfrac{40,000}{50} \times \$2.00 = 800 \text{ (hours worked)} \times \$2.00$$

$$= \$1,600$$

(3)   Relative work load $= \dfrac{\text{Work load}}{\text{Sales in \$100 units}}$

$$= \dfrac{40,000}{5,000} = 8 \text{ (i.e., credit}$$
$$\text{transactions per}$$
$$\$100 \text{ sales)}$$

$\dfrac{\text{Relative work load}}{\text{Productivity}} \times$ Effective pay rate = Payroll %.

$$\dfrac{8}{50} \times \$2.00 = .16 \times \$2.00$$

$$= \text{payroll expense of } \$.32$$

$$\$.32 \div \$100 = 0.32\%$$

Proof: $\$1,600 \text{ (payroll)} \div \$500,000 \text{ (store sales)} = 0.32\%$

4. (a) Reduce work load, possibly by persuading charge customers to purchase more at a time.

(b) Increase productivity by better work planning and supervision, or by using labor-saving equipment.

(c) Reduce the effective pay rate, either by cutting wages or by demanding more hours of work for same pay.

ASSIGNMENT 6:

In connection with the above problem, if the work load in December is expected to be 49,000, if sales are expected to be $700,000, and if a productivity of 55 is to be planned, what should be the credit department's December payroll budget, both in dollars and as a percentage of store sales? Express the relationships by means of the formula presented in the solution above.

DISCUSSION QUESTION:

Why is a knowledge of payroll in an expense center, expressed both in dollars and as a percentage of sales, not enough to control the expense adequately?

Managerial Decision

You have drawn up a chart for your automobile accessories and toy store showing for each of the past 52 weeks the relationship between transactions and clerk-hours and you have drawn a straight line that shows the normal clerk-hours for every transaction interval. You have been planning to use this chart in scheduling the number of employees to have each week this year. But an associate argues that this method will do nothing to cut down on selling payroll costs and that it will simply perpetuate last year's mistakes. Is he right — fully or partially? Would you use the chart for scheduling purposes, in spite of his criticism?

ADDITIONAL ASSIGNMENTS

7. Under which work centers would you put the following expense items?

1. Gasoline and oil for delivery trucks;
2. Cleaning the show windows;
3. Service manager's salary;
4. Pin tickets for marking merchandise;
5. Salaries of credit man and controller.

8. A store with three departments has sales and indirect expenses during the first 3 months of the spring season as follows:

Month	Store Sales	Store Expenses (Indirect)	Sales by Department		
			Dept. A	Dept. B	Dept. C
February	$43,000	$ 9,000	$13,000	$10,000	$20,000
March	55,000	10,000	15,000	15,000	25,000
April.	60,000	10,500	18,000	20,000	22,000

Indirect expenses are to be distributed to each department in proportion to *accumulated* sales for the season. That is, February expenses are to be prorated according to February sales, but March expenses according to the department sales accumulated from the beginning of the season.

Distribute the indirect expenses at the end of February, at the end of March, and at the end of April.

9. The sales transactions planned for May in the men's furnishings department are 3,750 and the productivity standard for the month is 3.75. The average sale is estimated at $4.00, and the effective pay rate at $3.00.

(a) Plan the necessary man-hours and the payroll for the month.

(b) Express the planned payroll percentages in terms of relative work load, productivity, and effective pay rate.

10. The following items of expense were charged to a selling department for a particular accounting period. Department sales were $60,000 and the gross margin was 30% for the period. What was the department's contribution margin (controllable margin)?

Sales salaries	$4,000	General administration	$ 300
Direct advertising	1,500	Rent	1,000
General advertising	600	Buyer's salary	500
Power, light, etc.	800	Sales supervision	700
Personnel	400	Depreciation (building)	100

DISCUSSION QUESTIONS:

Suppose that additional joint costs were allocated to the above department and that these additional expenses resulted in a negative operating profit. What should top management do about such a situation? Is it reasonable to evaluate a department's profitability and its employees' effectiveness based on a profit figure that is the result of both direct and indirect expenses? Elaborate.

Part V   UNIT PLANNING AND CONTROL

Staples are commonly controlled by means of periodic inventories. Orders are placed for the difference between the predetermined "maximum" and the sum of the quantity on hand and on order. The chief problem involved is to calculate the elements included in the *maximum*, especially the *reorder period* and the *reserve*.

DEFINITIONS

Minimum. Amount of stock planned to be on hand at the moment a reorder is placed. It is sufficient to cover probable sales during the delivery period and to provide for a safety factor.

Maximum. The amount of stock that should be on hand and on order just after a reorder is placed. As a formula,

Maximum = Delivery period + Safety factor + Reorder period

These may be expressed in terms of weeks' supply or in terms of units of goods. Since the minimum equals the delivery period plus the safety factor, the maximum (in weeks' supply) may also be expressed as the minimum plus the reorder period.

Safety Factor. A reserve for contingencies, especially for unforeseen increases in rate of sale. It may be expressed in terms of number of weeks' supply or as a specific quantity in units. When applied to a classification rather than a single item of merchandise, it also must include a provision for a basic assortment of colors, sizes, and so forth. Also called Reserve.

Reorder Period. The frequency planned for reordering a specific item.

Delivery Period. The expected period of time between ordering the merchandise and its receipt in stock. In planning, it is prudent to set the delivery period somewhat longer than the normal delivery time to allow for occasional delays.

Unit Open-to-Buy. The number of pieces of merchandise that are still to be ordered for delivery during a control period. It may be calculated as follows: Maximum in units – (On hand in units + Already on order in units).

A. MAXIMUM AND MINIMUM STOCKS

1. Maximum stocks.

● *Example:*

A staple item is to be ordered every 4 weeks. It takes 2 weeks for delivery and an extra week's supply is to be held as a reserve.[1] The buyer estimates that the article sells at a rate of about forty a week, regularly throughout the year. What maximum should be set for this item, so that the difference between the maximum and the quantity on hand may be ordered every 4 weeks. What rate of turnover would be realized on this item, if this method is used and if sales are forecast accurately?

Solution:

Maximum = Delivery period + Reserve + Reorder period
= 2 + 1 + 4 = 7 weeks' supply.
The maximum in units is 7 × 40 = 280.
If at a monthly count, 125 units are on hand,
155 more should be ordered.

Turnover: The stock would sell down to the reserve of 1 week's supply just before the reorder arrives. After the reorder arrives, stock would reach a high of 5 weeks' supply. Thus, it would average 3 weeks' supply: (1 + 5) ÷ 2. Sales for year (in weeks) ÷ average inventory (in weeks' supply) = annual stock-turn rate. Thus, 52 ÷ 3 = 17.3, the annual rate of turnover.[2]

ASSIGNMENT 1:

Under a tickler (periodic inventory) system of control, a maximum of ten units was set for a 15-week period, and inventory was taken every 3 weeks, the difference between the maximum and the inventory being ordered after each count. These inventory counts were as follows:

---

[1] The size of the reserve or safety factor should be related to the sales expectancy during the delivery and reorder periods, as will be explained in connection with problem 5.

[2] Alternate solution when data is in weeks' supply: Stock-turn rate = 52 ÷ (Reserve + ½ Reorder.) = 52 ÷ (1 + ½ of 4) = 52 ÷ 3 = 17.3.

On Hand

Beginning 6
End of 3rd week 4
End of 6th   "   2
End of 9th   "   5
End of 12th "   1
End of 5th   "   3

A record of sales was not maintained, but sales could be calculated by subtracting the closing inventory for the period from the maximum. Thus, the sales for the first 3 weeks were 10 – 4, or 6. It is estimated that the sales for the next quarter will be 25% ahead of the past period. It takes about 1 week to receive goods after a count is taken preparatory to a reorder. The buyer notes that his reserve is inadequate since he must have lost sales after the end of the 6th and 12th weeks when he had less than a week's supply on hand. He estimated that it should be about 2½ weeks' supply. What adjustment should he make in his maximum?

DISCUSSION QUESTION:

If a stock does not occasionally sell out before a reorder is received, does it mean that the reserve is too large?

2. Unit purchase planning — building up to a maximum.

● *Example:*

A standard cosmetic preparation is selling at the rate of twenty a week; twenty-five are on hand, and none are on order. It takes a week for delivery, reorders are placed every 2 weeks, and an extra week's supply is carried as a reserve. How many dozen should be ordered?

Solution:

Maximum = Delivery period + Reserve + Reorder period
Maximum = 1 + 1 + 2 = 4 weeks' supply
Maximum = 4 × 20 units = 80 units
Open-to-buy = Maximum – (On hand + On order)
= 80 – (25 + 0) = 55

The nearest reorder unit, then, is 5 dozen, or 60.

ASSIGNMENT 2:

A staple housefurnishings item sells at the rate of six a week. Delivery takes 2 weeks and reorders are placed once a month. An extra 2-weeks' supply is carried as a reserve to take care of unforseen increases in the rate of sale. Twenty are now on hand and six are on order. How many should be reordered?

DISCUSSION QUESTION:

How is it possible to estimate a future rate of sale for an item?

3. General operation of minimum-maximum system.

● *Example:*

A minimum or "low" of 12 is set for an item that takes one week to deliver. This is based on sales of 6 a week and allows for a reserve of one week's supply. Under the system followed, the maximum is set as always twice the minimum and an order is placed to bring the stock to the maximum. A ticket bearing the date 79 (79th day of the year) is turned in on date 100, the salesperson indicating that eleven pieces are actually on hand. Set a new minimum and determine the correct reorder quantity.

Solution:

The sales for the period between the date 79 and the date 100 are determined as follows:

$$\text{Maximum} = 2 \times \text{Minimum}$$
$$= 2 \times 12$$
$$= 24$$
$$\text{Sales} = \text{Maximum} - \text{On hand}$$
$$= 24 - 11$$
$$= 13 \text{ (sales for 3 weeks)}$$
$$\text{Sales for one week} = 13 \div 3$$
$$= 4\tfrac{1}{3}$$
$$\text{New Minimum} = 2 \times \text{One week's sales}$$
$$= 2 \times 4\tfrac{1}{3}$$
$$= 8\tfrac{2}{3}$$
$$\text{New Maximum} = 2 \times \text{Minimum}$$
$$= 2 \times 8\tfrac{2}{3}$$
$$= 17\tfrac{1}{3}$$
$$\text{Reorder quantity} = 17 - 11 = 6$$

ASSIGNMENT 3:

The card reproduced below is sent to the buyer on June 2. It is a part of a minimum control system in which the maximum is twice the minimum, and in which the safety factor is 1½ weeks' supply. Calculate the new minimum and reorder quantity.

Article: *Coffee pot*   Style *432*
Mfg. *J. Jones*   Delivery period   *2 wks.*
Date last minimum *May 12*
Present minimum *12*
Actually on hand *8*
Amount to be reordered ———

DISCUSSION QUESTION:

What would be the mechanics of making out such cards?

4. Minimum-maximum plan for a composite unit.

Example:

In a certain style of goods a buyer needs three colors (maroon, blue, and green) and four sizes (*A, B, C,* and *D*), and at least two pieces in each color and size. It takes 2 weeks to obtain delivery. He plans to replenish this style once every 4 weeks, and decides to allow 2 weeks' supply as a reserve for chance sale variations. The style is expected to sell at the rate of six a week.

1. What minimum should be set for the style?
2. What maximum should be set for the style?
3. If the buyer has forty units on hand, how many more should be ordered?

Solution:

1. Finding the minimum. With three colors, four sizes, and two pieces in each color and size, a basic assortment requires twenty-four units. An additional reserve of 2 weeks' supply or twelve pieces is required for sales variations. Thus, the total reserve is thirty-six. Since is takes 2 weeks for delivery (a supply of twelve), a reorder should be placed when the stock sells down to forty-eight. This is the *minimum.*
2. Finding the maximum. Since 4 weeks' supply is to be ordered at a time, twenty-four (4 × 6 sales a week) should be ordered normally when the stock falls to its minimum of forty-eight. Thus, the maximum should be seventy-two.

3. It is often impractical to reorder items just as their minimums are reached. Salespeople and stock clerks cannot always be relied on to report at the danger point; again, the buyer prefers to order all styles from the same resource together, not separately. Accordingly, the stock of all styles from a resource will be inventoried together at least once in 4 weeks and possibly once in 2 weeks. At the monthly counts, the buyer will order the difference between the maximum set and the amount on hand (and on order, if any). If counts are made every 2 weeks, orders will be placed only if the stock is so close to the minimum as to forecast that the minimum will be pierced before the next bi-weekly count. Thus, if at a monthly count forty are on hand, 32 will be ordered. If at a bi-weekly count sixty are on hand, none will be ordered, since the quantity is twelve above the minimum, enough for 2 more weeks' selling.

ASSIGNMENT 4:

A certain style of gabardine slacks is carried in brown, gray-green, and medium blue in all sizes, 28–40 inch waist. The buyer wants to keep at least two of each item in stock. It takes 2 weeks to obtain delivery and fill-in orders are to be placed approximately every 3 weeks. The reserve planned is 2½ weeks' supply. Sales are estimated at four a week. If forty-five are on hand and if the last order for twelve is still outstanding, how many more should be ordered?

DISCUSSION QUESTION:

Is it better to reorder at scheduled intervals or intermittently when the stock sells down to its minimum?

5. Planning the reserve by means of probability ratios.

Introductory note: In the problems above on maximum stocks, the reserve required to take care of chance fluctuations in the rate of sale was stated as a given number of weeks' supply. Statisticians have evolved a more analytical way of estimating fluctuations of data around a known mean that is called the Poisson Distribution. For example, sales of a staple and non-seasonal item may be reliably forecast at 520 a year. The weekly mean sales are thus ten. But due to the operations of chance, actual sales will not be ten every week. Some weeks they may be considerably more and some weeks considerably less. The Poisson Distribution reveals that there is one chance out of 100 that the sales in any one week would, on account of chance, exceed seventeen; seven more than the average of ten. Similar limits can be set for other proportions of probability, but it is generally considered "safe" to make allowances in planning for what is likely to happen in 99% of the cases. Some merchants however may "settle" for less protection, such as 95% (one lost sale in 20).[3]

The seven extra units or reserve required when planning 1 week ahead can be calculated mathematically by the following formula for 99% protection:

$$\text{Reserve} = 2.3 \times \sqrt{\text{Normal sales in planning period}}$$

Substituting the normal sales of ten,

$$\text{Reserve} = 2.3 \times \sqrt{10} = 2.3 \times 3.16 = 7.27 \ (7 \text{ approximately})$$

Normally, the planning period is generally more than 1 week. It represents the length of time it takes to make a correction in the planned stock on hand. This is the delivery period plus the reorder period. Thus, if delivery takes 2 weeks and reorders are to be placed every 4 weeks, once an order has been placed it will take 6 weeks before a further adjustment in the stock on hand can be made (4 weeks are to pass before another order is placed and it will take two weeks more to get the then-ordered goods in stock). Thus, the planner must allow for a reserve that is predicated on the possible chance increase in sales in 6 weeks.

If the average sales of ten a week are expected,[4] the normal expectancy for 6 weeks would be 60 units. But by chance they may be considerably more. How much more, to give protection 99% of the time, is determined by the formula above:

$$\text{Reserve} = 2.3 \times \sqrt{60} = 2.3 \times 7.7 \ (\text{approximately}) = 18 \ (\text{approximately})$$

This means that, with a normal sales expectancy of sixty in 6 weeks, there are 99 chances out of 100, that the sales will not exceed seventy-eight.

The basic concept in connection with the reserve is that it need not increase in direct proportion to the increase in sales during the planning period but rather only by the square root of the rate of increase in sales. Thus, once the reserve has been properly related to the sales, a fourfold increase in sales calls for only a twofold increase in the reserve.

● *Example:*

Reorders are placed every 4 weeks, delivery takes 2 weeks, and the estimated weekly rate of sale is 6.

---

[3] If only 95% protection is required, the reserve need be only

$$1.6 \times \sqrt{\text{Normal sales in planning period.}}$$

[4] It is not necessary to use the year's average as the norm. For example, the year's estimate may be 1,000 with 20% of the year's business expected in December, or 200 units. This figure can then be broken down into weekly expectancies, such as 60 (the first week in December), 65 (the second week), 55 (the third week), and 20 (the week after Christmas).

1. Calculate the "probability" reserve.
2. If sales should double to twelve a week, how much should the reserve be increased?
3. If sales are fifty-four a week, what should be the reserve?

Solution:

(1) Planning period = 4 weeks for reorder plus
$\qquad$ 2 weeks for delivery, or 6 weeks

$\quad$ Sales in period = 6 × 6, or 36
$\qquad$ Reserve = 2.3 × $\sqrt{36}$ = 2.3 × 6 = 14 (approximately)

(2) Sales in period 12 × 6 = 72
$\qquad$ Reserve 2.3 × $\sqrt{72}$ = 2.3 × 8.5 = 20 (approximately)

$\quad$ Note that sales are double, a ratio of 2.
$\quad$ The square root of 2 is about 1.4, and 14 times 1.4 equals 20

(3) Sales in period = 54 × 6 = 324
$\qquad$ Reserve = 2.3 × $\sqrt{324}$ = 2.32 × 18 = 42 (approximately)

$\quad$ Note that with sales 9 times what they were in (1), the reserve is
$\quad$ only 3 times as large.

ASSIGNMENT 5:

A certain book title sells at an average rate of three a week. Stock is filled in every 2 weeks and 1 week is allowed for delivery.

1. Calculate the reserve needed to allow for chance sales variations during the planning period.
2. Calculate the maximum stock in units.
3. How many should be reordered if eight are on hand and none are on order?

DISCUSSION QUESTION:

Is a reserve that provides 99% protection too large?

6. Maximum stocks with "probability" reserves.

Example:

In connection with example (1) above, assume that thirty units are now on hand. (1) What is the maximum and how many should be ordered? (2) What would be the stock-turn rate? (3) With sales of fifty-four a week, what is the maximum and the stock-turn rate?

Solution:

(1)   Maximum = Delivery period quantity + Reserve
                     + Reorder period quantity

Maximum = 12 + 14 + 24 = 50 units

Open-to-buy (reorder quantity) = maximum – (on hand + on order)

O.T.B. = 50 – (30 + 0) = 20 units

(2)   Average stock = Reserve + ½ reorder period quantity
                    = 14 + ½ of 24 = 14 + 12 = 26

Stock-turn rate = annual sales ÷ average stock = 6 × 52 ÷ 26 = 12

(3)   Maximum = 108 (delivery period quantity) + 42 (reserve)
                     + 216 (reorder period quantity) = 366

Average stock = 42 (Reserve) + 108 (which is ½ of the reorder
                     period quantity) = 150

Stock-turn rate = 2,808 (the annual sales) ÷ 150 = 18.7

ASSIGNMENT 6:

In a \$25-price line, delivery takes 3 weeks, and the assortment is filled in every 2 weeks. In addition to maintaining a reserve to take care of chance variations in sales, the buyer plans a basic assortment for this price line of seventy-two units to provide an assortment of sizes, colors, and styles. His planned sales for the coming 5 weeks total 400. He now has 120 on hand and 200 on order.

1. What should be the reserve, exclusive of the basic stock? With the basic stock?
2. What is the maximum?
3. What is the reorder quantity?
4. If sales should continue at the current rate, what would be the annual stock-turn of this price line?

DISCUSSION QUESTIONS:

1. Is it sound to regard a price line as though it were a single item, as long as an adjustment is made for a basic assortment?
2. What is the relationship of sales volume to stock-turn if reserves are properly set?

B. SEASONAL PLANNING

7. Ratio method of seasonal planning.

Example:

On the basis of last year's sales, it is expected that a certain staple item will sell as follows:

	Cumulative % of Season's Sales
1st three weeks of season	20.0%
4th week	27.0
5th week	32.4
6th week	37.7
7th week	42.9
8th week	48.2
9th week	52.0
10th week	57.6
Last three weeks	100.0

It is planned to keep stock on hand and on order (the maximum) equal to 5 weeks' supply.

Original planned sales for the season	2,000
Sales, first 3 weeks	500
Stock on hand, end of 3rd week	400
Stock on order, end of 3rd week	150

1. Find the O.T.B. for the 4th week.
2. If, during the 4th week, sales are 160 and receipts 130, find the O.T.B. for the 5th week.

Solution:

(1)   500 = 20%.

100% = 2,500, the revised sales plan.

48.2% – 20% = 28.2%, the percentage of season's business expected in the coming 5 weeks.

28.2% × 2,500 = 705, the maximum stock.

O.T.B. = 705 – (400 + 150) = 155

(2) On hand third week 400
     Receipts fourth week 130
     Total 530
     Sales 160
     On hand fourth week 370
     On order third week 150
     New orders fourth week 155
     Total 305
     Receipts fourth week 130
     On order fourth week 175
     On hand plus on order 545

Four-weeks' sales: 500 + 160 = 660 = 27% of season total.

Season total = $\dfrac{660}{0.27}$ = 2,444.

Next 5 weeks' expectancy: 52% – 27% = 25%.

25% of 2,444 = 611, the maximum stock.

O.T.B. = 611 – 545 = 66.

Note: The above method may also be used when the sales are planned in dollars, rather than in units — also for seasons of other lengths, such as 6 months.

ASSIGNMENT 7:

For a certain classification of merchandise, the buyer wants to set a reserve to protect his sales during the 5-week planning period. He reorders every 2 weeks and allows 3 weeks for delivery. He anticipates his season's business as follows:

     February (4 weeks) 10%
     March (5 weeks) 20
     April (4 weeks) 18
     May (4 weeks) 22
     June (5 weeks) 20
     July (4 weeks) 10
     Total 100%

During February, his sales were 200 units, and on March 1 the stock on hand was 300 and the stock on order, 150. How many should be ordered?

Note: His reserve is to be 2.3 times the square root of March sales (5 weeks).

DISCUSSION QUESTION:

For what types of merchandise and what types of stores is last year's seasonal pattern of sales for an item likely to be repeated?

8. Planning in terms of the ratio of an item's sales to total unit sales in a classification.

Introductory note: The cumulative ratio method used above is based on the assumption that the pattern of seasonal demand determined last year is to be repeated this year. If the pattern is not repeated, the forecasts are erroneous. Since the total of potential customers for an item is a factor in the actual selection of that item from an assortment, it is important to give some weight to the total unit sales of the classification of which the item in question is a part. Instead of determining the cumulative weekly or monthly ratios of the sales of the item to the total sales of the item for the season — as done above — item sales each week or month may be expressed as a percentage of the sales of all items in the classification for the same period. This ratio, when corrected, may be applied to the planned sales for all items for a period ahead. The sales of all items combined can be forecast with considerable accuracy by such means as described in section 16. The sales of the item within the classification may then be derived by the method exemplified below.

Example:

A buyer has the following data about the monthly sales of a specific item and the total unit sales within the classification of merchandise involved.

Last Year

Month	Item A	Total Unit Sales	Item A % to Total
1st	100	10,000	1
2nd	340	17,000	2
3rd	1350	22,500	6
4th	1000	25,000	4
5th	480	16,000	3
6th	160	8,000	2
Total	3430	98,500	

This Year

Month	Item A	Total Unit Sales	Item A % to Total
1st	180	9,000 (actual)	2
2nd	600	15,000 (actual)	4
3rd	1920	24,000 (actual)	8
4th		27,000 (estimated)	
5th		22,000 (estimated)	
6th		10,000 (estimated)	

Find the probable sales of item A during the last 3 months of the season on a basis of the total forecast for all items.

Month	This Year's Total Sales	Last Year's Item A %	Projected Item A Sales	Actual Item A Sales
1st	9,000	1	90	180
2nd	15,000	2	300	600
3rd	24,000	6	1,440	1,920
Total			1,830	2,700

$2,700 \div 1,830 = 1.47$. i.e., the actual sales are 47% higher than they would have been had last year's ratios been repeated.

Month	Projected Total Sales	Last Year's Item A %	Projected Item A Sales	Correction	Corrected Projection Item A Sales
4th	27,000	4	1,080	1.47	1,588
5th	22,000	3	660	1.47	970
6th	10,000	2	200	1.47	294

Note: At the end of the 4th month, the total sales for all items may be revised for the 5th and 6th months, a new correction factor calculated on a basis of 4 months, and a revision of item A sales made for the next 2 months.

ASSIGNMENT 8:

1. For the 4th month, if the actual sales for all items are 26,000 rather than 27,000, and the actual sales for item A are 1,620 instead of the projected 1,588, find the new projection of item A sales for the 5th month, assuming that the 5th month's sales projection for the classification is revised to 21,000, from 22,000.

2. What would be the projected sales ratio for the 5th month if the line ratio method were used, as in problem 7?

DISCUSSION QUESTIONS:

Why are the results with the two methods considerably different? Is it possible to forecast total unit sales more accurately than item sales? If so, why?

C. NORMAL REORDER QUANTITIES

9. Optimum reorder quantities for nonseasonal staples.

Example:

> A buyer is anxious to determine the best reorder quantity and reorder period for a toilet preparation. He expects to sell $1,000 worth at retail, during the year, at a markup of 40%. He is charged 6% on his merchandise investment for interest and 2% for insurance. The rate of depreciation is not great, but some items might become soiled or damaged and prices might drop. He therefore estimates depreciation at 2% of the investment. A careful accounting of the cost of placing the order and of receiving the order into stock (over and above fixed costs of maintaining invoice office and receiving room) reveals it to be about 50 cents.
> The investment or carrying charges totaling 10% weigh in favor of a high turnover with many but small reorders. The reorder costs of 50 cents an order weigh in favor of few reorders.

> 1. What is the ideal reorder quantity?
> 2. What is the reorder period that will keep costs at a minimum? Assume that no quantity discounts are involved.

Solution:

> 1. By trial and error, the answer could be found, but the following formula[5] will save a great deal of experimentation:

$$\text{Reorder quantity} = \sqrt{\frac{2 \times \text{Annual cost of sales} \times \text{Reorder cost}}{\text{Carrying rate}}}$$

$$= \sqrt{\frac{2 \times \$600 \times \$.50}{.10}} = \sqrt{\frac{\$600}{0.10}} = \sqrt{\$6,000} = \$77$$

> 2. If $77 worth are to be ordered at a time and $600 worth are needed in a year, 7.8 orders should be placed during a year. 52 ÷ 7.8 = 6.6. This would indicate that a reorder should be placed every 6 or 7 weeks.

---

[5] This formula may also be stated in terms of unit sales, rather than of dollar sales. It would then read as follows:

$$\text{Reorder quantity in units} = \sqrt{\frac{2 \times \text{Annual unit sales} \times \text{Reorder cost}}{\text{Cost per unit} \times \text{Carrying rate}}}$$

For example, if the unit cost in this example is $10, the unit formula will yield 7.7 units instead of $77.

To calculate the cost at this point:[6]

$$\text{Reorder cost, } 7.8 \times \$.50 = \$3.90$$

$$\text{Carrying cost, } 10\% \text{ of } \frac{\$77^5}{2} = \underline{\$3.85}$$

$$\$7.75$$

ASSIGNMENT 9:

A turkish towel sells at the rate of $30 a day at cost (306 days a year). The carrying rate is estimated at 7% and the reorder cost at 60 cents an order.

1. What is the ideal reorder quantity?
2. What is the ideal reorder frequency?

DISCUSSION QUESTION:

What practical limitations are there to the general use of this method in stores?

Managerial Decisions

1. You are introducing unit control into your men's wear store. Among other lines, you carry suits, shirts, men's socks, neckwear, and men's jewelry. In which of these lines would you record sales and derive inventories, and in which would you take inventories and derive sales?

2. In your drugstore, you have decided to count inventory and analyze purchases in order to derive unit sales. Which of the following three systems would you use: (a) to take inventory at regular, periodic intervals; (b) to set a minimum quantity to indicate the reorder point; or (c) to allot a specific space

---

[6] If $77 worth is received at one time and if another order is not received until the former $77 worth is sold, the average investment will be one-half of $77, or $38.50. It is true that a reserve will have to be established to take care of delivery delay and changes in sales, but the $38.50 represents the investment over and above the reserve that will have to be carried irrespective of the frequency of reorder.

To prove that $77 is the ideal reorder quantity, the cost for a slightly larger and slightly lower quantity may be calculated at $87 and $67.

$$\text{At } \$87: \$600 \div 87 = 6.9, \text{ the number of orders a year.}$$

$$\text{Reorder cost } 6.9 \times \$.50 = \$3.45$$

$$\text{Carrying cost } 10\% \text{ of } \frac{\$87}{2} = \underline{\$4.35}$$

$$\$7.80$$

$$\text{At } \$67: \$600 \div 67 = 8.9, \text{ the number of orders a year.}$$

$$\text{Reorder cost } 8.9 \times \$.50 = \$4.45$$

$$\text{Carrying cost } 10\% \text{ of } \frac{\$67}{2} = \underline{\$3.35}$$

$$\$7.80$$

to each item so that the difference between the allotted space and the actual inventory on hand will reveal the need for replenishment?

ADDITIONAL ASSIGNMENTS

10. The average weekly sales of an article are sixteen pieces and it takes 3 weeks to obtain a reorder. Orders are placed once in 4 weeks, and an extra 2 weeks' supply is held as a reserve. If seventy are on hand and twelve on order, how many should now be ordered?

11. The sales of a staple item over a 10-week period are as follows:

1st week 68	6th week 37
2nd week 49	7th week 82
3rd week 77	8th week 25
4th week 40	9th week 35
5th week 27	10th week 41

It takes 1 week to secure a reorder and the unit of order is one dozen. There are fifty pieces on hand and orders are to be placed about once a month. An extra week's supply is carried as a reserve. How many should be ordered?

12. In a house furnishings department, a minimum of ten cans was set on March 1 for a certain item of paint. At that time there were twenty cans in stock. Whenever the minimum was reached, eighteen cans were ordered. On June 1, an analysis revealed that reorders were placed on March 20, April 8, April 25, May 15, and May 29, and that there were seven cans then in stock. In each case, goods were received within 6 days of the reorder date. No want slips for this item were turned in during the period.

(a) What changes, if any, should be made in this method of control, and why?

(b) What changes, if any, should be made in maximum and minimum quantities?

(c) If this item is to be offered as a special starting June 16, and its sales are expected to increase 50% over the average rate of the preceding 3 months, what quantities should be ordered on June 1?

13. Using the average weekly rates of sale given in assignments 10 and 11, calculate the probability reserves by means of the formula 2.3 × √Normal sales in planning period. How do these compare with the ones used in problems 10 and 11? Recalculate the two assignments using the "probability" reserves. Are the results materially different?

14. Sales, 25 a week; delivery, 2 weeks; reorder period, 2 weeks; unit of delivery, 1; on hand, 150. The reserve is planned as suggested in assignment 13.

(a) Set the maximum stock and determine the stock-turn over a 4-week period.

(b) Once stock has been adjusted to sales, what will be the yearly turn?

15. Estimated annual sales of a staple item are $400; markup is 35%; carrying rate is 7%; reorder cost is $1.00.

    (a) What is the ideal reorder quantity?

    (b) What is the ideal reorder period?

20   How to Plan Model Stocks
and Control Fashion Assortments

Buying plans should be the outgrowth of an assortment plan that outlines the composition of the stock to be made available to customers at a specific time in the future. This assortment ordinarily consists of types, prices, colors, and sizes and often includes other selection factors as well. In the case of staples and styles that continue in demand for a long period, individual pattern and style numbers may also be included in the assortment plan.

Once such plans have been made as to the desired assortment at a target date, it is possible to plan unit purchases for fashion goods, even in advance of viewing market offerings. There are two major ways to do this: one is to refer to the planned future stock for each price line or other control unit and then to calculate open-to-buy in much the same manner as that customarily used in connection with dollar control. The second is to build up the stock in each control unit to a "maximum" that is adequate to cover the planned basic assortment for the target date, the delivery period quantity that will be available, the reorder period quantity, and the possible sales increases above normal expectations that should be provided for. This is essentially the method described in the last chapter in connection with staple stocks.

DEFINITIONS

Model Stock. A planned assortment of units of merchandise balanced to anticipated customer demand and resulting in the planned stock-turn.

Basic Stock (for a control unit). The smallest number of pieces within a grouping of merchandise to provide sufficient sizes, colors, style, numbers, etc., to satisfy customer demand. It may also provide for more than one piece in a style number, size, and color combination so as to avoid a "hole" in the stock whenever a sale is made.

Sales Analysis System of Unit Control. A system of stock control by which the sales are analyzed in units as they occur by such factors as classification, price line, material, color, size, and style number. A perpetual inventory system is often maintained.

Physical Inventory System of Unit Control. A system of stock control whereby the stock is counted at periodic intervals and the unit sales are derived from the inventory and purchase data.

Reserve Requisition Control. A unit control system whereby all requisitions from reserve to forward stock are treated as sales.

A. MODEL STOCKS

1. Model stock plan.

● *Example:*

It is desired to work out a model stock plan for a men's furnishings department with an estimated volume of $100,000 a year. Past experience and inter-store comparisons suggest that, except for the busy Christmas season, the stock should equal about 2 months' supply; thus the annual rate of stock-turn (except for the Christmas season) is 6. Of the annual volume, $23,000 is expected in the month before Christmas, since this is a highly seasonal department. Through the rest of the year, however, sales are fairly constant each month. There are ten classifications in the department and sales are expected to be distributed as follows:

	Sales	Markups
Shirts	40%	38%
Pajamas	4	38
Neckwear	22	37
Hosiery	15	37
Underwear	10	37
Handkerchiefs	2.5	43
Accessories	1.5	36
Suspenders and garters	1	41
Jewelry and belts	2	45
Gloves	2	40
Total	100% Average	37.8%

For each of these classifications, information is available on sales by types, price lines, styles, colors, and sizes (when pertinent). In the case of the neckwear stock, there are two types: four-in-hands and bow ties. The former accounts for over 95% of the unit volume. Four price lines are carried in four-in-hands. In order of dollar sales volume, these are: $5.00, $4.00, $7.00, and $10.00, but the unit volume at $5.00 and $4.00 is about the same.

In $4.00, $5.00, and $7.00 four-in-hands, there are fancy and plain colors with the fancy outselling plain about 4 to 1. Other fancies are carried at $10.00.

Bow ties are carried only at $3, but in three types: adjustable, straight, and tuxedo. The adjustable ties are carried in navy and fancy colors and the other two types only in black. Tuxedos sell in twice the quantity of straights and adjustables in twice the quantity of tuxedos.

1. Prepare a stock plan in dollars for each classification.
2. Prepare a unit model stock plan for the neckwear classification, breaking down the dollar figure set for this classification in (1) into types and price lines. Assume the average retail price in this classification to be $5.00. Thus, the dollar allotment may be changed into the number of ties to stock.

Solution:

1. Planned annual sales. $100,000
   Estimated sales Nov. 25–Dec. 25 23,000

   Estimated sales for 11 months . . . . $ 77,000
   Estimated sales per normal month 7,000
   Planned basic stock (2 months' supply) 14,000

In distributing the $14,000 to classifications, sales are used as a guide, but it is felt that the turn in the larger classification should be somewhat greater than that in the small ones. Thus, stock percentages vary from sales percentages.

Classifications	Sales	Stock	Stock
Shirts	40%	37%	$5,180
Pajamas	4	6	840
Neckwear	22	20	2,800
Hosiery	15	13	1,820
Underwear	10	10	1,400
Handkerchiefs	2.5	3.5	490
Accessories	1.5	2.5	350
Suspenders and garters	1.0	2.0	280
Jewelry and belts	2.0	3.0	420
Gloves	2.0	3.0	420
Total	100.0%	100.0%	$14,000

2. Neckwear:
   $2,800 ÷ $5.00 = 560, the approximate number of ties to stock; 92% (less than the sales percentage) of 560 is about 516, the approximate number of four-in-hands to carry, or 43 dozen. This

leaves only 4 dozen for bow ties. The breakdown of these figures by prices and color is presented in the following chart.

MODEL STOCK FOR TIES

Price Line	Type	Pattern Color	Stock Units	Stock Dozen	Stock at Retail	Cost Per Dozen	Total Cost
					Four-in-Hands		
$4.00		Fancy	156	13	624.00		
		Plain	48	4	192.00		
	Total		204	17	816.00	30.00	$ 510.00
$5.00		Fancy	156	13	780.00		
		Plain	48	4	240.00		
	Total		204	17	1,020.00	37.50	637.50
$7.00		Fancy	60	5	420.00		
		Plain	24	2	168.00		
	Total		84	7	588.00	50.00	350.00
$10.00	Total	Fancy	24	2	240.00	75.00	1,500.00
	Four-in-Hands Total		516	43	2,664.00		1,647.50
					Bow Ties		
	Adjustable	Navy – Polka Dot	12	1	36.00	22.50	22.50
$3.00		Fancy	12	1	36.00	22.50	22.50
	Straight Assorted 31"–32"–33"	Black	12	1	36.00	20.50	20.50
	Tuxedo Butterfly – Black		12	1	36.00	22.50	22.50
	Bow Total		48	4	144.00		88.00
	Planned Grand Totals		564	47	2,808.00		1,735.50

38.2% markup on retail.

ASSIGNMENT 1:

The planned stock in a women's shoe department at the beginning and end of a spring season was $56,000. Of this amount $5,000 was planned as the findings and slipper stock and $6,000 as clearance stock and specials. The balance was intended for the regular assortment of shoes.

On the basis of the sales in pairs during the preceding spring season, the following plans were made:

Price Line	Actual % of Unit Sales	Planned % of Unit Sales	Planned % of Unit Stock
$ 8.50	22.5	21.5	21.0
10.00	28.0	32.0	30.0
12.00	38.7	34.7	32.0
15.00	8.8	9.8	13.0
18.00	2.0	2.0	4.0
	100.0%	100.0%	100.0%

The planned distribution of sales varied from the past results because it was decided to increase sales at $10, as compared with sales at $8.50 and $12. Stock plans were varied slightly from sales plans in order to maintain good assortments in all price lines.

On the basis of the planned stock distribution, the average selling price per pair was determined and applied to the planned dollar stock of women's shoes. The number of pairs to stock at each price was then determined by applying the stock percentages.

Except for the two highest price lines, it was thought necessary to have a 56-pair schedule; that is, 56 pairs of shoes in each style were required in order to have a complete assortment of sizes and widths. For $15 shoes a 36-pair schedule, and for $18 shoes a 24-pair schedule, was deemed sufficient. On the basis of this plan, the number of styles to be carried at each price line was determined.

The next step was to distribute the number of styles in each price to include three classifications of shoes. In general, it seemed wise to have about 50% of the styles in Classification 1 shoes, about 30% in Classification 2 shoes, and 20% in Classification 3 shoes. The next question was to determine an adequate size distribution in each style. An analysis of past sales revealed the percentage of sales occurring in each size and width. On the basis of these percentages, the following size schedule was worked out for 56 pairs. The standard was not rigidly applied, but was varied according to last, pattern, style, and price of each style number. High-priced shoes, for example, were ordinarily sold in smaller sizes than were low-priced shoes.

STANDARD 56–PAIR SIZE SCHEDULE

Size	AAA	AA	A	B	C	D	E
4				1			
4½				1	1		
5		1	1	2	1		
5½		1	1	2	2		
6	1	1	2	3	2	1	
6½	1	2	2	2	1	1	1
7	1	2	2	1	1	1	
7½	1	1	1	1	1		
8	1	1	1	1	1		
8½	1	1	1	1			

If fewer than 56 pairs were carried in a style, the same proportions applied, except that it was sometimes desirable to have the 56-pair schedule represent the combined stock of two or three styles in a price line. For example, in the $18 price line, instead of having the 24 pairs in each style concentrated on the few best-selling sizes and widths, three styles could be combined and distributed over the 56-pair schedule. Thus, stock in the expensive shoes would be carried in all the sizes and widths in the 56-pair schedule, but not all sizes and widths would be carried for any one style number. The three styles would be alternated; for example, Style Number 100 might be carried in full sizes and Style Number 101 in the half sizes.

1. Plan the number of pairs of shoes to carry at each price line at the beginning of the season.
2. Plan the number of styles to carry in each price line and in each classification within each price line.
3. Prepare 36- and 24-pair size schedules for the higher-priced lines.

DISCUSSION QUESTION:

What merchandise classifications in women's shoes may prove to be more useful than the following possibility: morning, afternoon, and evening shoes?

2. Sales distribution for model stocks.

● *Example:*

An analysis of the sales of a certain type of men's shirts by size for the past season revealed the following:

Size	
14	95
14½	242
15	390
15½	484
16	290
16½	195
17	104
Total	1,800

It is believed that the assortment at each size was adequate and that the sales thus reflect demand. In buying shirts in the future, in what ratio should each size be bought, expressed both in percentage of total and in terms of a dozen? (Assume no stock on hand.)

Solution:

Size	Approximate Ratios
14	5.2% of 12 = 1
14½	13.4% of 12 = 2
15	22.0% of 12 = 2
15½	26.9% of 12 = 3
16	16.3% of 12 = 2
16½	10.5% of 12 = 1
17	5.7% of 12 = 1
Total	100.0% of 12 = 12

Note: To avoid an overstock of end sizes, some styles should not be bought in sizes 14 or 17 at all.

ASSIGNMENT 2:

In the department above, the sales by color were as follows:

White	310
Blue, solid or striped	824
Reds and tans	296
Miscellaneous	370
Total	1,800

In what color proportions should each dozen shirts be bought, assuming that the distribution of sales by color will be approximately the same this season as they were last season.

DISCUSSION QUESTION:

Even though buyers attempt to purchase sizes and colors in proportion to expected demand, they are commonly over-stocked on end sizes and secondary colors and do not have enough of the best sellers. Why is this probably true and how may it be avoided?

Managerial Decisions

1. You, the owner of a shoe store, have developed a model stock for your spring season. In what respects should your model stock for the fall differ?

2. During recent years the concept of a basic stock has been developed by merchandising experts. Should a merchant plan a basic stock as well as a model stock? How would they differ?

B. CONTROLLING FASHION STOCKS

3. Unit purchase planning with a planned closing stock.

● *Example:*

> In November, a buyer of boys' clothing is planning his spring purchases of suits to sell at $29.95. In view of current stocks and of sales and purchase expectations for the rest of the fall and winter season, he expects to have 24 of these suits on hand on February 1st next, and he wishes to have only 12 on hand by the end of the season, July 31st. Last year's sales during the 6-month period equaled 120 suits, and he expects sales this year to be about 10% ahead of last. Of the season's total sales, 10% is normally obtained in February and 14% in March. What are the planned purchases for the spring season? About how much should he order for February and for March delivery?

Solution:

> Planned purchases for season = 12 (closing stock) + 132 (planned sales) – 24 (opening stock) = 120. Since 10% of the season's volume is expected in February, and 14% in March, 12 might be ordered for February delivery and 17 for March. But, in practice, stock is generally built up early in the season, to provide ample stock at mid-season. The buyer, therefore, might decide to bring in one-half his requirements (60) before the mid-season, volume period, starting April 1st.

ASSIGNMENT 3:

> In a misses' dress department, a buyer wants 300 $25 street dresses on hand on June 1st; he expects to sell 350 during the month and to mark down 24 to lower prices. On May 1st, he has 335 on hand and 89 on order for May delivery. What is his planned purchase figure and his open-to-buy for the month?

DISCUSSION QUESTIONS:

> Should unit open-to-buy for outer apparel be calculated for each price line, for each size, for each color, for each style number? Which would be the most useful?

4. Planning purchases by sizes and colors — sales to date of delivery in same proportion as stocks desired at delivery date.

Example:

> For the $10 price line in classification *A* of a department, the plans in

units for September are as follows:

```
Stock end of month. . . . . . . . . . . . . . . . . . . . . . . . . . 700 pieces
Stock beginning . . . . . . . . . . . . . . . . . . . . . . . . . . . . 550  "
Sales. . . . . . . . . . . . . . . . . . . . . . . . . . . . . . . . . . . . 425  "
Markdowns into this price line from higher price lines . . . .  25  "
Markdowns out of this price line . . . . . . . . . . . . . . . .  50  "
```

The following information is available on August 15 on which to base the buying plans for deliveries the second week in September, since delivery takes 3 weeks.

1. 20% of September planned purchases allotted to 2nd week in September.

2. Stock commitments planned in the following proportions:

Colors		Sizes	
Black	30%	A	20%
Brown.	20	B	30
Blue	10	C	35
Other	40	D	15
	100%		100%

3. The following represents the stock on hand and on order on August 15:

Colors	On Hand	On Order	Sizes	On Hand	On Order
Black	125	65	A	75	45
Brown.	125	35	B	200	55
Blue	20	25	C	120	90
Other	230	75	D	105	10
	500	200		500	200

Prepare a buying plan for the buyer by colors and sizes covering the orders to be placed during the week of August 15 for delivery in the second week in September.

Solution:

Planned purchases = Sales + Markdowns out − Markdowns in + Planned increase in stock = 425 + 50 − 25 + 150 = 600 (units)

Planned purchases for 2nd week in September = 20% of 600, or 120 units.

Total commitments after orders are placed during the week of August 15:

500 (on hand) + 200 (formerly on order) + 120 (new order) = 820.

Colors	%	Units	Commitments Old		O.T.B.
Black	30	246	− 190	=	56
Brown	20	164	− 160	=	4
Blue	10	82	− 45	=	37
Other	40	328	− 305	=	23
	100%	820	− 700	=	120

Sizes	%	Units	Commitments Old		O.T.B.	O.T.B. Adjusted
A	20	164	− 120	=	44	41
B	30	246	− 255	=	−9	......
C	35	287	− 210	=	77	74
D	15	123	− 115	=	8	5
	100%	820	− 700	=	120	120

ASSIGNMENT 4:

1. At the end of the second week of a 4-week month (April), the following information is available in regard to a $5 price line in Classification *B* of a department:

	Number of Pieces
Stock on hand	120
Stock on order for prompt delivery	24
Sales last year, April	123
Sales last year, April to date	78
Sales last year, May	80
Sales this year, April to date	86

The following facts are also available in regard to the department and Classification *B*:

The planned department stock for May 1 is $24,400; sales in Classification *B* in May are approximately 10% of the department's sales; and an average stock-turn is planned for classification *B*. Sales in the $5 price line of Classification *B* are estimated at 50% of the classification's sales, but it is felt that twice the average turn should be obtained in this price line.

(a) Find the planned stock in units for May 1 for the $5 price line.
(b) Find the planned sales for the balance of April in view of last year's results and actual sales to date.
(c) Find the open-to-buy in units for the balance of April.

2. A physical inventory and check-up on outstanding orders by color and size supplies the following information:

GOODS ON HAND AND ON ORDER IN $5 PRICE LINE CLASSIFICATION B

Color	34	36	38	40	42	Total
Prints	10	6	4	3	7	30
Blue	8	2	5	12	7	34
Brown	11	10	16	3	0	40
Red	1	2	3	5	4	15
White	6	4	9	1	5	25
Total	36	24	37	24	23	144

An analysis of actual sales in the classification, supplemented by the fashionist's observation, indicates that the potential demand is about as follows:

Color		Size	
Prints	35%	34	15%
Blue	20	36	20
Brown	18	38	30
Red	15	40	25
White	12	42	10
Total	100%	Total	100%

Take the open-to-buy found in Part 1 and distribute it by color and size so as to bring the stock as nearly as possible into a model condition. In doing this, it is suggested that the open-to-buy be added to the stock on hand and on order and that this total be distributed according to color and size. (As an alternative method, the closing stock may be planned by color and size and sales estimated in each for the balance of the month. The former method involves less calculation.) It should be borne in mind that a higher-than-average turnover may well be planned for prints and for size 38, where the sales are large.

DISCUSSION QUESTION:

As a matter of policy, when the stock of certain sizes and colors is so large as to make it impossible for the open-to-buy to provide adequately for needed sizes and colors, should the open-to-buy be adhered to? Illustrate your discussion from the above problems.

5. **Planning purchase by sizes and colors — sales to date of delivery in different proportions than planned stocks at delivery date.**

Example:

1. The following figures for February are available for a $7.50 line in Class *B* of Department 44:

> Planned stock E.O.M.. . . . . 400 units
> Planned stock B.O.M.. 350   "
> Planned sales month (4 weeks). . . 200   "
> Planned markdowns out 25   "
> Planned markdowns in 15   "

Purchases to be distributed as follows:

> 1st week, 20%
> 2nd week, 25%
> 3rd week, 25%
> 4th week, 30%

Plan purchases for each week of February.

2. Since 2 weeks must be allowed for delivery, the planned purchases for the 1st week in February must be ordered the middle of January. At this time, the stock on hand is 300, and the stock on order for January delivery is 110. No orders have as yet been placed for February. Sales for the rest of January are estimated at 60.

Of the present stock, one-third is in black, and of the outstanding orders, 15% is in black, but during the early part of February the buyer wishes to have only 25% of his stock in black. Of his sales, probably 30% will be in black during the balance of January.

Of the present stock, 20% is navy, and 25% of the outstanding orders are navy, but during early February, 30% of the stock should be navy. During the balance of the month probably only 10% of the sales will be navy.

Of the present stock, 25% is brown, and of the outstanding orders, 30% are for brown. Of the sales to the end of the month, 35% will be brown. During early February, 20% of the stock should be brown.

How many black articles, how many navy, how many brown, and how many of the remaining colors should be ordered now for delivery during the first week in February?

Solution:

1. Planned purchases for February: 400 (E.O.M. stock) + 200 (Sales) + 25 (Markdowns out) – 15 (Markdowns in) – 350 (B.O.M. stock) = 260

1st week	20%	52
2nd "	25%	65
3rd "	25%	65
4th "	30% . . . . :	78
	Total.	260

2.

	Stock on Hand	Stock on Order	Sales	Estimated Stock, February 1
Total.	300	110	60	350
Black	100	16	18	98
Navy.	60	27	6	81
Brown.	75	33	21	87
Balance	65	34	15	84

Total commitments, 1st week in February:

350 (estimated on hand) + 52 (current order) = 402

Planned Distribution	%	Units	Estimated Stock, Feb. 1	O.T.B.	O.T.B. Adjusted
Total.	100	402	350	52	52
Black	25	101	98	3	0
Navy.	30	120	81	39	36
Brown.	20	80	87	–7	0
Balance	25	101	84	17	16

ASSIGNMENT 5:

On May 10, $10,000 worth of orders are to be placed for June delivery. Stock on hand is $25,000 and on order $15,000 for May delivery. The planned stock for June 1 is $20,000.

Under what conditions is it permissible to distribute $50,000 ($25,000 + $15,000 + $10,000) according to color requirements in June, subtracting from the total for each color the stock in that color *now* on hand and on order?

DISCUSSION QUESTION:

Can stocks be kept reasonably well balanced by color without going to the trouble of working out an open-to-buy for each color?

6. Markdowns and price lines.

Example:

A department expects to sell its units in the following proportions:

Price Line		Unit Sales
$ .89	. . . .	15%
1.00	. . . .	35
2.00	. . . .	30
3.00	. . . .	20
	Total.	100%

The $.89 price is solely a clearance price and goods are generally marked down from one regular price to the next lower one. In what proportions should the merchandise be purchased, assuming that purchases should be distributed according to sales?

Solution:

Price Lines	Sales at Regular Prices		Total Sales at Regular Prices		Purchases
$1.00	35%	÷	85%	=	41.2%
2.00	30	÷	85	=	35.3
3.00	20	÷	85	=	23.5
	85%				100.0%

If it is expected that the markdowns from $3 will be relatively heavy, the percentages may be adjusted somewhat. As the figures stand, the markdowns are about 8%.

ASSIGNMENT 6:

In a sport coat section, all markdowns are taken to special clearance prices rather than to regular prices. An analysis of sales in units reveals the following:

	Price	% of Unit Sales
Clearance	$ 5.00	10
Clearance	7.50	8
Clearance	10.00	11
Clearance	12.50	9
Clearance	15.00	2
Regular	16.75	4
Clearance	19.75	3
Regular	25.00	15
Regular	29.50	6
Clearance	32.50	2
Regular	35.00	10
Regular	39.50	8
Clearance	45.00	4
Regular	49.50	4
Clearance	55.00	1
Regular	65.00	3
Total		100%

In what proportion should the goods be bought for stock?

DISCUSSION QUESTION:

If most goods that are marked down are put into regular lower price lines rather than into special clearance prices, is an analysis of sales by price line a satisfactory guide for buying in the future?

7. Open-to-buy for a price line. Maximum method.

● *Example:*

The rate of sale of afternoon dresses in a $25 price line is estimated at 40 a week. In order to have an adequate assortment in this price line, the buyer estimates that at least 60 units will be required. In addition, he decides to carry an extra week's supply to allow for a possible increase in sales between delivery and reorder periods.[1] He plans to reorder every week but it takes nearly 3 weeks for delivery after an order is placed. On October 12, there are 115 dresses in stock and 80 are on order. Find the reorder quantity and the annual turnover.

Solution:

The basic assortment of 60 units plus 40 for sales fluctuations calls for a safety factor of 100 units.

$$\text{Minimum stock} = \text{Reserve} + (\text{Delivery period} \times \text{Weekly sales})$$
$$= 100 + (3 \times 40)$$
$$= 100 + 120$$
$$= 220$$

$$\text{Maximum stock} = \text{Minimum} + (\text{Reorder period} \times \text{Weekly sales})$$
$$= 220 + (1 \times 40)$$
$$= 220 + 40$$
$$= 260$$

$$\text{Reorder quantity} = \text{Maximum} - (\text{On hand} + \text{On order})$$
$$= 260 - (115 + 80)$$
$$= 65$$

$$\text{Sales at annual rate} = 40 \times 52$$
$$= 2,080$$

$$\text{Average stock} = \text{Reserve} + \tfrac{1}{2}\ \text{Normal reorder quantity}$$
$$= 100 + (\tfrac{1}{2}\ \text{of } 40)$$
$$= 100 + 20$$
$$= 120$$

$$\text{Annual turnover} = \frac{\text{Sales}}{\text{Average stock}} = \frac{2,080}{120} = 17.33$$

ASSIGNMENT 7:

In the $16.95 price line, the rate of sale is twenty-five a week. Reorders are placed every 2 weeks and reorders take 2 weeks. The lowest permissible assortment must provide six sizes with at least twelve dresses in each in order to provide styles and colors. A further reserve of one week's supply is required to provide for contingencies. If 100 are now on hand and twelve on order, how many should be ordered how?

---

[1] See section 19A for method of setting the reserves on the basis of a statistical distribution.

DISCUSSION QUESTION:

Compare this method with the closing stock method used in problems 1, 3, and 4.

8. Open-to-buy for a price line. Maximum based on stock-turn.

Example:

In the $6 price line for handbags, stock-turn of 13 times a year is desired. Delivery takes 3 weeks and reorders are planned for 2-week control periods, with the actual placement of orders distributed over these 2-week periods. Sales average about 40 a week, and 155 are now on hand and 75 are now on order. What is the open-to-buy for the 2-week control period just ahead?

Solution:

Maximum stock may be computed as:
Average stock for period + Delivery period + Reorder period.

```
Average stock period (in weeks supply) 52 ÷ 13 = 4
Delivery period . . . . . . . . . . . . . . . . . . . . . .= 3
Reorder period . . . . . . . . . . . . . . . . . . . . . .= 2
Maximum . . . . . . . . . . . . . . . . . . . . . . . . . .= 9
Maximum in units, 9 × 40. . . . . . . . . . .   360
On hand (155) + On order (75) . . . . . . .   230
O.T.B. . . . . . . . . . . . . . . . . . . . . . .   130
```

Note: If the bi-weekly reorders are to be placed all at once, the maximum should be computed as:

Average stock + Delivery + ½ Reorder quantity

This would make the maximum 8 weeks' supply, or 320, and the O.T.B. 90.

ASSIGNMENT 8:

In the $7.50 price line in a millinery store, a stock-turn of 17 times a year is desired. The manager plans his ordering by bi-weekly control periods, and it takes 2 weeks for delivery after a reorder is placed.
On March 1, this year, sixty $7.50 hats are in stock and forty are on order. The sales by weeks last year were as follows:

Week Ending	Number of Sales
March 9	18
" 16	20
" 23	15
" 30	25
April 6	22
" 13	28
" 20	45
" 27	30
May 4	24
" 11	20
" 18	19

To date, March 1, sales of $7.50 millinery are running about 5% behind last year. Easter of last year was April 21, and this year is April 12.

1. Plan the maximum stock for the $7.50 price line.
2. Find the open-to-buy.
3. If, on March 15, eighty hats are on hand and fifty on order, what is the open-to-buy?

DISCUSSION QUESTION:

If reorders are placed only at the beginning of each 2-week period, rather than distributed over the 2-week period, what would be the effect on the open-to-buy?

Managerial Decisions

1. You have decided to control your fashion stocks by analyzing sales daily and deriving inventory information. You wish, so far as possible, to obtain your sales data from saleschecks. What problems are you likely to encounter and how would you handle each? What are the pros and cons of using an electronic point-of-sale register rather than saleschecks?

2. A variety store records daily sales of frankfurters by means of a tally kept by the waitress at the counter. If you were the manager, would you continue this method of unit control? Why?

ADDITIONAL ASSIGNMENTS

9. Price line analysis for model stocks.

In an inexpensive dress department, sales during a 3-month period were as follows (the dresses have been put into stock in the percentages indicated in the second column):

Price Lines	Unit Sales at Each Price	Unit Retail Purchases at Each Price
$16.75	21.6%	38.1%
15.00	5.5	1.3
14.00	1.1	
13.95	2.8	2.5
12.85	6.6	
12.75	0.5	0.5
11.95	4.2	4.0
11.85	2.9	
10.00	31.2	53.6
9.85	0.9	
8.95	4.0	
7.95	12.7	
7.50	3.1	
6.95	0.5	
5.00	2.4	
Total.	100.0%	100.0%

1. Estimate the percentages in which the stock should be purchased.
2. Find the average sales price and the average price at which the goods were put into stock.
3. Find the percentage of markdowns.

10. Model stock problem (fall season).

You have just been appointed buyer of misses' dresses for the Blank Specialty Store. As your first assignment, the owner has asked you to analyze the daytime dress inventory and to take such measures as are necessary to bring the stock into a well-balanced condition. The following information is given.

The department features budget fashion merchandise between $15 and $35 retail, with 70% of the total volume being done in the price ranges up to and including $25. Past sales records indicate the following percentage breakdown by sizes:

Sizes	10	12	14	16	18	20
Percentage of Sales	6	21	25	24	15	9

The five outstanding fall colors in the order of their importance are black, brown, blue, red (including wine and rust), and green.

Blacks represent approximately two-thirds of fall sales, with the other four colors spread out fairly evenly. All other shades combined are no more important than any one of these colors in sales volume.

The following styles, based on their sales performance, are considered good running numbers. The starred items are to be advertised in 10 days:

A	719	D	575	J	1645
*B	149	*F	221	K	905

Each individual dress has been aged according to the week of the year it was received in stock. You are making this analysis the beginning of the 36th week, about September 1st.

The total planned stock figure this week for the polyester and blends classification is 4½ weeks' supply, or 195 units. The actual stock on hand and on order in this classification is indicated in the table below. The planned stock figure for the end of the 38th week should equal 4 weeks' supply.

The estimated sales for the coming 7 weeks are as follows:

Week	Units	Week	Units
36	35	40	50
37	40	41	55
38	45	42	60
39	50		

Sales from the middle of October through November are expected to average 60 per week. Reorders are to be placed every week; delivery takes 2 to 3 weeks.

SEPTEMBER DAYTIME DRESS
INVENTORY — POLYESTER AND BLENDS

SIZE 10 Style #	Color	Retail $	Age (week)	SIZE 12 (cont'd) Style #	Color	Retail $	Age (week)
A 461	black	25.	28	A 730	rust	25.	34
A 470	green	30.	31				
A 594	black	25.	28	B 172	black	20.	34
A 627	red	25.	30	B 195	gray	20.	35
A 719	black	25.	34	B 221	blue	20.	35
A 720	brown	30.	34				
				D 575	blue	20.	34
B 149	gold	20.	33	D 827	beige	25.	34
B 172	green	20.	34	D 830	blue	25.	35
C 214	black	20.	34	E 170	beige	30.	29
C 331	red	20.	34	E 175	black	25.	30
				E 175	brown	25.	30
D 575	black	20.	34	E 178	green	30.	30
				E 180	red	30.	32
SIZE 12				E 183	black	30.	32
A 461	black	25.	28	F 220	black	15.	32
A 465	green	20.	30	F 221	brown	15.	33
A 470	black	30.	31	F 222	blue	20.	29
A 594	brown	25.	28	F 225	black	20.	30

SEPTEMBER DAYTIME DRESS
INVENTORY — POLYESTER AND BLENDS (Continued)

Style #	Color	Retail $	Age (week)	Style #	Color	Retail $	Age (week)
SIZE 12 (cont'd)				*SIZE 14 (cont'd)*			
F 234	gray	15.	31	E 178	brown	30.	30
				E 181	black	30.	32
G 960	beige	35.	35	E 179	red	25.	30
G 1021	blue	35.	35	E 168	green	30.	34
				E 165	brown	20.	35
H 411	black	30.	36	E 195	blue	20.	34
H 414	green	20.	33				
H 516	rust	20.	33	F 220	blue	15.	32
H 519	brown	25.	34	F 225	brown	20.	30
H 534	red	30.	31	F 227	gold	20.	30
H 587	gray	20.	33	F 235	red	15.	31
H 619	brown	15.	31	F 275	green	20.	31
H 622	green	20.	31	F 269	black	20.	30
H 625	beige	30.	34				
H 700	beige	25.	34	G 960	brown	35.	35
				G 975	green	15.	29
J 1340	blue	20.	34	G 971	beige	30.	34
J 1395	black	20.	36	G 985	black	15.	29
J 1460	purple	30.	35	G 1036	red	20.	33
J 1620	black	20.	31				
J 1627	green	20.	28	H 411	blue	30.	36
J 1645	red	25.	34	H 519	brown	25.	34
J 1652	brown	20.	34	H 627	beige	20.	31
				H 503	gray	20.	33
K 900	gold	30.	35	H 414	blue	20.	33
K 905	beige	15.	35	H 690	brown	30.	31
K 923	rust	15.	29	H 775	green	15.	28
K 932	black	35.	30	H 309	black	25.	34
K 949	black	35.	32	H 462	red	20.	31
K 964	gray	30.	32	H 700	brown	25.	34
K 965	blue	25.	29	H 587	green	20.	33
SIZE 14				J 1340	brown	20.	34
				J 1443	purple	20.	31
A 627	blue	25.	30	J 1447	brown	20.	28
A 395	black	25.	32	J 1639	black	20.	29
A 703	brown	25.	31				
A 719	blue	25.	34	K 900	green	30.	35
A 635	green	25.	28	K 973	gray	20.	27
A 731	red	20.	31	K 949	blue	35.	32
B 149	brown	20.	33	*SIZE 16*			
B 137	black	20.	34				
B 671	red	25.	34	A 461	gold	25.	28
				A 470	blue	30.	31
C 214	green	20.	34	A 642	black	25.	34
C 439	black	25.	35	A 741	red	20.	35
C 473	rust	25.	34	A 562	gold	20.	34
				A 742	brown	25.	28
D 575	blue	20.	34				
D 583	blue	25.	35	B 249	purple	20.	31
D 591	brown	25.	32	B 203	green	20.	30
				B 137	black	20.	34
E 175	black	25.	30				

SEPTEMBER DAYTIME DRESS
INVENTORY — POLYESTER AND BLENDS (Continued)

SIZE 16 (cont'd)

Style #	Color	Retail $	Age (week)
C 349	black	25.	35
C 191	red	20.	31
C 604	black	25.	28
C 331	brown	20.	34
D 575	blue	20.	34
D 583	brown	25.	35
D 572	green	20.	31
E 170	beige	30.	29
E 175	black	25.	30
E 172	red	30.	31
E 181	gold	30.	32
E 165	blue	20.	35
E 162	red	30.	32
E 172	brown	15.	29
F 220	blue	15.	32
F 228	black	20.	31
F 262	green	35.	30
F 409	black	25.	29
G 960	brown	35.	35
G 1021	green	35.	35
G 987	blue	25.	34
G 963	brown	25.	29
G 943	green	25.	34
G 931	blue	20.	30
G 1025	gold	20.	33
K 900	blue	30.	35
K 932	black	35.	30
K 962	gray	30.	32
K 925	rust	25.	30
K 935	red	30.	32

SIZE 18

Style #	Color	Retail $	Age (week)
A 461	blue	25.	28
A 472	red	25.	34
A 470	black	30.	31
A 435	brown	25.	35
A 622	brown	20.	31
A 543	green	20.	35
A 719	gold	25.	34
A 641	black	25.	34
A 725	green	25.	28
B 195	brown	20.	35
B 143	blue	20.	35
B 171	green	20.	30
B 257	purple	20.	31
B 205	blue	30.	32

SIZE 18 (cont'd)

Style #	Color	Retail $	Age (week)
C 214	blue	20.	34
C 443	black	25.	34
C 472	gray	25.	34
C 187	green	20.	31
D 575	green	20.	34
D 826	blue	25.	34
D 561	beige	25.	31
D 603	black	20.	34
F 222	purple	20.	29
F 234	green	15.	31
F 226	green	20.	31
F 209	blue	15.	31
F 243	black	20.	30
J 1607	blue	25.	34
J 1641	red	25.	34
J 1460	purple	30.	35
K 907	green	20.	31
K 923	black	15.	29

SIZE 20

Style #	Color	Retail $	Age (week)
A 461	red	25.	28
A 772	brown	25.	31
A 632	green	20.	28
A 719	gold	25.	34
A 621	red	25.	30
B 142	green	20.	29
B 135	red	20.	27
B 160	red	25.	28
D 575	green	20.	34
D 506	brown	25.	28
D 770	green	25.	29
D 603	black	20.	34
E 175	brown	25.	30
E 185	green	30.	32
E 192	blue	20.	31
F 220	blue	15.	32
F 273	black	25.	29
F 225	blue	20.	30
G 935	green	20.	30
H 507	blue	20.	31
H 623	purple	30.	28
H 906	rust	25.	32
H 913	green	25.	20
H 631	rust	20.	30

Outstanding Orders
(For delivery in 1 and 2 weeks)

SIZE 10				SIZE 16		
Style #	Color	Retail $		Style #	Color	Retail $
A 435	black (2 dresses)	25.		J 1645	wine	25.
A 719	blue	25.		K 900	blue	30.
A 745	brown	20.		K 905	black	15.
B 149	green	20.		K 905	red	15.
D 575	green	20.		K 905	blue	15.
				K 962	green	30.
				K 949	blue	35.

SIZE 12				SIZE 18		
B 149	black (3 dresses)	20.		A 470	brown	30.
B 149	purple	20.		A 719	black	25.
C 331	gold	20.		A 719	blue	25.
F 225	wine	20.		B 149	blue	20.
J 1645	gray	25.		B 149	green	20.
J 1652	brown	20.		B 205	blue	30.
				C 604	brown	25.

SIZE 14				SIZE 18 (cont.)		
A 719	black	25.		D 575	rust	20.
A 719	brown	25.		D 603	green	20.
A 719	gray	25.		E 165	brown	20.
A 635	blue	25.		F 221	blue	15.
B 149	black	20.		F 221	green	15.
B 149	red	20.		F 221	blue	15.
B 671	green	25.		K 905	black	15.
C 473	wine	25.		K 905	brown	15.
D 575	brown	20.		K 923	brown	15.
D 583	brown	25.				
E 175	blue	25.		SIZE 20		
F 221	blue	15.		A 461	blue	25.
G 985	brown	15.		A 719	rust	25.
				B 142	red	20.
SIZE 16				B 149	black	20.
A 470	black (2 dresses)	30.		C 443	gray	25.
A 719	blue	25.		D 506	brown	25.
B 149	blue	20.		D 575	black	20.
B 137	brown	20.		F 220	black	15.
C 604	blue	25.		F 221	blue	15.
D 575	black (2 dresses)	20.		G 935	black	20.
E 165	beige	20.		H 913	blue	25.
F 221	blue	15.		J 1645	wine	25.
J 1645	black	25.		K 905	blue	15.
				K 923	green	15.

1. How many dresses should be ordered during the 36th week?
2. What is wrong with the present stock assortment and the outstanding orders by size, color, and price?
3. What sizes, colors, and prices should be ordered at once?
4. What styles should be reordered and in what size and color assortments?

11. Buying plan for a fitted suitcase classification of a leather goods department.

Stock on hand, January 31 . . . . $1,935
Sales during February and March last year 2,535
Planned sales, February and March this year 2,900
Stock desired, March 31 of this year 3,000

Stock, by pieces at each size and price, and sales last year for February and March were as follows:

Price	Stock January 31, This Year Sizes 18	20	22	24	Totals		Sales February and March, Last Year Sizes 18	20	22	24	Totals	
$ 20 . . .	3	0	1	2	6	$120	5	3	7	3	18	$360
25 . . .	1	3	1	2	7	175	3	2	4	2	11	275
30 . . .	1	0	3	0	4	120	1	2	1	1	5	150
35 . . .	0	1	0	0	1	35	2	0	5	2	9	315
40 . . .	2	0	1	1	4	160	0	0	1	0	1	40
45 . . .	1	1	2	1	5	225	1	1	1	1	4	180
50 . . .	0	0	2	0	2	100	1	1	0	1	3	150
55 . . .	0	0	0	0	0	0	0	2	0	2	4	220
60 . . .	0	0	0	0	0	0	0	0	0	0	0	0
65 . . .	0	1	3	0	4	260	0	0	0	0	0	0
70 . . .	1	0	1	1	3	210	1	0	2	2	5	350
75 . . .	0	1	0	0	1	75	0	1	1	1	3	225
85 . . .	0	1	1	1	3	255	0	0	1	1	2	170
100 . . .	0	0	1	1	2	200	0	0	0	1	1	100
Total . .	9	8	16	9	42	$1,935	14	12	23	17	66	$2,535

1. Distribute the total stock requirements (planned closing stock of $3,000, plus planned sales of $2,900) in proportion to last year's sales by price lines.
2. Distribute stock requirements in each price line by sizes.

3. Find the planned purchases by sizes.
4. What advantage would there be in planning closing stocks for each price line in different proportions from sales at each price line?

21   Invoice Mathematics

An invoice or bill sent by a vendor is payable at a time specified and is usually subject to certain discount deductions if the bill is paid promptly. These conditions are called the "terms" under which the goods are sold.

The usual objective of granting a cash discount is to offer the retailer a premium for paying promptly. The amount of time allowed to pay the bill (dating) varies among types of merchandise and depends on a number of factors, such as the approximate length of time it takes a retailer to re-sell a substantial part of the goods purchased, and the time required by the retailer to receive the goods from the factory, and to check, mark, and prepare the merchandise for sale.

Discounts are sometimes granted for buying in quantity or seasonally. Trade discounts are given because a buyer is a member of a particular functional group. This often occurs when goods are quoted at list prices that are suggested retail prices and buyers are granted substantial discounts, roughly equivalent to their markup requirements.

Still another phase of invoice calculation involves import duty and the determination of landed cost. Multipliers must be worked out so that a buyer can conveniently translate a quoted foreign price into terms of landed cost.

DEFINITIONS

Cash Discount. A discount allowed by a vendor for paying the invoice within an agreed time. *Example:* 2/10 means 2% is allowed if the bill is paid within 10 days of the date of the bill.

Trade Discount. A discount allowed only to certain classes of buyers, such as jobbers or other middlemen, and in some cases to retailers. Such discounts are deductible, no matter when the invoice is paid. Synonym: Functional Discount.

Discount Series. Trade discounts are often quoted in a series, such as 20%, 10%, 5%. Each discount in the series is deductible from the preceding net amount. *Example:* $100 less 20%, 10%, 5% means you may deduct 20% from $100, 10% from the balance of $80, and 5% from $72.

"On" Percentage. A single percentage which, when multiplied by the gross billed price, will give the net price. It is commonly used as a short-cut method when a series of trade discounts must be deducted.

List Price. The gross billed price, which is subject to a trade discount. In some cases, the list price is the retail price suggested by a manufacturer of a branded product.

Quantity Discount. A discount allowed when a given quantity is purchased. It is an inducement to buy a larger than average amount and may be deducted, regardless of when the bill is paid.

Anticipation. An extra discount commonly allowed by vendors when a bill is paid before the expiration of the cash discount period. Anticipation is often figured at the rate of 6% per annum. However, some vendors specifically state on their invoices that no anticipation is allowed and, in such cases, there is no advantage in prepaying the bill.

Ordinary Dating. A term of sale requiring that the invoice be paid within a specified number of days from the date of invoice. Normally the date of the invoice is the same as the date the goods are shipped by the vendor. *Example:* 2/10, net 30 days means that the discount period expires in 10 days and that the full amount is due 30 days from invoice date.

E.O.M. Dating. Dating that requires the retailer to pay within a certain number of days from the end of the month in which the goods are billed. *Example:* 2/10 E.O.M. dating, when the invoice date is April 10, indicates required payment on May 10th (10 days from the end of April). *Note:* When a bill is dated the 26th of the month or later, E.O.M. dating commonly begins from the end of the following month. *Example:* 2/10 E.O.M. dating, when the bill is dated April 26th, means that payment must be made by June 10th (or 10 days from the end of May) in order to take the discount.

Advance Dating. Dating that is some time after actual shipment, giving additional time in which payment may be made and cash discount deducted. The time for payment of the invoice is computed from the advance dating, rather than from the invoice date. *Example:* Date of invoice August 20th, as of October 1st.

Extra Dating. The granting of a specified number of days in addition to the ordinary dating terms. It is another device for giving the payer extra time to pay the bill and deduct cash discount. *Example:* 2/10 – 30 extra, or 2/10 – 30 X, means 2% may be deducted if the bill is paid in 40 days from invoice date.

R.O.G. (Receipt of Goods) Dating. Dating is computed, not from the date of the bill, but rather from the day the goods are received by the store. This dating is often given to buyers, located at a distance from the market, who receive the bill a few days after shipment, but who may not receive the merchandise for a considerably longer time.

C.O.D. (Cash on Delivery). The buyer must make payment when the goods are delivered.

F.O.B. (Free on Board) Point. Indicate the point at which legal title to the goods passes from seller to buyer. In addition, it usually indicates the point to which the vendor has agreed to pay transportation charges. For example, F.O.B. Factory means that title passes when the goods leave the factory and that the store must pay transportation charges from the factory to the store. F.O.B. Store, on the other hand, means that title passes when the goods arrive and that the shipper will pay transportation charges to the store.

The Net Period. The time allowed to pay a bill without deduction of discount. If an invoice is not paid when the net period expires, a vendor has the right to initiate legal action against the retailer in order to force payment. *Note:* When the net period is not specified, it is customary to assume that it is 20 days after the expiration of the cash discount period. *Example:* If terms are 2/10, the buyer may pay in 30 days without incurring any penalty, although he loses the cash discount.

Net Terms. A condition of sale calling for the payment of the billed amount of the invoice at a specified date with no cash discount deduction. If the date is not specified, payment in 3 days from the date of invoice is generally considered acceptable.

Customs Duties. Taxes levied on imported goods. These duties are for revenue and for the protection of domestic manufacturers and growers.

Specific Duty. A specific amount stated in dollars and cents per pound, gallon, bushel, or other unit of measurement.

Ad Valorem Duty. Stated as a percentage of the "dutiable" value of imported goods.

The Dutiable Value. The value of the merchandise on which the *ad valorem* duty is based. It is ordinarily the cost of the goods in the foreign country plus cost of packing materials and labor required to get the goods ready for foreign shipment.

Consular Invoice. An invoice prepared by the American consulate in the foreign country from which goods are imported. The U.S. consulate checks whether customs regulations and laws have been complied with and whether sufficient duty will be imposed.

Commercial Invoice. The bill for the goods bought abroad. It contains the following information:

1. Name of boat
2. Date and port of shipment
3. Name and address of shipper
4. Invoice number and order number

5. Name and address of importer
6. Marks and numbers placed on package
7. Number and kind of packages and contents of each
8. Weight and measurement of each package
9. Detailed description of each article
10. Price per unit and total price
11. Term of sale
12. Insurance placed
13. Documents attached and number of copies of each
14. Statement showing country of origin
15. Cable-code words referring to each article, order, and invoice itself
16. Signature of vendor or officer of vendor's firm

Foreign Cost. The cost of the merchandise in the foreign country.

Landed Cost. The cost of imported merchandise landed on the dock in our own country (or at the store) and includes foreign cost plus all other importing costs and duties expressed in dollars, not in foreign currency.

Commissionaire. A foreign resident buyer who assists in locating resources and placing orders in a foreign country. He charges a fee that is included in the landed cost.

The Multiplier or Landed Rate. A figure that, when multiplied by the foreign cost (in foreign currency), gives the landed cost (in American currency). It is helpful in estimating quickly the cost of the goods landed in the United States from the quoted foreign price.

The Rate of Exchange. The number of dollars or cents exchangeable for a unit of foreign currency at a given time.

A. DATING

1. Cash discount with ordinary dating.

● *Example:*

An invoice dated September 15 carries terms of 3/10, net 30. When must it be paid to avoid loss of the discount, and when to avoid becoming overdue?

Solution:

1. The bill must be paid on or before September 25 to deduct the 3%.
2. October 15 is the final due date.

ASSIGNMENT 1:

An invoice dated June 4 carries terms of 3/10, net 60.

(a) What is the last day the discount may be deducted?

(b) When does the net period expire?

2. Cash discount and E.O.M. dating.

● *Example:*

An invoice dated October 3 carries terms of 3/10, E.O.M. When does the discount expire? When does the net period expire?

Solution:

If the bill is paid within 10 days from the end of October or by November 10, 3% can be deducted. Since the net period is not stated, it probably expires 20 days later, or November 30.

ASSIGNMENT 2:

An invoice for $3,000 dated July 16 carries terms of 5/10, E.O.M.

1. When does the discount period expire?
2. If the discount is taken, how much should be remitted to the vendor?
3. When does the net period expire?

3. E.O.M. dating when the bill is dated after the 25th of the month.

● *Example:*

An invoice dated May 26 carries terms of 4/10, E.O.M. When does the discount period expire?

Solution:

The invoice is considered to be dated June 1; therefore, the discount period expires July 10.

ASSIGNMENT 3:

A bill dated January 28 bears terms of 3/10, E.O.M. When does the discount period expire?

4. Advance dating.

● *Example:*

> An invoice is made out April 3 and carries terms of 3/10, post-dated 60 days. When does the discount expire?

Solution:

$$
\begin{aligned}
4/3-4/30 &= 27 \text{ days} \\
5/1-5/31 &= 31 \text{ days} \\
6/1-6/2\ \ &= \underline{\ \ 2 \text{ days}} \\
&= 60 \text{ days}
\end{aligned}
$$

> The discount period expires 10 days later, or June 12.

ASSIGNMENT 4:

> An invoice dated June 12 carries terms of 5/10, post-dated 90 days. When does the discount period expire?

5. Extra dating.

● *Example:*

> An invoice dated June 17 carries terms of 3/10–60 extra, net 90. When do the discount and net periods expire?

Solution:

The discount period is 70 days long.

$$
\begin{aligned}
6/17-6/30 &= 13 \text{ days} \\
7/1\ -7/31 &= 31 \text{ days} \\
8/1\ -8/26 &= \underline{26 \text{ days}} \\
&= 70 \text{ days}
\end{aligned}
$$

The discount period expires August 26, and the net period expires 20 days later or September 15.

ASSIGNMENT 5:

> An invoice dated March 14 carries terms of 5/10–30 extra, net 60.

> 1. When does the discount period end?
> 2. When does the net period end?

6. R.O.G. dating.

● *Example:*

An invoice dated November 3 carries terms of 2/10, net 30 R.O.G. The merchandise was received on December 24. What is the last day to take the discount and the final due date?

Solution:

The discount period expires 10 days after the receipt of the goods or January 3. The net period expires 20 days later, or January 23.

ASSIGNMENT 6:

A store sent in an order on February 1. The merchandise was shipped by the vendor on March 15 and received by the store on March 30. The invoice carried terms of 6/10, net 30 R.O.G. When do the discount and net periods expire?

7. Averaging due dates.

● *Example:*

A store purchases merchandise on a frequent but irregular basis from a local jobber on terms of 3/10, net 30. To avoid making a separate payment for each invoice, an average expiration date is calculated. The following are the invoices and dates for August.

7/4	$ 750
7/11	$1,000
7/15	$1,250
7/19	$ 900
	$3,900

Solution:

The average date is determined as follows:

Date	X	Amount	=	Weighted date
4	X	750	=	3,000
11	X	1,000	=	11,000
15	X	1,250	=	18,750
19	X	900	=	17,100
		3,900		49,850 ÷ 3,900 = 13

The average date is the 13th, plus a 10-day discount period, means paying on or before the 23rd of August.

ASSIGNMENT 7:

If the following invoices bearing terms of 5/10, net 30 are to be paid together, when should they be paid to earn the discount? How much should be remitted?

Date	Amount
March 25	$ 950
March 30	750
April 6	800
April 10	1,000

Managerial Decisions

A manufacturer offers you a concession either in the form of a lower billed cost or a higher cash discount. In either case, the dollar amount of the concession is the same. Which form of concession would you choose? Why?

B. ANTICIPATION

8. Figuring interest at 8% per annum.

Example:

At 8% per year, how much interest should be paid for the use of $1,900 for 45 days?

Solution:

In figuring interest it is customary to assume a 360-day year. Therefore, each 30 days is 1/12 of a year. In this problem 45 days is equal to 3/24, or 1/8 of a year.
Hence:

$$\frac{1}{8} \times 0.08 \times \$1,900 = \text{interest due}$$

$$0.01 \times \$1,900 = \$19 \text{ interest due for 45 days.}$$

ASSIGNMENT 8:

Figure the interest on $5,400 at 7.5% for 53 days.

9. Figuring anticipation.

● *Example:*

An invoice for $1,000 is dated July 13 and carries terms of 8/10–30 extra, net 60. If it is paid on July 23, how much should be remitted, assuming that anticipation at 6% a year is permitted?

Solution:

The discount may be deducted up to 40 days after July 13. It is paid in 10 days or prepaid by 30 days. The store may deduct the 8%, as well as 6% interest for 30 days, or 0.5%.[1] Therefore, the total deduction is 8.5%, or $85. Total remittance should be $915.

Alternate Solution:

$1,000 – $80 =		$920.00
	= Less 0.5% of $920	4.60
	= Total remittance	$915.40

ASSIGNMENT 9:

An invoice for $1,500 is dated June 29 and carries terms of 6/10 E.O.M., net 60. If the invoice is paid July 11, how much should be remitted, assuming that 6% anticipation is permitted?

10. Choosing terms.

● *Example:*

A manufacturer offers a choice of terms.

1. 7½/10–60 extra, net 90 (6% anticipation permitted)
2. 8/10, net 30

Which is more advantageous?

Solution:

If payment is made the 10th day, 1% anticipation may be added to 7½%, totaling 8½% total reduction. Also, if payment is made after 10 days, then (1) is obviously better.

---

[1] Some stores calculate the anticipation as the number of days between the date of payment and the final due date. In the example, these stores would deduct anticipation for 50 days rather than 30 days.

ASSIGNMENT 10:

A buyer is offered a choice of the following terms:

(1) 6½/10–30 extra
(2) 7/10, net 30

Which is more advantageous and why?

11. Cash discount in terms of interest per annum.

Example:

What is the annual interest rate corresponding to terms of 2/10, net 30?

Solution:

For the privilege of retaining the money an extra 20 days, one pays 2%. Twenty days is 1/18 of a year, and the annual rate would be 0.02 × 18, or 36% per year. (Actually if the discount is taken, only 98% of the amount is paid and the technically correct interest rate is 37.73% (36%/98%).)

ASSIGNMENT 11:

What is the interest rate corresponding to terms of 3/10, net 60?

12. Adjusting discount rates ("loading discounts").

Example:

A manufacturer offers terms of 6/10, net 30 on merchandise costing $1,000. A buyer desires terms of 8/10, net 30. What price revision must be made to allow the 8% discount and retain the original net price?

Solution:

Under the original terms the manufacturer would receive $1,000 less 6%, or $940. Assuming that the revised billed price is 100%, then with the new discount the net price will be 100% – 8%, or 92%. To find the revised price divide $940 by 92%. The new price is $1,021.74.

ASSIGNMENT 12:

A billed price of $2,500 less 2% is equivalent to what billed price less 4%?

Managerial Decision

You have a small dress shop and have been paying your bills on the tenth of each month. Would it be worthwhile to pay all your bills in ten days, rather than to wait until the 10th of the month?

C. TRADE DISCOUNTS

13. A series of trade discounts.

● *Example:*

> A manufacturer offers trade discounts of 10%–5% on merchandise having a list price of $100. Find the net price.

Solution:

$$\$100 - 10\% = \$90$$
$$\$90 - 5\% = \$85.50, \text{ the net price}$$

ASSIGNMENT 13:

> Trade discounts are offered of 15%–10%–5% on merchandise having a list price of $2,000. Find the net price.

14. Figuring the "on" percentage.

● *Example:*

> A buyer who repeatedly handles the same series of trade discounts wants to find the "on" percentage to save time. The trade discount is list price less 9%–5%.

Solution:

> The list price is 100%. Then $100\% - 9\% = 91\%$. $91\% - 5\% = 85.45\%$, which is the "on" percentage; or multiply the complements of the discounts together: $91\% \times 95\% = 85.45\%$.

ASSIGNMENT 14:

> Find the "on" percentage corresponding to the list price less 15%–10%–5%.

15. Deducting trade and cash discounts.

● *Example:*

> An invoice of $1,000 carries a series of trade discount of 10%–5%–

2% and terms of 2/10, net 30. If payment is made the 10th day, what should be the remittance?

Solution:

$$\$1,000 - 10\% = \$900$$
$$\$900 - 5\% \text{ of } \$900 = 855$$
$$\$855 - 2\% \text{ of } \$855 = \$837.90$$
$$\$837.90 - 2\% \text{ of } \$837.90 = \$821.14$$

or

$$\$1,000 \times 90\% \times 95\% \times 98\% \times 98\% = \$1,000 \times 82.114\% = \$821.14$$

ASSIGNMENT 15:

The list price of an invoice is $1,500. The trade discount series is 15%– 10%–5%. The cash discount is 3/10, net 30. If the bill is paid the 10th day, how much should be remitted?

16. Theory of high cash discount rates.

Example:

An invoice for $1,500 carries terms of 8/10, net 30 and is dated September 1. If it is paid on September 21, how much should be remitted?

Solution:

The bill was paid in 20 days, not in 10 days. Theoretically, the cash discount of 8% has been lost. However, a cash discount as high as this is probably in reality a trade discount and should be taken anyway. It may be proper, however, to include payment of interest at 6% per annum for the 10 days the payment is late. Deducting 8% from $1,500 gives $1,380 and adding 1/8 of 1% yields $1,382.30.

ASSIGNMENT 16:

An invoice for $950 is dated February 12 and bears terms of 12/10, net 60. The bill is paid on March 24. How much should be remitted?

Managerial Decision

How would you handle a large cash discount percentage when you fail to pay an invoice before the expiration of the cash discount date? (Consider other possibilities than the one given in example 16.)

D. DUTY AND LANDED COSTS

17. Figuring ad valorem duty.

● *Example:*

The foreign cost of an item imported from England is 2£. Packing materials and labor costs are 1£, *ad valorem* duty is 25%; and the rate of exchange is $2.82. What is the duty in American currency?

Solution:

Ad valorem duty is based on foreign cost plus packing and labor charges: 2£ + 1£ × $2.82 = $8.46; and $8.46 × 25% = $2.115.

ASSIGNMENT 17:

A store imports items from Denmark, which cost 25 kroners; packing and labor costs are 10 kroners, *ad valorem* duty is 60%, and the rate of exchange is $.15. What is the duty in American currency?

18. Specific duty.

● *Example:*

A store imported 600 ounces of perfume from France, which cost 100 francs per ounce. The duty is 50 cents per ounce. What was the total duty?

Solution:

Specific duty is based on numbers of units brought in, not on value. Therefore, the duty is 600 × $.50, or $300.

ASSIGNMENT 18:

A merchant imported 500 pieces of merchandise from New Zealand. The value was 2£ per unit. Packing and labor charges were 1£ for the shipment. Specific duty is 65 cents each and the *ad valorem* duty is 50%. The rate of exchange is $2.77. What is the total duty?

19. Landed cost and multiplier.

● *Example:*

A store imported 500 pieces of merchandise from Canada. The foreign cost was $4.50 each in Canadian dollars; packing and labor charges were $25; freight charges were $200; insurance and commissionaire's fees were 5% of the foreign cost; *ad valorem* duty was 20%; and the rate of exchange was $1.03. What was the landed cost and the multiplier?

Solution:

$$\text{Foreign cost} = 500 \times \$4.50 = \$2,250 \qquad \text{Canadian}$$

Packing and labor =	25
Freight =	200

Insurance and commissionaire's fees

$\$.05 \times 2,250 =$	112.50
Duty = $\$2,275 \times 0.20 =$	455
Landed cost	$3,042.50 Canadian

$$\$3,042.50 \times \$1.03 = \$3,133.78 \ (\text{U.S.})$$
$$\$3,133.78 \div \$2,250 = 1.3928, \ \text{the landed rate or multiplier.}$$

Note: The duty in U.S. funds is $455 \times 1.03 = \$468.65$.

ASSIGNMENT 19:

The foreign cost of goods bought in France was 10,000 francs; packing and casings, 250 francs; shipping costs, 1,000 francs; insurance and fees, 15% of foreign cost; miscellaneous charges, 2,000 francs; specific duty of 5 cents per unit on 1,000 units; *ad valorem* duty of 45%; and rate of exchange of 23 cents. Find the landed cost and the multiplier.

20. Utilizing the multiplier.

● *Example:*

On a trip to England a buyer is quoted a price of 5 shillings a unit for a certain good. The landed rate or multiplier is $.4642. He is required to maintain a retail markup of 40%. At what price must he sell the article?

Solution:

To find the landed cost in American currency, multiply 5 shillings by $.4642, which gives $2.32. Since 40% is the markup, then, 60% will be the cost. Therefore, $2.32 \div 0.60 = \$3.87$, which is the needed retail.

ASSIGNMENT 20:

In Brazil a buyer is quoted a price of 40 cruzeiros per unit on a certain article. The multiplier is $.1385. He needs a 45% markup on retail. What would be the retail price per unit in American currency?

Managerial Decisions

Would you include the buyer's salary and traveling expenses while abroad in ascertaining the landed cost of the goods purchased on the trip? Why?

ADDITIONAL ASSIGNMENTS

21. A vendor offers an item for $7.75 with terms of 4/10, net 60. The buyer is required to secure terms of 6%. What would be the adjusted price to allow the vendor to receive the same discounted price and the buyer to receive his 6% discount?

22. An invoice dated September 15 carries terms of 8/10, net 30 and is paid October 15. The amount is $1,500. How much should be remitted?

23. A bill dated July 26 and paid August 5 for $5,000 carries terms of 5/10-60 extra, net 90 F.O.B. store. Freight charges of $50 were paid by the store. Find the amount of the remittance.

24. A manufacturer offers a choice of the following terms: (a) 2½/10-60 extra, (b) 3/10, net 30. Which should a buyer choose?

25. How much should be remitted on an invoice of $750 carrying terms of 3/10-90 extra, net 120, dated May 4 and paid May 14?

26. What is the equivalent "on" percentage for a series of trade discounts of 20%-15%-10%-5%?

27. Terms of 4/10, net 60 are equivalent to what annual interest rate?

28. A store imported 500 items from Great Britain. The foreign cost each is 4£, packing and labor is 2.5£, specific duty is $1 each, *ad valorem* duty is 30%, and the rate of exchange is $2.82. What was the total duty in American currency?

29. A buyer purchases 1,000 units of a product from Denmark. If the landed rate is $.2543, the cost 50 kroners each, and a markup of 45% is desired, what is the required retail price in American currency?

30. A store has purchased 3,000 items from a vendor in Mexico for 100 pesos each. The packing and labor costs are 1,200 pesos, commissionaire's costs are 20% of foreign costs, miscellaneous costs are 1,300 pesos, specific duty is 30 cents each, *ad valorem* duty is 30%, and the rate of exchange is 8 cents. What is the landed cost in American currency?

31. Two hundred and fifty items of merchandise valued at £500 are purchased in Bermuda. Packing and material costs are £10, miscellaneous costs are £25, *ad valorem* duty is 55%, the rate of exchange is $2,8164, and the required markup is 40%.

(a) Find the landed cost.
(b) Find the required retail price of each item.